Against Adaptation

THE LACANIAN CLINICAL FIELD

Against Adaptation

LACAN'S "SUBVERSION" OF THE SUBJECT

Philippe Van Haute

TRANSLATED BY
Paul Crowe and Miranda Vankerk

OTHER
Other Press
New York

Copyright © 2002 Philippe Van Haute

ISBN   978-1-59051-665-8

Production Editor: Robert D. Hack

This book was set in 11 pt. Berkeley by Alpha Graphics of Pittsfield, New Hampshire.

Library of Congress Cataloging-in-Publication Data

Haute, Philippe van, 1957-
    Against adaptation : Lacan's "subversion" of the subject / Philippe Van Haute.
        p. cm.—(The Lacanian clinical field)
    Includes bibliographical references and index.
    ISBN 1-892746-65-4
    1. Psychoanalysis.   2. Lacan, Jacques, 1901–   I. Title.   II. Series.
BF173 .H418 2001
150.19'5'092—dc21

                                                    2001036422

For Lut, Dawit, and Eyob

Who cannot see the distance that separates the unhappy consciousness—of which, however strongly it is engraven in Hegel, it can be said that it is still no more than the suspension of a corpus of knowledge—from the "discontents of civilization" in Freud, even if it is only in a mere phrase, uttered as if disavowed, that marks for us what, on reading it, cannot be articulated otherwise than the "skew" relation that separates the subject from sexuality?

—Jacques Lacan

Sometimes one seems to perceive that it is not only the presence of civilization but something in the nature of the function itself which denies us full satisfaction and urges us along other paths. This may be wrong, it is hard to decide.

—Sigmund Freud

Contents

Foreword

Authors who set out to write an introduction to the work of Lacan inevitably face a difficult choice—they can either give a general introduction that deals with the entirety of Lacan's work, or they can concentrate on one or more programmatic texts and attempt to provide a thoroughgoing commentary on them. We already have several introductions of the first type at our disposal.[1] Their generality is their strength, but also their weakness. They give an overview of the whole *oeuvre* of Lacan (and where necessary of the developments that have taken place within it), but precisely because of this they have the tendency to abstract themselves from the concrete texts that make up that *oeuvre*. This procedure has a twofold result: in the first place, it can lead to the somewhat over-hasty conclusion that Lacanian psychoanaly-

---

1. One thinks, for example, of the particularly successful introductions of B. Fink (1995, 1997).

sis forms a closed system that one can either take or leave. In the second place—and perhaps more importantly—it can unintentionally reinforce the impression many have that the texts of Lacan are unintelligible. Indeed, these texts are infamous for their obscurity and their degree of difficulty; and it is true that many of Lacan's texts are difficult to access without the guidance of a commentary. Given that general introductions seldom or never contain extended textual analyses, however, they are often of no real help in reading Lacan's work itself. Thus, readers are left with the disagreeable feeling that the texts of Lacan will remain impenetrable for them no matter how many introductions they might read, and they conclude that this *oeuvre* must be particularly esoteric. If we wish to deliver Lacan from this disrepute, then it is undoubtedly necessary to write introductions and commentaries that pay more attention to the concrete texts and how they can be made intelligible.

Lacan has written several texts of a programmatic nature,[2] and these offer a good picture of the issues and content of his thought. A commentary on these texts, then, is exceptionally well suited to achieve the goal that stands before us: to write an introduction that also puts the reader in a position to understand

---

2. One thinks, for example, of "The Function and Field of Speech and Language in Psychoanalysis" (Lacan 1956), E 30–113, EF 237–322; "The Direction of the Treatment and the Principles of its Power" (Lacan 1958), E 226–280, EF 586–646; "The Subversion of the Subject and the Dialectic of Desire in the Freudian Unconscious" (Lacan 1960), E 292–325, EF 794–827. ["The Subverison of the Subject and the Dialectic of Desire" will hereafter be referred to as "Subversion." We will cite the English translation of *Écrits* (Lacan 1977) as "E" followed by page and line numbers, while the French text (1966) will be cited as "EF" followed by page numbers only. In places the author's interpretation of the text makes it clear that Sheridan's translation is misleading. In such cases we indicate that the translation is modified and add the text in the original French.—Trans.]

a particular text as thoroughly as possible. We have opted to comment on Lacan's famous "The Subversion of the Subject and the Dialectic of Desire in the Freudian Unconscious,"[3] and our reasons for doing so are twofold.

First, the text functions as a hinge between Lacan's work of the fifties and that of the sixties. In it, Lacan considers to some extent both the concepts that he developed at the beginning of the fifties—in particular, the categories of the imaginary and the symbolic—and those that he worked out chiefly in the sixties, such as the object *a*, the real, and the phantasy.

Second, in this text Lacan introduces his famous "graph of desire," an attempt to render the structure of the subject of desire more perspicuous by graphic representation. Our text is structured around the progressive construction of this graph of desire, allowing the introduction of various fundamental Lacanian concepts (the object *a*, the phantasy, the phallus, and so on) in relation to each other. We address these concepts and their place on the graph by way of a commentary on the text. It goes without saying, however, that we do not therefore limit ourselves to the passages that have a direct bearing on the graph. On the contrary, we have tried to give a commentary on the whole of Lacan's text.[4]

The graph is constructed in four separate stages, each stage implying a further deepening of the problem of subjectivity and

---

3. "Subversion" is a reworked version of a lecture Lacan gave at a colloquium on dialectic organized by Jean Wahl (September 19–23, 1960). The text appeared for the first time in *Écrits* (Lacan 1966).

4. Other commentaries are available on Lacan's graph of desire, some more extensive than others. For example M. Adriaensen, "Topische coördinaten voor een dialectiek van het verlangen. Een grafisch model," in Adriaensen 1992, pp. 11–56; C. Conté, "La clinique du graphe—$OD," in Conté 1992, pp. 133–152; Dor 1985, pp. 179–248.

of desire. We cannot underline forcefully enough that these four stages have no genetic significance. The graph of desire articulates the *structure* of desire and of subjectivity, and Lacan in fact rejects any psychogenetic approach to subjectivity in favor of a structural determination of it. The graph is the result of this theoretical choice.

With the aim of keeping the text as readable as possible, we have excluded nearly all quotations. We do, however, quote the passages upon which we comment *in extenso* in the footnotes. The structure and the thematic of our own text is defined by Lacan's text. This, however, has not prevented us from reordering Lacan's text in relation to certain themes—for example, the Name-of-the-Father (*le Nom-du-Père*) and the phallus—which Lacan deals with at several different points in his text. We have grouped together the various passages relating to these themes at those points in the argument where they are most significant for the construction of the graph of desire—for it is the construction of the graph that defines the basic structure of Lacan's argumentation in "Subversion." In this way it has been possible to comment on the greater part of Lacan's text *ad litteram* and to clarify the structure and coherence of Lacan's thought.[5]

Our reading of "Subversion" will above all answer the question of what Lacan understands by the "subversion of the subject" and how this thematic goes together with the idea of a "dialectic of desire." We will thus cast light on the importance of Lacanian metapsychology for psychoanalysis (both theoretical

---

5. I have left out of consideration the passages in which Lacan expressly enters into a debate with philosophy (particularly with Hegel). I address them only briefly in the footnotes. An extensive commentary on the relevant passages would make my exposition unnecessarily complicated. For further comment on these passages and on the relation between Lacan and Hegel, see Borch-Jacobsen 1991, Van Haute 1990.

and clinical) on the one hand, and for a philosophical problematic of the subject on the other. That is to say, our reading of this text allows us to clarify the crucial and decisive significance of the "metaphor of the Name-of-the-Father" and of the castration complex for Lacanian thought. And indeed, in the course of the exposition it will become clear that the "metaphor of the Name-of-the-Father" and the castration complex form the culminating point of Lacanian psychoanalysis, for it is from them that the various other concepts that determine its structure receive their ultimate significance.

Lacan developed a *psychoanalytic* theory of desire. Consequently, this theory is something more and something other than an abstract philosophical idea; rather, it has its ultimate touchstone in Lacan's discussion of psychopathology. Accordingly, we will close our exposition with a discussion of Lacanian psychopathology as it is worked out in "Subversion." This discussion will not only allow us to see the way in which the "metaphor of the Name-of-the-Father" and the castration complex play a decisive role throughout Lacan's treatment of psychoanalytic psychopathology, but will also make it possible to expose the fundamental significance of Lacan's "dialectic of desire."

The manner in which Lacan construes the graph of desire is interesting for yet another reason. It illustrates, in a striking manner, the ontological dualism that can, without a doubt, be considered *the* basic assumption of Lacanian psychoanalysis.[6] This ontological dualism is related to the fact that Lacan thinks of language and the body as originally external to each other. In a mythical originary moment, the body encounters language

---

6. Lacan borrows this ontological dualism from the work of Alexandre Kojève (Kojève 1980). For more on this problematic, see my *Psychoanalyse en filosofie* (Van Haute 1990).

as something external to it, something that takes it up in a dynamic that is originally alien to it. The debate over this ontological dualism is of crucial importance if we are to correctly situate the stakes and the significance of Lacanian psychoanalysis. For it is on the basis of this ontological dualism that Lacan develops a vision in which man appears as a being of desire that is fundamentally maladapted. From the beginning of his intellectual career, Lacan underlined that there is a "primordial Discord" between man and nature (Lacan 1949, p. 4). He thus opposes any vision of man (psychoanalytic or otherwise) in which adaptation—and more generally a fundamental co-adaptation between the human subject and its environment—functions as the explicit or implicit starting point for the understanding of subjectivity.[7]

Finally, let us turn back to the fundamental choice that underlies this book. We have chosen to introduce the work of Lacan through a commentary on one of his most significant texts. As a result of this choice, we deal with certain developments in the later work of Lacan either not at all, or at least only summarily,[8] and the same is true for his earlier texts (see Ogilvie

---

7. Here it is primarily a question of Lacan's critique of ego psychology, as we will discuss in more detail later. However, Lacan also criticizes Hegelian philosophy on the same grounds. Lacan's rejection of any thinking that makes adaptation central still retains its relevance today. Cognitive psychology and cognitivism, for example, make coadaptation between man and his environment the core of their vision of man. Certain authors in the phenomenological tradition also appear susceptible to Lacan's critique. This problematic would take us too far astray here, however, and we will not pursue it further.

8. It goes without saying that "Subversion" does not constitute an endpoint in the development of Lacan's thought. Where it seemed necessary, we have referred briefly in the footnotes to later developments in his thought (for example, in relation to female sexuality). We also give bibliographical references for those who wish to go more deeply into these problematics.

1987). Undoubtedly, this has its disadvantages. We believe, however, that too few concrete analyses of Lacan's texts have been
published. It is only on the basis of such textual analyses that
we can gain a real view of the precise significance of the subtle
(and sometimes not so subtle) shifts that occur in his work; only
thus can it really be made clear that the significance of certain
Lacanian concepts—for example, *jouissance*—changes according to context. Only thus, finally, can the impression be dispelled
that Lacanian psychoanalysis forms a system that one can take
or leave. Concrete textual analyses, and their comparison, teach
us to recognize the thought of Lacan as the fruit of an unfin-
ished debate—a debate as much with his contemporaries as with
himself, and one that remains of great importance today for both
psychoanalysis and for philosophy.

Acknowledgments

This study is a completely reworked and expanded version of the text given at the invitation of Paul Moyaert at a workshop for the Centre for Psychoanalysis and Philosophical Anthropology (K. U. Leuven/ K. U. Nijmegen) on March 28, 1998, in Leuven. From the beginning Paul Moyaert encouraged me to publish this text in book form. He has read the various versions of the manuscript with unflagging attention. His incisive comments on the manuscript, and the countless discussions that we have had over the years about Lacan and psychoanalysis, were always illuminating for me. He is in no small degree responsible for this book coming to be.

Rudi Visker read through the final version of my manuscript with meticulous care, and my discussions with him about Lacan, psychoanalysis, and philosophy in general have been a constant source of inspiration for me. Without his help I would most likely have never seen certain problems, let alone worked them out.

I thank Fons Van Coillie and Lily de Vooght for their critical observations on earlier versions of this manuscript, and for the interest they showed throughout the writing of it.

My discussions with Thomas Geyskens have been very helpful in the explanation of certain difficult passages, especially in the writing of the last chapter on Lacanian psychopathology.

I thank my students for being prepared to keep listening to my attempts to create order from my chaos.

Last, but by no means least, I thank my wife and children. They gave me constant support and showed unbelievable patience during the period in which I worked on this book, and I do not know how I can thank them enough.

The Lacanian Clinical Field: Series Overview

JUDITH FEHER GUREWICH

Lacanian psychoanalysis exists, and the ongoing series, The Lacanian Clinical Field, is here to prove it. The clinical expertise of French practitioners deeply influenced by the thought of Jacques Lacan has finally found a publishing home in the United States. Books that have been acclaimed in France, Italy, Spain, Greece, South America, and Japan for their clarity, didactic power, and clinical relevance will now be at the disposal of the American psychotherapeutic and academic communities. These books cover a range of topics, including theoretical introductions; clinical approaches to neurosis, perversion, and psychosis; child psychoanalysis; conceptualizations of femininity; psychoanalytic readings of American literature; and more. Thus far, the series is comprised of twelve books.

Though all these works are clinically relevant, they will also be of great interest to those American scholars who have taught and used Lacan's theories for over a decade. What better opportunity for the academic world of literary criticism, philosophy, human sciences, women's studies, film studies, and multicultural studies finally to have access to the clinical insights of a theorist known primarily for his revolutionary vision of the formation of the human subject. Thus The Lacanian Clinical Field goes beyond introducing the American clinician to a different psychoanalytic outlook. It brings together two communities that have grown progressively estranged from each other. For indeed, the time when the Frankfurt School, Lionel Trilling, Erich Fromm, Herbert Marcuse, Philip Rieff, and others were fostering exchanges between the academic and the psychoanalytic communities is gone, and in the process psychoanalysis has lost some of its vibrancy.

The very limited success of ego psychology in bringing psychoanalysis into the domain of science has left psychoanalysis in need of a metapsychology that is able not only to withstand the pernicious challenges of psychopharmacology and psychiatry but also to accommodate the findings of cognitive and developmental psychology. Infant research has put many of Freud's insights into question, and the attempts to replace a one-body psychology with a more interpersonal or intersubjective approach have led to dissension within the psychoanalytic community. Many theorists are of the opinion that the road toward scientific legitimacy requires a certain allegiance with Freud's detractors, who are convinced that the unconscious and its sexual underpinnings are merely an aberration. Psychoanalysis continues to be practiced, however, and according to both patients and analysts the uncovering of unconscious motivations continues to provide a sense of relief. But while there has been a burgeoning of different psychoanalytic schools of thought since the desacralization of Freud, no theoretical agreement has been reached as to why such relief occurs.

Nowadays it can sometimes seem that Freud is read much more scrupulously by literary critics and social scientists than by psychoanalysts. This is not entirely a coincidence. While the psychoanalytic community is searching for a new metapsychology, the human sciences have acquired a level of theoretical sophistication and complexity that has enabled them to read Freud under a new lens. *Structural linguistics and structural anthropology have transformed conventional appraisals of human subjectivity and have given Freud's unconscious a new status. Lacan's teachings, along with the works of Foucault and Derrida, have been largely responsible for the explosion of new ideas that have enhanced the interdisciplinary movement pervasive in academia today.*

The downside of this remarkable intellectual revolution, as far as psychoanalysis is concerned, is the fact that Lacan's contribution has been derailed from its original trajectory. No longer perceived as a theory meant to enlighten the practice of psychoanalysis, his brilliant formulations have been both adapted and criticized so as to conform to the needs of purely intellectual endeavors far removed from clinical reality. This state of affairs is certainly in part responsible for Lacan's dismissal by the psychoanalytic community. Moreover, Lacan's "impossible" style has been seen as yet another proof of the culture of obscurantism that French intellectuals seem so fond of.

In this context the works included in The Lacanian Clinical Field should serve as an eye-opener at both ends of the spectrum. The authors in the series are primarily clinicans eager to offer to professionals in psychoanalysis, psychiatry, psychology, and other mental-health disciplines a clear and succinct didactic view of Lacan's work. Their goal is not so much to emphasize the radically new insights of the Lacanian theory of subjectivity and its place in the history of human sciences as it is to show how this difficult and complex body of ideas can enhance clinical work. Therefore, while the American clinician will be made aware that Lacanian psychoanalysis is not primarily a staple of literary criticism or philosophy but a praxis meant to cure patients of their psychic distress, the academic community will be exposed for the first time to a reading of Lacan that is in sharp contrast with the literature that has thus far informed them about his theory. In that sense Lacan's teachings return to the clinical reality to which they primarily belong.

Moreover, the clinical approach of the books in this series will shed a new light on the critical amendments that literary scholars and feminist theoreticians have brought to Lacan's conceptualization of subjectivity. While Lacan has been applauded for having offered an alternative to Freud's biological determinism, he has also been accused of nevertheless remaining phallocentric in his formulation of sexual difference. Yet this criticism, one that may be valid outside of the clinical reality—psychoanalysis is both an ingredient and an effect of culture—may not have the same relevance in the clinical context. For psychoanalysis as a praxis has a radically different function from the one it currently serves in academic discourse. In the latter, psychoanalysis is perceived both as an ideology fostering patriarchal beliefs and as a theoretical tool for constructing a vision of the subject no longer dependent on a phallocratic system. In the former, however, the issue of phallocracy loses its political impact. Psychoanalytic practice can only retroactively unravel the ways that the patient's psychic life has been constituted, and in that sense it can only reveal the function the phallus plays in the psychic elaboration of sexual difference.

The Lacanian Clinical Field, therefore, aims to undo certain prejudices that have affected Lacan's reputation up to now in both the academic and the psychoanalytic communities. While these prejudices stem from rather different causes—Lacan is perceived as too patriarchal and reactionary in the one and too far removed from clinical reality in the other—they both seem to overlook the fact that the fifty years that cover the period of Lacan's teachings were mainly devoted to working and reworking the meaning and function of psychoanalysis, not necessarily as a science or even as a human science, but as a practice that can nonetheless rely on a solid and coherent metapsychology. This double debunking of received notions may not only enlarge the respective frames of reference of both the therapeutic and the academic communities; it may also allow them to find a common denominator in a metapsychology that has derived its "scientific" status from the unexpected realm of the humanities.

I would like to end this overview to the series as a whole with a word of warning and a word of reassurance. One of the great difficulties for an American analyst trying to figure out the Lacanian "genre" is the way these clinical theorists explain their theoretical point of view as if it were coming straight from Freud. Yet Lacan's Freud and the American Freud are far from being transparent to each other. Lacan dismantled the Freudian corpus and rebuilt it on entirely new foundations, so that the new edifice no longer resembled the old. At the same time he always downplayed, with a certain coquetterie, his position as a theory builder, because he was intent on proving that he had remained, despite all odds, true to Freud's deepest insights. Since Lacan was very insistent on keeping Freudian concepts as the raw material of his theory, Lacanian analysts of the second generation have followed in their master's footsteps and have continued to read Freud scrupulously in order to expand, with new insights, this large structure that had been laid out. Moreover, complicated historical circumstances have fostered their isolation, so that their acquaintance with recent psychoanalytic developments outside of France has been limited. Lacan's critical views on ego psychology and selected aspects of object relations theory have continued to inform their vision of American psychoanalysis and have left them unaware that certain of their misgivings about these schools of thought are shared by some of their colleagues in the United States. This apparently undying allegiance to Freud, therefore, does not necessarily mean that Lacanians have not moved beyond him, but rather that their approach is different from that of their American counterparts. While the latter often tend to situate their work as a reaction to Freud, the Lacanian strategy always consists in rescuing Freud's insights and resituating them in a context free of biological determinism.

Second, I want to repeat that the expository style of the books of this series bears no resemblance to Lacan's own writings. Lacan felt that Freud's clarity and didactic talent had ultimately led to distortions and oversimplifications, so that his own notoriously "impossible" style was meant to serve as a metaphor for the difficulty of listening to the unconscious. Cracking his difficult writings involves not only the intellectual effort of readers but also their unconscious processes; comprehension will dawn as reader-analysts recognize in their own work what was expressed in sibylline fashion in the text. Some of Lacan's followers continued this tradition, fearing that clear exposition would leave no room for the active participation of the reader. Others felt strongly that although Lacan's point was well taken it was not necessary to prolong indefinitely an ideology of obscurantism liable to fall into the same traps as the ones Lacan was denouncing in the first place. Such a conviction was precisely what made this series, The Lacanian Clinical Field, possible.

Introduction:
Freud's Copernican Revolution

The psychoanalytical tradition has betrayed Freud:[1] this thought is undoubtedly the point of departure for Lacanian psychoanalysis. This betrayal makes a "return to Freud" more than necessary. More specifically, such a "return" has to show clearly the manner in which Freudian psychoanalysis subverts the traditional philosophical notion of the subject—a notion that is codeterminative for science and for academic psychology.[2]

Lacan claims that psychoanalytic orthodoxy has aimed at a reinforcement of the ego in both theory and practice.[3] The

---

1. E 293/15–27, EF 794. We will come back to these passages later.

2. "Hence, let it be noted, my entirely didactic reference to Hegel, by which I wished to say something, for purposes of the training that I have in mind, about the question of the subject, in so far as that question is properly subverted by psychoanalysis" (E 293/11–14, EF 794).

3. When Lacan speaks of "psychoanalytic orthodoxy" he is mainly thinking of "ego-psychology." Lacan criticizes ego-psychology in several places in "Subversion," and it is clear from the context that Lacan more or less identifies "American psychoanalysis" with ego-psychology. This was probably correct at the time Lacan wrote this text; however, it is obvious that Lacan's critique of ego-psychology cannot be taken seriously as a critique of contemporary American psychoanalysis. While dated, however, his polemics against

ego of the analysand must be reinforced so that it will be in a position to manage conflicts and creatively adapt itself to reality. To the question of which reality the analysand must therefore adapt itself to, and how this can happen, the tradition has an answer that is as surprising as it is simple: "reality" is the given social reality in which the analysand exists. "Adaptation" to this reality takes place through an identification with the analyst, who is supposed to adequately incarnate the aim of the analysis—the well-adapted subject. According to Lacan, analysis thus becomes a subtle suggestive technique without any scientific content.[4]

According to Lacan, academic psychology can provide no solace here;[5] for it assumes the unity of the subject whose vari-

---

ego-psychology remain interesting to the extent that they allowed him to articulate his theory of the inadaptation of the human subject, and the critical potential of that theory cannot be underestimated. It is for this reason only that we detail his arguments against the ego-psychology of his time at places in our analysis.

4. "What qualifies me to proceed in this direction [i.e. of determining the "subversion" of the subject by psychoanalysis] is obviously my experience of this praxis. What has decided me to do so, those who follow my teaching will bear this out, is a theoretical nullity [i.e. the central position of the ego and its reinforcement] coupled with abuses in the way in which it is passed on [in that psychoanalytic "knowledge" is passed on the basis of an identification with the analyst, and psychoanalysis thus becomes a technique of suggestion that can only be repeated in a sterile fashion], which, while presenting no danger to the praxis itself, result, in either case, in a total absence of scientific status" (E 293/15–20, EF 794).

5. "At a second stage, we encounter what has already been constituted, by virtue of a scientific label, under the name of psychology. . . . Its criterion is the unity of the subject, which is one of the presuppositions of this sort of psychology, it being even taken as symptomatic that its theme is always more emphatically isolated, as if it were a question of the return of a certain subject of knowledge (*connaissance*), or as if the psychical had to obtain its credentials as a double of the physical organism" (E 293/35, 294/8, EF 795).

ous properties and functions it studies, without pausing even for a moment to consider the scientific validity of this assumption. The emphasis on the unity of an essentially "knowing" subject goes together with the idea that the psyche has to be understood as a functional double (*doublure*) of the organism. The psyche must assist the organism in its attempt to adapt itself to reality. Just like psychoanalytic orthodoxy, academic psychology believes that psychic life must be understood primarily and fundamentally as "adaptation," or in terms of an "adaptive" problematic.

Lacan radically rejects this assumption. The relation between the human subject and its environment, in the broad sense of the word, cannot be thought in terms of adaptation. This is one of the fundamental insights that dominates Lacanian psychoanalysis. It claims in this way to have broken with the traditional philosophical and scientific study of the human subject. Thus we must first ask ourselves how Lacan situates psychoanalysis within the traditions of science and philosophy.

Western and non-Western traditions alike have always understood psychic experience as a state of knowledge (*état de la connaissance*).[6] Thus Plato viewed "enthusiasm" (*enthousiasmos, mania*), which denotes a state of confusion, as a specific form of knowing. Again, in Buddhism, one progresses through various grades of *samadhi*, thereby bringing to rest the intellectual activity of knowing and attaining a state of blessed equilibrium;

---

6. "We must take as our standard here the idea in which a whole body of traditional thought comes together to validate a term, 'state of knowledge' (*état de la connaissance*), that is not without foundation. Whether it is a question of the states of enthusiasm described by Plato, the Buddhist degrees of *samadhi*, or the *Erlebnis*, the experience obtained under the influence of hallucinogenic drugs, it is necessary to know how much of these is authenticated by any theory" (E 294/9–15, EF 795).

these *samadhi* states themselves, however, are conceived of as a source of activity and insight. Others recommend the use of drugs because they give us access to experiences—and so to forms of knowledge—that would otherwise remain closed to us. However, the fact that one talks in this connection of "states of knowing" should prompt us to caution, implying as it does that these experiences are not considered valuable in themselves. "Enthusiasm" in Plato, and the grades of *samadhi* in Buddhism, are only significant within the theoretical system in which they have their place. In other words, the experience is governed by a theory that determines what counts as valuable.[7]

A reference to the philosophy of Hegel might be instructive here.[8] Hegel's *Phenomenology of Spirit* (1977) describes the progressive realization of absolute knowledge. In this connection, Lacan writes that Hegel attaches no importance to the despair of "unhappy consciousness" as such, for example, in his description of this process of development of consciousness to absolute knowledge. Such affective states are in themselves not decisive. What *is* fundamentally at issue is the place of this fig-

---

7. ". . . it is necessary to know how much of these [experiences] is authenticated by any theory" (E 294/14–15, EF 795).

8. "It is clear that Hegelian knowledge (*savoir*), in the logicizing *Aufhebung* on which it is based, sets as little store by these states in themselves as modern science, which can recognize in them an object of experience, in the sense of an opportunity to define certain co-ordinates, but in no way an ascesis that might, let us say, be epistemogenic or noophoric. It is certainly on this account that reference to them is pertinent to my approach" (E 294/18–24, EF 795). Hegel is, more generally, Lacan's privileged interlocutor in his attempts to determine the radicality of the Freudian revolution. For Lacan considers Hegelian thought to be the crowning achievement of the modern metaphysical tradition, and believes accordingly that the determining presuppositions of this tradition emerge nowhere more clearly than in the work of Hegel. This is where what Lacan himself calls an "entirely didactic reference to Hegel" (E 293/11, EF 794) finds its justification.

ure of consciousness in the "genesis of Spirit." "Unhappy con-sciousness," and the despair by which it is characterized, bor-rows its significance from its place in an essentially rational process of genesis, of which it is but one moment. In an analo-gous manner, science is not interested in psychic experiences as such. When taken as the object of empirical research, it is not the drug-experience as such that is the object of interest, for example, but its influence on the perception of color. In other words, the drug-experience as such only has importance insofar it can be brought into relation with other parameters on which it has an influence. In no case is the experience in itself understood as a source of knowledge, and in a certain sense it is no different in psychoanalysis.

As much as many may believe that Freudian "depth psy-chology" concerns itself with just such "depth experiences," a minimal familiarity with Freud suffices to show that this no-tion does not in fact feature anywhere in his *oeuvre*.[9] Psy-choanalysis is no mysticism. It is not in search of any "insights" that might emerge from such experiences. For example, when his first hysterical patients enter a state of reduced conscious-ness and are overcome by hallucinatory experiences, what in-terests Freud are not these experiences or states themselves, but what the patient *says* about them.[10] The experiences of the

---

9. "For I suppose my listeners are sufficiently informed about Freud-ian practice to grasp that such states play no part in it—but what is not fully appreciated is the fact that the practitioners of this supposedly depth psychol-ogy do not think of using them to obtain illumination, for example, do not even attribute to these states any value in relation to the direction indicated by such a depth psychology" (E 294/25–30, EF 795).

10. "For that is the meaning, which is not insisted on, of that distance from which Freud proceeds when it comes to hynoid [sic] states, even when it is merely a question of explaining the phenomena associated with hysteria.

patient have to be articulated, so that the hidden "logos" of which they are the expression can be brought to light. For Lacan, moreover, the fact that the unconscious "logos" at work in those experiences can be brought to light by way of *language* immediately implies that the unconscious, too, also belongs to the order of language in one way or another. Only because and insofar as the unconscious itself already is "language" can it be deciphered through the painstaking labor of free association.[11] In other words, psychoanalysis wants to let an unconscious logic—the logic of the unconscious—speak. In consequence, it cannot be understood as a sort of initiation rite that lends access to an archetypical experience (e.g., cosmic experience), or anything similarly inexpressible. Lacan writes that if—*ex absurdo*—we suppose that someone did succeed in expressing something of this order in the course of analysis, this would result in the immediate annihilation of all psychic structures. For it would be a matter of nothing other than a sort of megalomania, in which one wanted to transcend every limita-

---

The stupifying [sic] fact is that Freud prefers the discourse of the hysteric" (E 294/31–34, EF 795).

11. "I have some difficulty in getting a hearing in circles infatuated with the most incredible illogicality [a polemical reference to the French psychoanalytic milieus of the day] for what is involved in questioning the unconscious as I do, that is to say, to the point at which it gives a reply that is not some sort of transport of delight [a polemical reference to Jung according to whom the effect of bringing the unconscious to speech is a powerful *Erlebnis*], or flat rejection, but rather that 'it says why' [analysis is not a matter of reaching a state of rapture, but of exposing the unconscious "logic" that is at work in symptoms and the like]. If we take the subject anywhere it is to a deciphering that already presupposes this sort of logic [namely that of the deciphering and thus of language] in the unconscious: in which, for example, an interrogative voice, even the development of an argument, is recognized" (E 294/37, 295/5, EF 796).

tion, and the boundaries between the unconscious and consciousness were abolished.[12]

Following in the wake of science and the philosophical tradition, psychoanalysis is not interested in inexpressible affective depths and experiences of this sort. However, this does not mean that the relation between philosophy, science, and psychoanalysis can be understood in terms of a continuity. In this regard Freud spoke of a "Copernican revolution."[13] According to Lacan, this revolution implies that psychoanalysis has introduced a decisive break in the way in which the scientific and philosophical tradition has up until now thematized the subject and subjectivity. In what, precisely, does this decisive break consist?

According to Freud, modern humanity has endured three fundamental narcissistic wounds.[14] Copernicus deprived humanity of its central place in the universe; Darwin showed that humanity is the result of a long and complicated process of evolution—not the crowning achievement of divine creation, but only

---

12. "In other words, psychoanalysis that is sustained by its allegiance to Freud cannot in any circumstances offer itself as a 'rite of passage' to some archetypal, or in any sense ineffable, experience: the day when anyone expresses a view of this order that is not simply a dead loss will be the day when all limits have been abolished. And we are still a long way from that" (E 295/9–14, EF 796).

13. "This is merely an approach to our subject. For it is a question of grasping more precisely what Freud in his doctrine himself articulates as constituting a 'Copernican' step" (E 295/15–17, EF 796).

14. "Is it enough that a privilege should be consigned to it, namely the one that put the earth in the central place? The subsequent dislodging of man from a similar place by the triumph of the idea of evolution gives one the feeling that this would involve a gain that would be confirmed by its consistency. But can one be sure that this is a gain, that it is real progress?" (E 295/18–23, EF 796).

a somewhat better evolved species. By Freud's reckoning, psychoanalysis is the third in this series of wounds. No matter how much Darwin forced humanity to fundamentally recast its views of its origins, this did not stop it from believing that it coincides with itself as self-consciousness. The Freudian revolution puts an end to this naive belief. For Freud teaches us that man "is not master in his own house." The subject is not to be understood as essentially self-consciousness; instead, it is delivered over to unconscious forces that elude its grasp.

Lacan asks, however, whether these three wounds are as fundamental as we would like to believe. Have they in fact shaken the self-conception of the subject as fundamentally as Freud would have it? Thus has Darwinism, for example, really freed humanity from its belief that it holds a central position in reality? How could it, when Darwin places man at the top of the evolutionary pyramid?[15] And, for that matter, is it really so certain that heliocentrism serves us any better in this regard? The emphasis that heliocentrism places upon the problem of the center—does the earth or the sun stand in the center of the universe?—leads us to forget that pre-Copernicans may well have believed themselves the center of the universe even less than moderns do.[16] Pre-Copernicans did indeed consider the earth

---

15. "In any case it is not because of Darwin that men believe themselves to be any the less the top dogs in creation, for it is precisely of this that he convinces them" (E 295/30–32, EF 797).

16. "Does nothing make it appear that the other truth, if we may so term revealed truth, is seriously affected as a result? Do we not believe that, by exalting the center, heliocentrism is no less of a lure than seeing the earth as the center of the Universe, and that the fact of the ecliptic no doubt provided a more stimulating model of our relations with the true, before it lost much of its interest by being no more than the earth nodding its assent?" (E 295/23–29, EF 797).

the center of the universe, but earthly existence itself was under-stood from within a larger totality of meaning, represented sym-bolically by the starry sky. In this sense, the central place of the earth was less absolute than it seems at first. In other words, humanity saw itself as taken up in a symbolic order that tran-scended it, and this order defined its existence. Given this, can one in all seriousness affirm that the appearance of the autono-mous subject of science, which displaced the earth from the center, is to be thought of as a narcissistic wound?

If the expression "Copernican revolution" is to be mean-ingful vis-à-vis psychoanalysis, it must, following Lacan, respond to a logic even more hidden than perhaps Freud himself thought.[17] According to Lacan, this hidden logic pertains to the relation between knowledge and truth that was set in motion precisely by the introduction of heliocentrism. We know that Copernicus's *De Revolutionibus* (Copernicus 1974) was preceded by a preface, in which the Lutheran theologian Osiander asserts that the Copernican system has no claim to reality whatsoever—it is merely a mathematical fiction that allows us to better cal-culate the movement of heavenly bodies. In opposition to this mathematical knowledge stands the religious-metaphysical truth, according to which the earth does in fact stand in the center of the universe.[18] It is also worth noting that Copernicus,

---

17. "The linguistically suggestive use of Copernicus' name has more hidden resources that touch specifically on what has just slipped from my pen as the relation to the true, namely, the emergence of the ellipse as being not unworthy of the locus from which the so-called higher truths take their name. The revolution is no less important for concerning only the 'celestial revolu-tions'" (E 295/33–38, EF 797).

18. "For if the work of Copernicus, as others have remarked before, is not as Copernican as is customarily believed, it is in this that the doctrine of double truth continues to offer shelter to a knowledge that until that time, it

in the best Platonic tradition, takes circular movement to be the most perfect. Just as the religious metaphysical model holds that the sun turns about the earth in a uniform circular motion, so in the mathematical "fiction" the motion of the earth as it turns about the sun is also uniformly circular. Consequently, circular motion dominates the mathematical fiction as much as it does the religious-metaphysical truth. The priority of circular motion is a metaphysical assumption that characterizes the whole system. Scientific knowledge and religious-metaphysical truth could peacefully coexist without ever coming into conflict.

After Kepler, this situation could continue no longer. The thought that heavenly bodies describe an elliptical path is at odds with one of the most fundamental metaphysical assumptions determining the work of Copernicus. Here knowledge comes into conflict with the truth, and the theory of double truth becomes untenable. Kepler's discoveries about the planetary laws of motion do not square with what was considered an essential property of reality as such, and knowledge (science) and metaphysical-religious truth can thus no longer be seen as simply existing alongside each other in an external manner.[19] The "Copernican revolution" unavoidably confronts humanity with the question of

---

must be said, had every appearance of being quite content with it" (E 296/4–7, EF 797).

19. "To stop at this stage [the introduction of the ellipse] no longer means simply revoking some idiotic notion deriving from the religious tradition [the theory of the double truth?], which, as can be seen well enough, is none the worse for it, but rather of binding more closely the régime of knowledge to the régime of truth. For if the work of Copernicus, as others remarked before, is not as Copernican as is customarily believed, it is in this that the doctrine of double truth continues to offer shelter to a knowledge that until that time, it must be said, has every appearance of being quite content with it" (E 295/39, 296/7, EF 797).

how knowledge and truth stand in relation to one another. If Freud can justifiably talk of a "Copernican revolution" in relation to psychoanalysis, then for Lacan this is precisely because and insofar as psychoanalysis similarly problematizes the relation between knowledge and truth in a novel way.[20] Let us see what Lacan means by this.

According to Lacan, philosophy as much as science has relentlessly striven to close any gap between knowledge and truth, or at least to make the gap appear merely accidental and provisional.[21] Once more, a reference to Hegelian philosophy can be

---

20. "Yet if the historical birth of science is still a sufficiently burning question for us to be aware that at that frontier [between knowledge and truth] a shift took place [in the transition from Copernicus to Kepler], it is perhaps there that psychoanalysis is marked out to represent an earthquake [in the relation between knowledge and truth] yet to come" (E 296/11–14, EF 797).

21. In what follows I limit myself to philosophy, since Lacan remains quite summary and allusive in relation to science. Just like philosophy, science has, according to Lacan, attempted to close as quickly as possible the gap between truth and knowledge (E 296/8–10, EF 797). Science always attempts to exclude any so-called subjective factor ("the abolished subject of science," E 297/15, EF 798). The subjectivity of the researcher plays no role in modern science, nor in principle ought it play any role. The subject is bracketed, as an interfering factor in the progressive development of science. The objectivity of scientific knowledge, on the contrary, guarantees its truth. Lacan's very summary discussion of scientific endeavor in "Subversion" is undoubtedly a reference to Heidegger's discussion of the same topic, for example in "The Age of the World-Picture," in Heidegger 1977. Modern science, Heidegger writes there, arises at the same time as the Cartesian *cogito*, which only accepts as true what it can represent (*Vor-stellen*) to itself. The certainty of representation becomes the ultimate yardstick of the truth. This implies that every "subjective deviation" in the usual sense of the word is from the very beginning excluded from the process of knowledge. Or better perhaps, from now on the subject possesses, at least in principle, an adequate criterion (the certainty of representation) by which it can neutralize such "subjective deviations." What the subject knows with certainty is true and vice versa. And as a result, any essential tension between truth and knowledge is denied.

instructive in understanding what Lacan intends here.[22] In the *Phenomenology of Spirit* every figure of consciousness is followed and replaced by a new figure of consciousness, until eventually absolute knowledge is attained. Every figure of consciousness is sooner or later confronted with its own incompleteness and internal contradictions. Consciousness is then required to take on a new form in order to adapt itself to the newly discovered truth. Thus the stoics, for example, believed in a purely internal freedom that is in no respect related to external reality. The interiority of consciousness and the external determination of reality are here thought, as it were, independently of each other. However, this is an untenable position, and sooner or later consciousness is required to abandon it. Consciousness must draw external reality into its own determination, but at the same time it does not want to give up its own freedom. Consciousness thus posits itself as skeptical consciousness; it replaces the absolute positivity of

---

22. "For let us look again from this angle at the service we expected from Hegel's phenomenology, for it represents an ideal solution—a solution, one might say, involving a permanent revisionism, in which truth is in a state of constant re-absorption in its own disturbing element, being in itself no more than that which is lacking for the realization of knowledge. The antinomy that the Scholastic tradition posed as a matter of principle is here taken to be resolved by virtue of being imaginary. Truth is nothing other than that which knowledge can apprehend as knowledge only by setting its ignorance to work. A real crisis in which the imaginary is resolved, thus engendering a new symbolic form, to use my own categories. This dialectic is convergent and attains the conjuncture defined as absolute knowledge. As such it is deduced, it can only be the conjunction of the symbolic with a real of which there is nothing more to be expected. What is this real, if not a subject fulfilled in his identity to himself? From which, one can conclude that this subject is already perfect in this regard, and is the fundamental hypothesis of this whole process. He is named, in effect, as being the substratum of this process; he is called *Selbstbewusstsein*, the being conscious of self, the fully conscious self" (E 296/15–33, EF 797–798).

thought with the infinity of negation. In this way the skeptic realizes that of which stoicism was only the concept, for true freedom of thought is never realized in an impotent apposition of thought and reality, but in the effective negation of the successive particular determinations with which consciousness is confronted. However, this skeptical position will also turn out to be inadequate. It is overcome in the "unhappy consciousness," which will itself in turn succumb to its own contradictions.[23] For Lacan, what is most important here is that in the *Phenomenology of Spirit,* knowledge (the way consciousness understands itself) is constantly disturbed by a truth that forces it to form itself into a new figure of consciousness. Truth and knowledge are not related to each other externally here, as in Copernicus's theory of double truth.[24] To the contrary, knowledge is driven forward from within by a truth that it does not yet know lies within

---

23. Lacan describes this process in the terms of his own theory as follows: ". . . a real crisis in which the imaginary is resolved, thus engendering a new symbolic form, to use my own categories" (E 296/23–25, EF 798). It belongs to the structure of every figure of consciousness to posit itself in the first moment as absolute, and so remain blind in the face of its own contradictions. In every figure of consciousness, consciousness believes itself for an instant to have reached its own truth. This unjustified belief in its own completeness is termed by Lacan the "imaginary." This misrecognition is, however, constantly broken up by the work of the truth ("a real crisis"), which leads to the formation of a new figure of consciousness ("a new symbolic form"). Lacan talks about a "symbolic form" because every figure of consciousness gives form to reality in some way. We shall later return to examine in more detail the terms "imaginary," "symbolic," and "real."

24. Lacan himself refers to the old scholastic idea that human reason can never completely grasp divine truth ("The antinomy which the Scholastic tradition posed as a matter of principle is here taken to be resolved by virtue of being imaginary" E 296/20–21, EF 798). By this, Lacan means that the partial or incomplete character of the separate figures of consciousness in Hegel's *Phänomenologie des Geistes* ("imaginary" because it goes together with

its reach.[25] Truth and knowledge are intrinsically interwoven in such a manner that knowledge will constantly incorporate the truth that disturbs it, until both are absorbed into each without remainder. Thus truth is the driving force of the process; truth carries knowledge towards its completion and forces it to adapt itself constantly.[26] According to Lacan, the absolute knowledge that is thus attained is like a symbolic system that expresses the essential structures of reality in its entirety. This final state cannot be described as anything other than perfect self-consciousness. Absolute knowledge is the subject that fully coincides with itself. What thus appears as the *telos* of the "science of experience of consciousness" must at the same time be thought of as its fundamental presupposition. The completely realized self-consciousness is inscribed from the beginning as the aim of the development of consciousness.[27]

---

a misconception of its partial character) is progressively overcome by the realization of an Absolute Knowledge. The opposition between knowledge and truth, which was a matter of principle for the scholastics, now appears to be simply a provisional ("imaginary") moment in a development directed towards its abolition.

25. "Truth is nothing other than that which knowledge can apprehend as knowledge only by setting its ignorance to work" (E 296/21–22, EF 798).

26. "[I]t represents an ideal solution—a solution, one might say, involving a permanent revisionism, in which truth is in a state of constant re-absorption in its own disturbing element [the truth disturbs knowledge, but is also constantly reabsorbed in it], being in itself no more than that which is lacking for the realization of knowledge" (E 296/16–19, EF 797). The last part here refers to the idea that for Hegel, there is no definitive and principle disparity between knowledge and truth. Precisely for this reason, the truth can be defined as that which knowledge (provisionally) lacks in order to be complete.

27. "This dialectic is convergent and attains the conjuncture defined as absolute knowledge. As such it is deduced, it can only be the conjunction of the symbolic with a real of which there is nothing more to be expected. What is this real, if not a subject fulfilled in his identity to himself? From which, one can conclude that this subject is already perfect in this regard, and

The significance of the Copernican revolution Freud effected can now be further determined.[28] We already said that according to Lacan, psychoanalytic orthodoxy as much as academic psychology wants to think psychic life primarily as, or in terms of, "adaptation."[29] This implies that both disciplines suppose an essential conformity between psychic life and the reality to which it must adapt itself. Psychic life and reality are in principle attuned to each other. Every disturbance to this relationship is secondary to the pre-given harmony, and can be removed and rendered harmless in principle if not in fact. In more Hegelian terms, we could also say that in principle, knowledge can always incorporate the truth that disturbs it. According to Lacan, then, neither psychoanalytic orthodoxy nor academic psychology recognizes a difference in principle between knowledge (psychic life) and the truth by which it is driven onward (the reality to which psychic life must adapt itself).[30]

---

is the fundamental hypothesis of this whole process. He is named, in effect, as being the substratum of this process; he is called *Selbstbewusstsein*, the being conscious of self, the fully conscious self" (E 296/25–33, EF 798).

28. "In any case, my double reference to Hegel's absolute subject and to the abolished subject of science provides the illumination necessary to an accurate formulation of Freud's dramatism: the reentry of truth into the field of science at the same time as it gains recognition in the field of its praxis: repressed, it reappears" (E 297/14–18, EF 798–799).

29. Thus, according to Lacan, psychoanalysis has nothing to gain by attempts to further develop metapsychology with the aid of concepts borrowed from academic psychology. Such lateral borrowings only serve to reinforce the already existing tendency to form psychoanalysis into an ideology of adaptation. In this way the Freudian heritage is simply misunderstood (E 297/9–13, EF 798).

30. Of course, this last point must be connected with the fact that academic psychology bends to the requirements of the other sciences, which, as we saw, seek to exclude any subjective factor.

Freud breaks radically with this paradigm of a primary accord between truth and knowledge. The experience of the unconscious makes this break necessary, for it forces us to postulate an essential difference between knowledge and the (unconscious) truth of the subject. More precisely, psychoanalysis teaches that knowledge can never completely neutralize that truth. The difference between the two is thus more than merely factical in nature; it is, rather, definitive for the very essence of subjectivity. Freud further connects this fundamental difference with the fact that the subject is in the grip of an unconscious truth it cannot control. The conflictual relation between truth and knowledge thus posited by Freudian psychoanalysis also forces us to reject any ideology of adaptation; human being is fundamentally ill-adapted or "out of joint." Between human being and its world yawns an unbridgeable gap.

Freud relates this fundamental impossibility of adaptation to the problematic of sexuality, which for him forms the core of the unconscious.[31] According to Freud, there is something in human sexuality that fundamentally disorders us, and makes of

---

31. "Who cannot see the distance that separates the unhappy consciousness—of which, however strongly it is engraven in Hegel, it can be said that it is still no more than the suspension of a corpus of knowledge—from the 'discontents of civilization' in Freud, even if it is only in a mere phrase, uttered as if disavowed, that marks for us what, on reading it, cannot be articulated otherwise than the 'skew' relation that separates the subject from sexuality?" (E 297/19–25, EF 799). The "unhappy consciousness" of Hegel's *Phänomenologie des Geistes* is constantly in search of itself, and yet never coincides with itself (with its own essence). Nevertheless, this impossibility is only transitory. It is only a provisional moment ("a suspension of a corpus of knowledge") that will be overcome in the further development of consciousness. What Freud writes about sexuality, however, is of another order. A disparity exists between the subject and sexuality ("the 'skew' relation that sepa-

us essentially maladapted beings, out of joint with the reality we live in. This disorder and maladaptation are precisely what fundamentally characterize us as human. In order to understand human being as human being we must start out from this disorder, and not from the problematic of adaptation, which in this perspective can only appear as at most secondary. According to Lacan, this is what is really at stake in Freud's "Copernican revolution." It is also the ultimate meaning of Lacan's subversion of the subject.

Freud's insight that the unconscious is fundamentally sexual implies that the content of the unconscious points to nothing other than our bodily existence. We also know, however, that Lacan connects the unconscious with language. How can these two insights—that the unconscious is of the order of language, and that it is also bodily and sexual—be reconciled with each other? How does this problematic fit with what we have called Freud's "Copernican revolution"? And what are the consequences of this for psychoanalytic theory and practice? These are the questions we will try to answer in this book.

---

rates the subject from sexuality") and it essentially disorders the subject. For Lacan this is the core of Freud's message, even if it seems that Freud cannot formulate this message without immediately taking away its force ("a mere phrase, uttered as if disavowed"). In *Civilization and Its Discontents* (1930) Freud does indeed write, "Sometimes one seems to perceive that it is not only the presence of civilization but something in the nature of the function itself which denies us full satisfaction and urges us along other paths." However, Freud immediately adds what seems to be a disavowal of the previous claim: "This may be wrong, it is hard to decide" (p. 105). The idea that "there is no sexual relation" is probably already at work in the background of Lacan's argument here. We will return to this notion later.

1

The Primacy of the Symbolic and the Unconscious

FREUD AND LACAN ON THE UNCONSCIOUS AND LANGUAGE

Lacan's best known thesis, and the one for which he won fame far beyond strictly psychoanalytic milieus, is undoubtedly this: "The unconscious is a chain of (linguistic) signifiers."[1] And indeed, Lacan never stops repeating that the unconscious is of the order of language. This idea, he continues, is as much in agreement with the basic theses of the *oeuvre* Freud bequeathed us as it is with psychoanalytic experience. Of course, Lacan is conscious that this idea as such cannot be found in Freud's texts. In fact, the very opposite is the case: for Freud language belongs to the (pre-)conscious system, and the unconscious is characterized by the absence of linguistic structures. According to Freud (1915), the unconscious consists of *Sachvorstellungen* (thing-presentations), which have to be strictly distinguished from *Wortvorstellungen* (word-presentations). We turn first to a clarification of this essential distinction in Freud.

According to Freud, clinical experience teaches us that the unconscious and its products (dreams, symptoms, etc.) do not know the test of reality. Who has not chuckled on reading, in Freud's *Traumdeutung*, about the little boy who dreams that he

---

1. "Since Freud the unconscious has been a chain of signifiers that somewhere (on another stage, in another scene, he wrote) is repeated, and insists on interfering in the breaks offered it by the effective discourse and the cogitation that it informs" (E 297/34–37, EF 799). We will comment upon the second part of this sentence later on in our text.

urinates against a wall with such enthusiasm that a whole lake is formed behind him (Freud 1900, p. 368)? The dream clearly takes no notice of the fact that such a feat is not possible in reality. In the same way, one of Freud's analysands can dream unperturbed that Freud has a trunk (Freud 1900, p. 413).[2] The dream takes no notice of the fact that in humans such an appendage is anatomically impossible. From such data Freud infers that the unconscious, of which the dream (but also, for example, the symptom) is the deformed translation, knows no reference to reality. According to him, the unconscious consists of "thing-presentations." By this he means presentations or psychic inscriptions that do not, as it were, *present* anything—presentations that are not intentionally directed to a reality outside of us. In other words, they are not presentations *of* something else, to which they refer.[3] In a certain sense, then, the unconscious refers only to itself, without taking account of external reality. For Freud, this explains why the productions of the unconscious sometimes seem so bizarre to waking life. Given that the conscious ego always implicitly takes account of reality, what arises from the unconscious can only appear to this ego as unusual and extravagant.

According to Freud, the reference to reality only comes into being at the level of the (pre-)conscious system. Moreover, this reference cannot be thought apart from the connection between "thing-" and "word-" presentations that comes about precisely in this system. "Thing-presentations" take on intentional character as a result of this connection with language. For Freud,

---

2. We will return later to examine this dream more fully.

3. In fact, Freud writes *Sachvorstellungen* not *Vorstellungen der Sache*. The latter would mean that the unconscious presentations still refer to reality. On this point, see Vergote 1997, p. 77ff.

language unavoidably and structurally speaks *about* something—something which is not itself language, and which, for the time being, we have somewhat uncritically termed "reality beyond ourselves." In this context we can turn back to the analysand who dreamt that Freud had a trunk. It is possible that the analysand, while dreaming the dream (i.e., before consciously remembering this dream), had little or no difficulty with such a remarkable phenomenon. Once the dreamer has woken, however, this dream-presentation will inevitably appear impossible, for in waking life this presentation is subject to the structuring of language that brings with it the reference to outside reality. In that reality, only elephants have trunks.

Against this, one could object that Freud compared the dream with a rebus, in which every picture can be replaced by a word. Freud also seems to understand the formation of the dream in terms of linguistic metaphors such as "translation" (of unconscious ideas into dream images [Freud 1900]). Moreover, the dream is not the unconscious itself, but a product of the unconscious, which arises on the border between the unconscious and the pre-conscious system. How then can we claim that the dream teaches us that the unconscious does not recognize language? Freud's answer to this question is clear. Even if the dream employs language to express the unconscious (one thinks, for example, of the comparison of the dream with a rebus), it does so by treating words as things. The dream employs words in their sheer materiality—and thus independently of their referential potential—in order to connect the elements of the dream. Thus, it is not without significance that the analysand who dreamt that Freud had a trunk was originally French-speaking. In French the word for "trunk" is *trompe*, which refers to *tromper*, to deceive. According to Freud, the dream expresses the following (transferential) meaning: *Vous* [Freud] *me trompez* ("You

[Freud] are deceiving me"). The connection between *trompe* and *tromper* arises simply on the basis of the material similarity between the words. If the dream thus employs language to bring the unconscious to expression, then one must immediately add that here, according to Freud, language is too much under the influence of the primary processes of the unconscious to fulfill its referential role. For Freud, this means that language does not yet function as language in the proper sense here: the unconscious does not know language, and nor therefore does it know the test of reality.

This short exposition of Freud allows us to understand the sense in which it is not part of the Freudian legacy, in the strict sense, to claim that the unconscious belongs to the order of language. At the same time, it shows us that this discussion is perhaps more complicated than it seems at first sight, and indicates which of Freud's texts Lacan bases himself on in calling his insights "Freudian." Let us start with this last point, and once more take the dream of Freud's French-speaking analysand as our example. The trunk is an image that seems to be produced by the signifier *trompe*. Lacan then asks: How could this signifier bring about this effect, if it were not already in some sense present in the unconscious and at work there? This question goes closely together with the question of precisely what we understand language to be. In other words, is not Freud's rejection of the linguistic character of the unconscious codetermined by a specific conception of language, a conception that in turn must be subjected to critical inquiry?[4] Now, not only is it clear for Lacan that Freud's ideas on language are untenable; he is also convinced

---

4. It is certainly not our intention here to investigate Freud's conception of language *in extenso*. We merely want to throw some light on the particular logic of Lacan's interpretation of Freud.

that the ideas of structural linguistics would have put Freud in a position to formulate the thesis that the unconscious is of the order of language for himself, without having to fundamentally adjust his ideas on the unconscious. According to Lacan, the structural linguistics of de Saussure (1978), Benvéniste (1966), and Jakobson (1963) allows us in a certain sense to understand Freud better than he understood himself. It makes it possible to see that Freud's fundamental insights are not in direct conflict with the idea that the unconscious must be understood as a "chain of signifiers."

A FEW GENERAL REMARKS ON LACAN'S THEORY OF LANGUAGE[5]

The unconscious, according to Lacan, has to be understood as a chain of signifiers. The central term in this definition is of course, *the signifier*. This term has to be understood in an active sense:

---

5. We do not wish to give an exhaustive commentary on Lacan's theory of language, any more than Freud's. For this we refer the reader to the literature. Here, we limit ourselves to what is strictly necessary in order to clarify "Subversion." In this regard, we want chiefly to make clear how Lacan can identify the primary processes of the unconscious with linguistic processes. To this end we draw our inspiration from the following paragraph from "Subversion": "In this formula, which is mine only in the sense that it conforms as closely to Freud's text as to the experience that it opened up, the crucial term is the signifier, brought back to life from the ancient art of rhetoric by modern linguistics, in a doctrine whose various stages cannot be traced here, but of which the names of Ferdinand de Saussure and Roman Jakobson will stand for the dawn and its present-day culmination, not forgetting that the pilot science of structuralism in the West has its roots in Russia, where formalism first flourished. 'Geneva 1910' and 'Petrograd 1920' suffice to explain why Freud lacked this particular tool. But this defect of history makes all the more

the (linguistic) signifier must be thought of as something that cuts actively into something else that is not yet structured, in the strict sense, and in so doing gives rise to meaning. A few examples will illuminate this idea. It is known that Lacan attaches great importance to fatherhood, and to what he calls the "Name-of-the-Father" (Lacan 1957–58, pp. 180–181; E 310/24–29, EF 813). But what is a father? At first sight it seems the answer to this question is readily available. Is not the father simply the begetter of the child? Nevertheless, it would appear from anthropological research that the matter is somewhat more complicated than we usually think. Certain primitive tribes ascribe pregnancy not to coitus with this or that man, for example, but rather to an encounter with spirits in an out-of-the-way place. One need not infer from this that the members of the tribe have no notion of the connection between coitus and pregnancy. This seems rather unlikely. What is at stake here is not so much the question of whether the members of the tribe do or do not know that there can be no pregnancy without coitus, but rather that of whether there exists in the symbolic system a signifier that expresses the idea that the one with whom the woman has coitus is also the father of the child that she bears. In other words, it turns out that the connection between procreation and fatherhood is decided on the level of the

---

instructive the fact that the mechanisms described by Freud as those of the 'primary process,' in which the unconscious assumes its rule, correspond exactly to the functions that this school believes determines [sic] the most radical aspects of the effects of language, namely metaphor and metonymy—in other words, the signifier's effects of substitution and combination on the respectively synchronic and diachronic dimensions in which they appear in discourse" (E 297/38, 298/14, EF 799–800). In what follows we leave out of consideration Lacan's relationship to structural linguistics and Russian formalism, because this would lead us too far from our path and deserves a separate study. For more information on this point see Broekman 1973.

symbolic system; it is a question of whether there is a signifier in the symbolic system that articulates this connection. According to Lacan, it follows from this that the signifier is not merely the reproduction of a previously given order. On the contrary, it actively institutes a function—fatherhood—that clearly cannot be directly derived from the facts of experience.

A second example[6] might further clarify the meaning and importance of the signifier—the distinction between "man" and "woman." Few will want to contest that there is indeed such a distinction. Nevertheless, if we try to found this difference exclusively in reality, we will be disappointed. As much as we might endeavor to justify this distinction in terms of various feelings, patterns of thinking, and so on, we will never find anything more than *gradual* differences. Yet we are not a bit "man" and a bit "woman" (or vice versa), but either "man" or "woman"—we are one or the other. This absolute difference does not exist in (lived) reality, which knows only gradual distinctions. Even a reference to biological data is of little help here. Certainly, it is difficult to deny that relevant biological differences exist between "men" and "women," but even these differences seem to offer no satisfactory explanation for the fact that we admit, *without hesitation*, to belonging to one or the other category. That I am a "man" or a "woman"—the one or the other—is not a pure biological given. On the contrary, such a strict order, on the basis of which we have simply to "choose" one or the other category, only comes about when the symbolic system "impresses" itself, as it were, upon (biological) reality and upon lived experience. The strict difference between "man" and "woman" comes to us from lan-

---

6. In what follows we give as an example of signifiers the words "man," "woman," etc. Later we will have to nuance this. Signifiers are not in the first place words, but the significant differences that are articulated by phonology.

guage, as do all other distinctions by which reality is for us ordered and receives its meaning (for example, the distinction between human and animal, between human and gods, etc.). In Lacan's terms, these distinctions come to us from the order of signifiers, and they must therefore be understood as an actively structuring principle. Lacan has a name for this articulated system of differential (linguistic) distinctions that lays down for us the law in accordance with which we can perceive reality as meaningful: *the symbolic*. The symbolic is the order of language and of the law.[7] Lacan often calls this order *the Other* (*l'Autre*).[8]

Thus it also becomes clear why we said, in our exposition of Freud above, that the expression "reality outside of us" requires further consideration, and cannot simply be accepted as it stands. The world in which we carry on our everyday existence is always already structured by the signifiers of language. The world in which we shape our lives receives its form from our expectations, intentions, representations, and so on, and these are themselves structured in turn by the symbolic systems that determine us (for example, in articulating the difference between man and woman). At the very least, then, the opposition between language and the thing about which it speaks is more complex than we suggested above, and than Freud sometimes seems to think. The world about which we speak and in which we live is no "brute" reality; it is itself already mediated and structured by the signifiers of language,

---

7. Later we will specify this as the law of the father.

8. The term "Other" in Lacan does not refer exclusively to the order of language and the law as such. Lacan also often uses this term to indicate the unconscious. For the unconscious is also of the order of language. Furthermore, he also calls other "persons" *l'Autre* insofar as they represent the order of language and the law.

which allow it to appear as a meaningful and differentiated environment (*Umwelt*).

The signifier actively institutes meaning. Language does not simply reflect reality; it is not the expression of a previously given order. The reality in which we carry on our existence must, on the contrary, be understood in a pregnant sense as the effect of the order of signifiers. In this context, Lacan points out that signifiers are essentially determined diacritically or differentially. In other words, they signify primarily on the basis of their difference from other signifiers and not, for example, by referring to a non-linguistic reality. Let us return to our example of the difference between "man" and "woman." It is clear that the signifier "man" only has meaning as opposed to the signifier "woman"—for what could "man" mean without "woman"? The signifiers "man" and "woman" receive further meaning from a complex network of references in which signifiers such as "human," "animal," and "plant," for example, hold a central place. The meaning of a signifier is in the first place dependent upon the linguistic context of which it is a part. Moreover, the fact that a signifier only receives meaning from a complex network of signitive references immediately implies, for Lacan, that the meaning of a signifier changes according to the context in which it is taken up. When an analysand says in an analytical session, *Je vais à la mer* ("I am going to the sea"), the analyst might hear, *Je vais à la mère* ("I am going to the mother"), basing her interpretation on other associations that the analysand has formulated in the course of this or other sessions. A second example can perhaps make the point somewhat clearer. Some years ago, for professional reasons, I opened a bank account in Holland, and the bank clerk asked if I had any "titles." I replied that I did, but immediately added that I wanted to keep them in Belgium, where I was living at the time. The man looked at me strangely, and asked me if the "titles" were not valid in Holland. After a bit of talking back and forth, it turned out that he had meant academic titles, while I, because of my Belgian background, had understood "titles" in the sense of the French *titres* ("financial securities").[9] Just as the associative context determined the meaning of the signifier *mer/mère* ("sea"/"mother") in the first example, so here the meaning of the signifier "title" changes depending on whether it is to be understood in an academic context or an economic one. The production of meaning is thus in principle a process that cannot be closed off. There is no ultimate context that could, as it were, embrace all contexts and so bring the production of meaning to completion.

To some extent, we can also understand now why Lacan says that his thesis "the unconscious consists of a chain of signifiers" is in agreement with the basic theses of the Freudian *oeuvre*. According to Freud, the unconscious is not of the order of language because the unconscious does not know any reference to reality, and it is precisely language that introduces this reference. Lacan's differential definition of the signifier, however, implies that language cannot be understood primarily as a reference to a reality outside of it, as Freud had thought. On the contrary, the meaning of a term is determined by its place *in the system*; it is the product of the "play of signifiers." Just as the Freudian "thing-presentations" combine with each other and generate effects without taking reality into account, so too the Lacanian "play of signifiers" is not determined by

---

9. [To understand this example the reader should know that both the author and the bank clerk were speaking Dutch. The confusion arose because more legal terms derived from French are used in the Dutch spoken in Belgium (Flemish)—Trans.]

a self-sufficient, pre-given referent. Both the Freudian and the Lacanian unconscious, as it were, put external reality out of play.

However, Lacan goes still a step further. According to Freud, the primary processes of the unconscious are governed by two fundamental mechanisms: *condensation* and *displacement*. According to Lacan, condensation and displacement can be understood according to the models of *metaphor* and *metonymy* respectively. Or better, displacement is a metonymical process and condensation is a metaphorical process. Lacan believes that in this way, a linguistic status can be ascribed to the unconscious without breaking with the fundamental characteristics by which Freud tries to understand it. Let us unpack this idea a little further.

According to Freud, condensation and displacement are the two fundamental principles that determine the activity of the unconscious. They are at work in all the formations of the unconscious (the symptom, slips of the tongue, etc.), though Freud described them chiefly in relation to dreams. *Condensation* refers to the fact that one simple dream image can represent several associative chains at the same time. So, for example, it often happens that a certain figure in a dream turns out on closer analysis to represent several persons. I dream about my brother, but in the course of the analysis it turns out that my brother represents not only himself, but also an older sister and a childhood friend. *Displacement*, on the other hand, refers to the fact that presentations that seem at first sight like details, insignificant for the meaning of a dream, often in fact stand in for a complex course of ideas decisive for its interpretation. For example, there might appear in a dream a completely unknown man with just the sort of beard that my father had when I was a child. What seems initially unimportant (the beard) might, on closer inspection, be decisive for the understanding of the dream (the beard evokes my father and my complex relationship with him).

Thus the Freudian principles of displacement and condensation. How, then, does Lacan bring these two principles into relation with metaphor and metonymy respectively? We already know that according to Lacan, language is a differential network of signifiers that refers in the first place to itself. Meaning is an effect of language, and not vice versa. Metaphor and metonymy must therefore be understood primarily as relations between signifiers as such. They cannot, according to Lacan, be founded in the signified, or in a self-sufficient referent that can explain the signified. We shall address metonymy first.

According to Lacan, *metonymical* processes are related to the way signifiers are linked together within a common, contiguous context. Very generally, one could say that metonymy indicates one and the same object with another word, which nevertheless belongs to the same semantic context. In his article "The Agency of the Letter in the Unconscious" (Lacan 1957a), in which he presents his theory of language in a systematic manner, Lacan gives the following example of metonymy: "thirty sails" standing for "thirty ships" (p. 156; see also EF 601). In the expression "thirty ships," "ships" is replaced by "sails" on the basis of the fact that both terms belong to the same semantic context. In the expression "to be on the couch," "on the couch" stands for "in psychoanalysis"; the signifiers are here connected in a new way on the basis of the fact that "couch" and "psychoanalysis" belong to the same contiguous context. Finally, the expression "I am having a glass," for example, is a metonymy that stands for "I am drinking a glass of beer." Here, too, it is the semantic proximity that allows the signifiers to be linked together in a new way, so that one and the same referent is signified by more than one word.

According to Lacan, then, no new meaning arises in metonymy; the signified of the original and the metonymical expression remain the same, because the signifiers that refer to it are bound to each other through a relation of contiguity.[10] However, we may not conclude from this that a metonymical link between signifiers can simply be traced back to a link in reality outside of language. The connection between signifiers is not governed by a self-sufficient referent. Thus, for example, when we replace "thirty ships" with thirty sails, this does not guarantee that in actuality we will also see "thirty sails"; ships can very well have more than one sail. The connection between the two signifiers is therefore not governed by the self-sufficient presence of the signified, something that, as we saw, is rendered impossible in any case by the differential determination of the signifier. Signifiers signify only by force of their difference from other signifiers.

This implies that in the final instance there are no positive terms in language. Every signifier is only a moment in an endless series, and it will (must) be supplemented by still other signifiers, which again and again fail to definitively determine the signified. For our example, this means that since the replacement of "ship" by "sail" cannot be founded in reality without remainder, there will always be new signifiers necessary to express the referent "ship." According to Lacan, metonymy thus refers to a general property of language, by virtue of which every signifier is necessarily followed by another. There is no ultimate signifier that can bring this movement to an end, and every manifestation of meaning is limited and incomplete.

---

10. This contiguity can take various forms: part-whole, cause-effect, contents-container, and so forth.

Lacan therefore connects metonymy with the diachronic dimension of language, for metonymy points to a linking of signifiers that in principle unrolls in time.[11]

How, then, does Lacan understand *metaphor*? Very generally, metaphor refers to a process of substitution by which two signifiers from two *heterogeneous* semantic fields are substituted for each other. Thus, the expression "John is a real lion," in which the signifier "lion" takes the place of the signifier "courageous," is a metaphor. Traditionally, this process of metaphorization is often understood in the following way: one signifier ("courageous") is crossed out, and another signifier ("lion") is put in its place—that is, the second signifier is linked with the signified of the signifier that has disappeared. Thus, according to this traditional vision, metaphor in fact says the same thing as the original expression, but in another way. Lacan flatly rejects this conception; metaphor does not say the same thing in a different manner. "John is a lion" says something more and something other than "John is courageous." Let us see why.

We know that there is always one signifier too few to definitively determine the signified, so that the signified is never a finished, identifiable identity. It is therefore impossible for the signified to function as the sufficient ground of the metaphorical substitution of two signifiers. The metaphorical term (in our example, "lion") does not replace a signifier that could be used literally in its place—indeed, the differential character of the signifiers makes the determination of a literal mean-

---

11. Cf. ". . . metaphor and metonymy—in other words, the signifier's effects of substitution and combination on the respectively synchronic and diachronic dimensions in which they appear in discourse" (E 298/12–14, EF 800; see n. 5 for the whole passage).

ing impossible. As a result, the expression "John is a lion" can never be completely reduced to the expression "John is courageous," nor does the latter expression express the actual and true (literal) meaning of the metaphor "John is a lion." The metaphor, as a result, creates a new meaning irreducible to the original.[12]

In "The Agency of the Letter in the Unconscious" Lacan offers the following example of metaphor from Hugo: *Sa gerbe n'était pas avare, ni haineuse* ("His sheaf was neither miserly nor spiteful" [Lacan 1957a; E 156–157, EF 506–507]). Here "sheaf" stands for "Boaz," the farmer from the Old Testament book of Ruth. The tradition deals with this metaphor in terms of the substituted term ("Boaz") and seeks an equivalence of meaning between "Boaz" and "sheaf." Lacan, however, takes the expression as it is written. At first sight the expression seems to be absolutely meaningless; no sheaf ever showed any emotions. This apparent lack of meaning, however, gives back to the signifiers their full signifying force. In this manner it creates a signifying effect that can in no way be recuperated, that is, cannot be traced back to another expression that would give its literal meaning. Nothing predisposes the signifier "sheaf" to take the place of "Boaz," but once this substitution is made, an underivable meaning arises. In this way, metaphor points to the potential of (the system of) signifiers to autonomously break through constituted meanings—independent of any reference to a previously given signified—and so say something completely new. This last point

---

12. If no signifier has a fixed meaning on the basis of which the metaphorical substitution can be explained and authorized, then for Lacan this also means that metaphor can only be defined as the *sheer* substitution, grounded only in itself, of one signifier by another.

makes it clear why Lacan relates metaphor to the synchronic dimension of language.[13] Metaphor does not relate to the way in which signifiers are coupled with each other, but to the potential of (the system of) the signifier to disorder every constituted connection and meaning.

We can now also understand why and how Lacan links condensation with metaphor and displacement with metonymy. Condensation has the consequence that an element in a dream turns out on closer inspection to stand for several elements at once. It is not a question here of how the elements of the dream are linked together, but of the fact that one dream image represents several images from several contexts articulating the life of the analysand. This process then is more metaphoric in nature.[14] Displacement, on the other hand, refers to the fact that an apparently unimportant detail can represent a complex se-

---

13. ". . . metaphor and metonymy—in other words, the signifier's effects of substitution and combination on the respectively synchronic and diachronic dimensions in which they appear in discourse" (E 298/12–14, EF 800; see n. 5).

14. Of course, I would not want to claim that the equation of metaphor with condensation and metonymy with displacement is in any sense self-evident. I want only to make the logic of Lacan's argumentation somewhat clearer. For example, It remains very much a question whether Freud could assent to Lacan's thesis that in condensation / metaphor a new meaning arises. On the contrary, according to Freud, condensation brings a pre-existing latent dream-idea to expression in a concealed fashion. Consequently, the art of interpretation consists in bringing this latent dream-idea to the surface and so "undoing" the condensation, as it were. Such a reading of interpretation is excluded from the first in the Lacanian conception of metaphor: the meaning that arises here is irreducible to a previously given signified. This problematic is undoubtedly related to the problem of the status of interpretation. In this regard we can perhaps formulate the following hypothesis: Freud interprets more on the level of the meaning, while Lacanian interpretation refers rather to the level of the "pure" signifier abstracted from its possible meanings. More generally,

ries of ideas. One might think of the example of the beard of my father, which I mentioned above. The substitution here comes about through the fact that both elements (father-beard) stand in a relation of proximity within one and the same context. Displacement is thus more of the order of metonymy.

Before passing over to the next section, in which we shall take up the "elementary cell" (*cellule élémentaire*) of Lacan's "graph of desire," I want to give one more brief, concrete illustration of Lacan's abstract theory of language, and of his idea that the unconscious is of the order of the signifier. Freud tells the story of an obsessive neurotic man who was fascinated by black beetles, which he dared not pick up. When he was a child, there lived with his family a maid whose few words of French included the expression *Que faire?* ("What are you doing?"). Freud drew a connection between the French *Que faire?* and the German *Käfer* ("beetle"), which turns out to also be used as a pet name for a woman. According to Lacan, the symptom is thus determined by a signifier that generates effects in its sheer materiality. *Que faire* is replaced by *Käfer,* which in turn means "beetle" and is used as a pet name for a woman. What Freud calls a "condensation" (various associative chains coming together in the anxiety about beetles) Lacan interprets as a metaphor; two signifiers from two heterogeneous contexts are substituted for each other on the basis of their simple material similarity, and in this way are responsible for the formation of the symptom.

---

it is clear that the Freudian conception of condensation is more a matter of the "contraction" of various elements (for example, a figure in a dream that is a collection of characteristics of different figures) than a metaphor in the strict linguistic sense.

THE ELEMENTARY CELL OF THE GRAPH OF DESIRE: THE SYMBOLIC AND THE REAL

The previous section made it somewhat clearer what Lacan means when he claims that the signifier determines our existence and gives it form. How, then, should we think of the fundamental relationship between the subject and language? Lacan articulates this relationship in a particularly striking way in what he calls the "elementary cell" of the *graph of desire*. Lacan has good reason here to speak of an *elementary* cell, for the theoretical decisions this cell contains are determinative for the further construction of the graph. It is thus in our interest to dwell in detail on this first building block of the graph, with the aim of bringing its full theoretical scope to light.[15]

Lacan draws the "elementary cell" of his graph as follows:

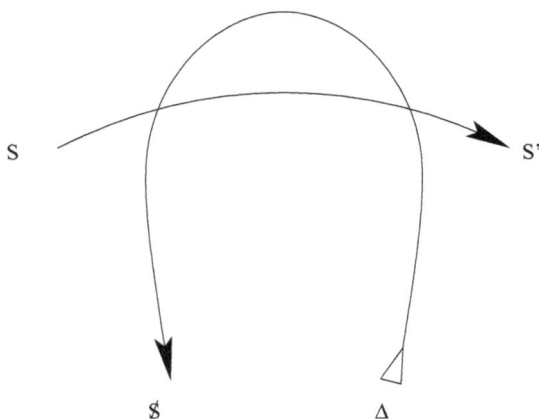

---

15. "This is what might be said to be its elementary cell. . . . In it is articulated what I have called the 'anchoring point' (*point de capiton*), in which the signifier stops the otherwise endless movement (*glissement*) of the signi-

Here Δ refers to the mythic moment in which the subject still has not entered the order of language—the human being as a simple being of needs, with vague, unstructured presentations (of hunger and thirst, light and dark, warm and cold, etc.) that are as such not yet taken up in the order of language and meaning. Lacan writes in this regard of "the mass of the pre-text, namely, the reality that is imagined in the ethological schema of the return of need." Elsewhere, Lacan speaks of "the flux of lived experiences" (*le flux du vécu*; Lacan 1956–57, p. 48); the immediacy of the experience of myself in relation to the environment, prior to any linguistic mediation. Δ, in other words, refers to the pure movement of life.

This notion of a "subject" that still swims in the stream of the pre-textual already allows us to some degree to address a second basic category of Lacanian thinking. We already know that the symbolic is the order of language and of the law. We also know that language, as a system of differentially determined signifiers, does not allow for a closure of the production of meaning. This implies that something is left out of every linguistic formulation, something that cannot be taken up in this order. By definition, every linguistic formulation leaves over something that cannot be integrated into the order of the symbolic. Lacan speaks in this regard of the *real*, which structurally resists any recuperation into the world of meaning. By

---

fication. The signifying chain is regarded as being supported by the vector $\overrightarrow{S.S'}$.—even without entering into the subtleties of the retrograde direction in which its double intersection with the vector $\overrightarrow{\Delta.\mathcal{S}}$ occurs. Only in this vector does one see the fish it hooks, a fish less suitable in its free movement to represent what it withholds from our grasp than the intention that tries to bury it in the mass of the pre-text, namely, the reality that is imagined in the ethological schema of the return of need" (E 303/8–17, EF 805).

extension, the human being simply as a being of needs, prior to entering the order of signifiers, can also be called *real*. The real must further be distinguished from what we usually understand by the term "reality"; this last category refers to the reality in which we carry on our everyday existence, and, as we earlier emphasized, that reality is essentially structured by the symbolic.[16]

We described the starting point of the "elementary cell" of the graph as "mythic" because, according to Lacan, the subject is in a manner of speaking "always already" taken up in the order of the symbolic. Even before our birth we are spoken about. Parents-to-be constantly fantasize about their unborn child: they talk about the name that they will give it, often even before it is conceived; they express expectations and anxieties about its future; or they discuss at length the way they will bring it up, partly in light of their own experience. This is more than mere idle fantasy. Not only is the child thereby taken up in the discourse of its parents before it even begins its biological existence, but also—and most importantly—the way in which the parental discourse functions will be determinative for its future. Our place in the symbolic system is already decided, to a large degree, before we are born. It is not something we can freely distance ourselves from, or something we can just lay aside. On the contrary, it is crucial in giving form to our existence—indeed, in a certain sense it *is* this existence itself. One might think, for example, of the situation of a child who bears the name of a famous forefather, and is invested with all sorts of expectations that this name immediately evokes for the parents as much as the child.

---

16. And the imaginary, as we shall later see in more detail.

All this, however, takes nothing away from the theoretical importance of the "elementary cell" of the graph, in which Lacan seems (forced) to presume a sort of pre-subject that has not yet entered the order of language. Quite to the contrary, this elementary cell throws light on a presupposition of Lacanian thought— a presupposition that would otherwise perhaps remain concealed, but the importance of which it is difficult to overestimate. This presupposition concerns the relationship between body and language, or better, the initial exteriority of the body with respect to language. We can make this even clearer by pursuing our discussion of the "elementary cell" of the graph in the light of the passage that we have been dealing with.[17]

The human being as a being of needs (Δ) cannot express its needs other than through language. For in order to satisfy needs we require the help of the Other, who will herself immediately interpret the utterances of the child in terms of the order of signifiers. When a child cries, the mother says, "She must be hungry," "She needs a fresh diaper," or "She is unhappy." In the elementary cell of the *graph* this concatenation of signifiers is represented by the vector $\overrightarrow{S.S'}$. In this context, Lacan compares the pre-linguistic subject that inscribes itself in language to a fisherman, who casts a fishing-line (the vector $\Delta.\$$) into the world of language ($\overrightarrow{S.S'}$) and, as it were, "catches" a signifier ("the fish it hooks").[18]

The articulation of the needs is not, however, a neutral operation. Rather, language introduces a clear and articulated structure into the more or less confused sensations and feelings

---

17. See n. 15.
18. It perhaps makes more sense within this metaphor to say that the fish (signifier) bites the line (actively). For needs are primarily named by the Other. It would thus seem to be a matter of an active structuring of the needs.

by which the needs at first manifest themselves. Anyone who has followed a wine-tasting course knows that a significant part of the course content consists in learning to give a name to the various flavors that one tastes when drinking wine.[19] Once one has this skill in hand, one very soon notices that the names rebound upon how and what one tastes. The wine connoisseur tastes more and tastes otherwise than the normal untrained person. Of course, the latter nonetheless also notices differences between different sorts of wine. However, the capacity to also be able to clearly articulate these differences in language gives the tasting a quality it did not possess of itself, and that cannot be derived directly from the immediate experience.[20] According to Lacan, the expression of needs in the order of language and culture leads to a diversification and multiplication that cannot be entirely explained by biology. Similarly, for example, humans are not only in search of a sufficient number of calories in order to survive, and perhaps not even primarily so. One look at the menu of any restaurant suffices to confirm that the demand for food is very diversified, and goes far beyond the level of biological functionality.

"Δ" indicates the human being as a being of needs that seeks satisfaction; it indicates the pure movement of life. In the first moment, this being wants nothing more than to return to the state that existed before the needs manifested themselves ("the intention that tries to bury it—the signifier—in the mass of the pre-

---

19. I am indebted to Fons van Coillie for this example.

20. This example, of course, ties up perfectly with what was said above about fatherhood in certain "primitive" cultures. Coitus gets a different meaning as soon as it is brought into relation with fatherhood; it does not have this meaning of itself. Consequently, the signifier introduces something new, which cannot be derived directly from the biological order. The same applies, as we have already seen, to the distinction between "man" and "woman."

text"). It simply seeks satisfaction.[21] However, the being of needs unavoidably encounters language (the vector $\overrightarrow{S.S'}$) along its way ("its free movement"), which subsumes its needs in a dynamic that cannot be reduced to biological necessity and often takes no account of it. Consequently, the relation between language and body is characterized by an essential exteriority. More specifically, the relation between these two orders cannot be thought of as a relation of expression; the symbolic is not the translation of a pre-given natural order. On the contrary, for Lacan language is like an alien body that grafts itself onto the order of the body and of nature.[22]

---

21. According to Lacan, this intention is presented in a far more striking manner by the vector $\overrightarrow{\Delta.S}$ than that which withdraws through the movement from Δ to S ("what it withholds from our grasp"; E 303/15, EF 805). Here Lacan seems to mean the real; once it has been marked by the order of signifiers, the subject only has access to itself by means of language, and henceforth can only appear to itself in language. The "real" subject—the subject as it exists in itself, independently of linguistic mediation—is irrevocably lost.

22. But exactly how "alien"? Already in the foregoing the ambiguity of some of Lacan's formulations has emerged, at least implicitly. Does language introduce a completely new order, one in no way determined by external reality, or does the order that is introduced by language and by the symbolic fit in with what is pre-given, without, however, being reducible to it? Thus one can, for example, say that the *absoluteness* of the difference between "man" and "woman" is an effect of the symbolic, but it seems to be much more difficult to say that this difference *per se* is in no way dependent upon the biological reality that it orders. The stakes in this debate are not insignificant. If we say that language imposes an order upon the biological and the real in a completely autonomous fashion, then it follows from this that the "movement of life" in no way extends to the production of meaning. In the other case— language recalibrates, in an irreducible way, meanings that were already formed in an inchoate way in the "movement of life"—we have to say that language is both an extension of bodiliness and a break from it. This last possibility would, however, substantially relativize the exteriority of language to the body, which would still seem to be one of Lacan's basic assumptions. We will return to this problematic in our conclusion.

We now understand, further, why the two vectors of the elementary cell of the graph have a different direction, and why they cross each other twice ("the retrograde direction in which its double intersection with the vector $\overrightarrow{\Delta.\$}$ occurs").[23] Language is not simply the extension of the world of immediate experience ("the stream of experience") and of needs. The symbolic follows a peculiar dynamic, which cannot be derived from biological reality or from the immediacy of experience. Accordingly, the two vectors do not follow the same direction—rather they intersect one another. By inscribing itself in language in this way, the being of needs becomes a subject. This subject, however, is essentially a split or crossed-out subject that can never coincide with itself ($\$$). As soon as the subject is marked by the signifier, every determination of it leaves a remainder; the subject as subject of the signifier—and strictly speaking there is no other—never simply coincides with itself. This implies that access to the immediacy of the "stream of experience" is denied to the subject once and for all. As subject of the signifier, all the subject can do is to strive after this lost immediacy from within the order of language, and all it achieves by this is to re-establish its own partition (Van Haute 1998). The exteriority of language with respect to the body takes on an extra dimension; not only is language not the extension of the body, but the entry into the order of language must always be understood as a loss. This loss can be made up for in very different ways on the level of phantasy,[24] but inevitably these can only refer to the idea

---

23. The double intersection also points to the problem of the "anchoring point," which we still have to discuss further.

24. We write "on the level of the phantasy" because we have never really known this completeness and immediacy. For the human being has al-

of a fullness and immediacy that is no longer affected by the differentiating and fragmenting force of the signifier. We will now illustrate this idea further by way of the relationship between the body and the unconscious in Lacan.

THE BODY, LANGUAGE, AND THE UNCONSCIOUS

We may not infer from the initial exteriority of the body in relation to language that the subject of the unconscious is not essentially bodily. All it does mean is that so far as the unconscious is concerned, the body cannot be the biological body, and that every biologizing interpretation of the Freudian doctrine of the drive must be rejected. Once one assigns the unconscious a linguistic status, then for Lacan every reference to biology in relation to the unconscious loses all meaning,[25] and as a result, the "psychoanalytic body" cannot be conceived of in terms of instinct. On the contrary, it is a question of the body insofar as it has received a certain signification.

---

ways already taken up the order of language and of the law. Thus what we lose through the entry into the symbolic is something we never really possessed. Later we shall examine this point more fully in connection with the problematic of the *jouissance de l'Autre/de la mère*.

25. "Freud's biologism has nothing to do with the moralistic abjection that wafts up from the psychoanalytic kitchen . . . that margin beyond life that language gives to the human being by virtue of the fact that he speaks, and which is precisely that in which such a being places in the position of a signifier, not only those parts of his body that are exchangeable, but this body itself" (E 301/15–26, EF 803). We have omitted the reference to the death drive and to the object *a* in this passage, since we will return to examine this more extensively in relation to the structure of the drive.

In this connection, one thinks first of all of the so-called "part-objects" (breast, feces, etc.).[26] According to Freud, these "part-objects" are the proper objects of the drive, and the relation with the Other is also primarily structured around them. A classic example of this is the feces, which can take on a number of significations in the context of toilet training. The child might consider them a gift to the mother in order to assure itself of her love; the feces might also be understood as something over which it has control independent of the mother, and which it uses to affirm this independence. For us, what is important above all else here is that such objects play a crucial role in a relation of exchange with the Other,[27] and as such, they can be loaded with a number of significations that essentially codetermine this relation. Clearly, these objects do not play this role on the basis of their biological function. Rather, their importance is determined exclusively by the way the symbolic has determined the meaning of our bodily relation to the Other for us.

This is illustrated in a striking way by the phantasmatic equivalencies and relations between these objects that Freud (1917) says arise in the unconscious. Freud writes that in the products of the unconscious (symptoms, phantasies), "feces" (money, gift), child, and penis can be difficult to distinguish, and are easily exchanged for one another. According to Lacan, these equivalencies can only be understood in terms of the metaphoric-metonymical operation of language. Thus Freud points out that the equation

---

26. Later we will examine in more detail the status and importance of these part-objects in relation to the object *a*. For a commentary on the notion of the part-object in Freud, see Laplanche and Pontalis 1988, pp. 301–302.

27. Lacan seems to refer to this point in the passage we are commenting upon when he talks about "those parts of his body that are exchangeable" (E 301/26, EF 803).

between "child" and "penis" must be related to the fact that both are indicated by the same symbol in the language of the dream as well as in everyday language (Freud 1917, pp. 126–127); both the little child and the male sexual organ are often called *die / das Kleine* ("the little one"). The part-objects can thus only play their role because and insofar as they refer to the order of language.[28]

According to Lacan, then, the "psychoanalytic" body is the body insofar as it has received a certain signification from language. More is at stake here than just the so-called part-objects, however. In and through our concrete relations with the Other, the body receives a determinate signification for us, and it will also inevitably be subject to certain commands and prohibitions that essentially determine the way we relate to ourselves and our environment. For example, it is easy to see that a child who constantly hears that its sexual organs are "dirty" will relate to itself (and to the Other) in a different way than a child whose parents value the sexual organs positively, as possible sources of pleasure. In this way, language marks off parts of the body and invests them with a determinate signification. Language, Lacan writes, establishes a certain margin over against the biological body. As a result of the installation of the body in language, the body itself functions as a signifier, and therefore cannot be understood only in terms of the laws of biology.[29] We can perhaps best illustrate this by reference to the psychoanalytic interpretation of children's drawings. Psychoanalysis under-

---

28. Further on, however, we will see that this does not mean for Lacan that these "part-objects" may themselves be understood primarily as signifiers.

29. ". . . that margin beyond life that language gives to the human being by virtue of the fact that he speaks, and which is precisely that in which such a being places in the position of a signifier, not only those parts of his body that are exchangeable, but this body itself" (E 301/23–26, EF 803).

stands the manner in which children draw themselves and their environment as a symbolic expression of their bodily being-in-the-world. The various elements from which the drawing is built up, however, can only be understood from their relation to each other—they are like signifiers, the signification of which is contextually determined. It is clear, moreover, that biological regulation is put out of play, as it were; body parts are missing or artificially enlarged, or their interrelation is represented in a manner that makes a mockery of any biological functionality. Thus Lacan compares the unconscious body image with a coat of arms, in which heterogeneous elements generate a determinate signification on the basis of their relations with each other.[30]

All of this cannot be understood in isolation from Lacan's lifelong discussion with so-called object-relations theory.[31] According to this theory,[32] the libido seeks not so much pleasure

---

30. E 302/18–21, EF 804. We will discuss the complete passage in which this reference to heraldry and children's drawings occurs in the next paragraph (see n. 31).

31. "For, of course, psychoanalysis involves the real of the body and the imaginary of its mental schema. But to recognize their scope in the perspective that is authorized by development [this is a reference to the psychogenetic perspective in which the object-relations are usually thought—we will come back on this directly], we must first perceive that the more or less departmented integrations that appear to order it function in it above all like heraldic elements, like the body's coat-of-arms. This is confirmed by the use one makes of it to read children's drawings" (E 302/15–20, EF 804; punctuation modified).

32. For a good overview of the various object-relations theories, see Buckley 1986. We limit ourselves to the very orthodox formulation of this theory in the work of Fairbairn, to which Lacan's criticism seems to be especially applicable. In this regard one can read the two articles of Fairbairn in the anthology just cited. It is still very much a question whether Lacan's criticism would also be applicable to Kleinian object-relations theory, for example; this problematic, however, goes beyond the intention of this book.

as a suitable object to satisfy it; the ultimate goal of the libido is the object (Fairbairn 1986). The point of departure of Freudian psychoanalysis is thus reversed, for according to Freud, the libido primarily seeks pleasure, and the object is subordinated to this. The object is essentially contingent and exchangeable for Freud; it is only important insofar as it is in a position to bring pleasure. The theorists of object-relations, on the other hand (Fairbairn, Fenichel, and others), reverse this relation between the experience of pleasure and the search for an object. They unambiguously adopt a psychogenetic standpoint, in which the libido has to be understood as a psychic power initially relating only to part-objects. According to these authors, however, the libido is by nature directed to a relationship with a total object of the other sex. This relation comes about on the ground of a complex developmental process, in which various stages (oral, anal, etc.) must run their course and be integrated with each other.[33] The search for pleasure plays a subordinate role in this process—pleasure is nothing other than a secondary and derived phenomenon that guides the development of object-relations.[34] Paramount for us here, however, is the fact that in the perspec-

---

33. Thus Fairbairn, for example, understands the phallic phase as "the product of an identification of the genital organs with the breast as the original part-object of the oral attitude—an identification which is characteristically accompanied by an identification of the genital organs with the mouth as a libidinal organ" (Fairbairn 1986, p. 76). It is to this sort of view that Lacan is referring when he says, "But to recognize their scope in the perspective that is authorized by development [i.e., the psychogenetic perspective to which we referred], we must first perceive that the more or less departmented integrations that appear to order it [this being a reference to the idea that the libidinous relation to the various partial-objects must be progressively integrated into the relation with a total object] . . ." (E 302/16–18, EF 804).

34. "[L]ibidinal pleasure is fundamentally just a sign-post to the object" (Fairbairn 1986, p. 76).

tive of object-relations theory, the development of the subject is basically viewed in the perspective of a possible totalization. The subject originally relates only to part-objects, but it must progressively move towards grasping itself as a whole, capable of relating autonomously to the genital Other in his or her totality. This means not only—nor even primarily—that the subject is capable of a satisfying sexual ("genital") relation with the Other. Much more, it means that the subject must be capable of a mature, non-incorporative and "giving" attitude towards the Other, of which genital sexuality makes up an integral part.[35]

Lacan thus claims that in this perspective, biological and psychological maturation are clearly thought of as mirror images of each other. Psychological development corresponds to the biological development that bears it along. The progressive integration of the drives and the progressive development of the ego are both directed at the realization of a "mature dependence in a giving relationship with a (genital) other," in which pleasure and love are brought into mutual accord.[36]

However, if we have to conceive of the body as a signifier, this immediately implies that the development of the subject cannot be understood in terms of a progressive integration of psychic functions, running parallel with a gradual totalization

---

35. Thus Fairbairn (1986) writes, "The gradual change which thus occurs in the nature of the object-relationship is accompanied by a gradual change in libidinal aim, whereby an original oral, sucking, incorporating and 'taking' aim comes to be replaced by a mature, nonincorporating and 'giving' aim compatible with developed genital sexuality" (pp. 77–78).

36. When Lacan writes, in his later work, that "there is no sexual relationship," then by "sexual relationship" he understands precisely the idea of a mutual integration of pleasure and love that is described by the theorists of object-relations as the goal of a teleological development. We shall return to this later.

of the partial drives and objects.[37] Such a view takes no account of the specific operation of the order of signifiers in terms of which the body becomes psychically meaningful. For Lacan, the various parts of the body in fact function as signifiers, and for precisely this reason, any integration is merely provisional and precarious. The order of signifiers excludes from the beginning any definitive integration and totalization (and as a result any teleology); in fact, it takes up the various parts of the body in a dynamic that always stands free in some way from biological regularity and biological functionality. The "psychoanalytic body" is like a coat of arms that, as with any coat of arms, refers to the history of the subject. This history is no teleological process with a quasi-biological foundation. On the contrary, it comes about through contingent encounters and events that can constantly receive new meanings from the order of signifiers. New events lead to new meanings, and these in turn can also have an effect on the unconscious body image. As a result, this body image is the record of the way in which the body is inscribed in the symbolic in the course of our personal history, and not the underlying principle of a teleologically understood development.[38]

---

37. Indeed, Lacan immediately ties this impossibility of a totalization to the linguistic status of the body. Thus, following the passage in which he asserts that the psychoanalytic body has to be understood as a signifier, he says, "Thus it becomes apparent that the relation of the object to the body is in no way defined as a partial identification that would have to be totalized in such a relation . . ." (E 301/26–29, EF 803).

38. Thus what we said above about children's drawings does not simply pertain to one developmental stage, but expresses rather a structural given. Lacan refers to children's drawings in order to say something about the "psychoanalytic body" *in general*.

2

The Subject of the Unconscious

THE SUBJECT OF THE ENUNCIATION AND THE SUBJECT OF THE STATEMENT

We have already remarked that according to Lacan, it is impossible for the subject to coincide with itself. But is this really such a revolutionary thought? To begin with, it is very doubtful that there has ever been a philosopher—be it Hegel, Descartes, or Spinoza—who has ascribed to the individual human subject the capacity to realize total self-possession. Furthermore, it is difficult to deny that a considerable portion of the philosophy of the twentieth century (one might think, for example, of Merleau-Ponty, Sartre, and many others) has taken the finitude of the subject as an express theme of reflection. Where, then, lies the specificity of Lacan's conception of subjectivity, so that he can speak of a "subversion of the [classical] subject"? Lacan himself poses this question explicitly:[1] When the unconscious is of the order of language, what sort of subject can be at work? This question becomes all the more pressing when we realize that this subject itself cannot give an answer to this question. For psychoanalytic experience teaches us that this subject not only does

---

1. "Once the structure of language has been recognized in the unconscious, what sort of subject can we conceive for it? . . . Namely, [what is] the right way to reply to the question, 'Who is speaking?,' when it is the subject of the unconscious which is at issue [?] For this reply cannot come from the subject if he does not know what he is saying, or even if he is speaking, as the entire experience of analysis has taught us" (E 298/15, 299/11, EF 800).

not know *what* it is saying, but often does not even know *that* it is saying something. Of course, it is true that the meaning of symptoms, slips of the tongue, and so on, is not immediately clear for the analysand. More than this, however, we are often not even conscious that certain behaviors, emotions, or thoughts *have* a symptomatic value; we do not realize that in these behaviors, emotions, and thoughts, something is said to which the conscious subject has no access.

One might think of a married man who is constantly getting into serious arguments with certain women. For him, these conflicts are at first only due to factors like the annoying character of the woman in question. In the course of an analysis, however, it may become clear that they all occur with women with whom he might fall in love. Thus it is not so much the irritating character of these women that is at issue, but his own anxiety for new loves that he did not count on (or did not want to have to count on). And so it is that before analysis, the analysand in this example is not conscious of the fact that his aggression towards certain women says something about himself that escapes him.

The subject of the unconscious, then, cannot answer the question of its own status. However, we do know that the unconscious has to be understood as a chain of signifiers—the unconscious is of the order of language. Lacan claims that it is therefore logical that we should begin with the I as a signifier in treating the problem that concerns us here.[2] In other words, we

---

2. "We can try, with methodological rigor, to set out from the strictly linguistic definition of the I as signifier, in which there is nothing but the 'shifter' or indicative, which, in the subject of the statement, designates the subject in the sense that he is now speaking. That is to say, it designates the subject of the enunciation, but it does not signify it. This is apparent from the fact that every signifier of the subject of the enunciation may be lacking in the statement . . ." (E 298/17–22, EF 800).

must begin with a strict linguistic definition of the subject: the I as "shifter" or "indexical." Very generally, shifters (or indexicals) are terms that indicate something in relation to the subject that performs the enunciation: "here," "now," "there," and so on. The meaning of these words can only be determined from the communicative context as such. I only know what "here" means when I know who pronounces it, and where. The same applies also to personal names, and more especially to the first person singular pronoun ("I"), to which Lacan refers here.[3]

In deciding the referent of "I," we depend exclusively on the communicative context. According to Lacan, this shifter thus *indicates* the subject of the enunciation, without, however, *signifying* it.[4] By this, Lacan means that the personal pronoun "I," while designating the subject of the enunciation, has *only* this indicative function; it is empty of content, and does not itself tell us anything about its possible meanings. Its meaning only becomes clear, on the other hand, on the basis of what follows in the statement in which it is used. The shifter "I" has no meaning and no determinable content unless I add something like "am a diligent student."

In this connection, Lacan distinguishes the *subject of the enunciation* (*sujet de l'énonciation*) from the *subject of the statement* (*sujet de l'énoncé*), where the subject of the enunciation is what is posited as present by means of a shifter like "I." The subject of the statement, on the other hand, refers to the subject as it appears to itself and to the other (for example, as someone

---

3. ". . . the 'shifter' or indicative, which, in the subject of the statement, designates the subject in the sense that he is now speaking" (E 298/19–20, EF 800).

4. "[I]t designates the subject of the enunciation, but it does not signify it" (E 298/20–22, EF 800).

who believes herself to be a diligent student). It pertains to the subject objectified in a statement[5]—the subject with determinable content—as opposed to the subject of the unconscious, which constantly escapes itself.[6] Every statement creates a certain identity—it says something about somebody—and we can thus better understand why Lacan, at this stage in his exposition, makes an appeal to the shifter "I." For in order to exist in a tangible form, the subject of the signifier (the subject of the unconscious) has to be represented in the statement; on the other hand, given that it immediately escapes from any definitive determination, that subject has to be represented by signifiers that respect its indeterminacy. The shifter "I" is just such a signifier, in that it has a merely indicative function, and in no way anticipates its possible meanings.[7]

According to Lacan, the subject of the enunciation can also be present in the subject of the statement in ways other than via the shifter "I." An interesting example of this is what French grammarians have called the *ne explétif,* for example as it occurs in the statement *Je crains qu'il ne vienne* ("I'm afraid he is com-

---

5. We will discuss the status of this "subject of the statement" more fully later, in connection with our exposition of the imaginary.

6. Later Lacan will talk in an analogous context about the subject that "binds itself into the signification" (E 299/23–25, EF 801) and so listens to the pre-conscious in place of the unconscious. We will come back to this.

7. Moreover, the merely indicative function of the shifter "I" seems superfluous, as Lacan goes on to point out in the passage we are discussing (see n. 2), because it can simply be left out in the articulated statement. ("This is apparent from the fact that every signifier of the subject of the enunciation may be lacking in the statement . . ." [E 298/21–22, EF 800].) When, for example, I say to someone, "Open the window," the first part of the sentence ("I say to you") is presupposed. Thus the factual presence of the shifter "I" is not necessary for the meaning of the sentence.

ing").[8] In a few lines of parody, Lacan dispenses with the established notion that this *ne explétif* is simply superfluous ("expletive") and that its use is arbitrary. The *ne explétif*, on the contrary, expresses something very personal, which has to be ascribed to the order of the enunciation. Lacan writes that he hopes that the weight that he assigns to this *ne* will bring these grammarians to another view, "before it becomes obvious" (*avant qu'il ne soit avéré*) that they understand nothing about it. Here Lacan points out that it is precisely the presence of this particle *ne* that gives his statement the character of an attack. If we were to remove the *ne*, he continues, then the subject of the enunciation would immediately disappear into impersonality. We would be left with a simple assertive sentence, in which nothing personal could any longer be heard. Lacan concludes by saying that he fears nevertheless that these grammarians will mock him for his views (*Mais je crains qu'ils n'en viennent à me honnir*), and here too, the *ne* is far from superfluous. On the contrary, it expresses an emotion of fear, and omitting it would reduce the statement to a timid assertion. In either case, then, the absence of the *ne explétif* would nullify the personal emphasis, such that

---

8. "I think, for example, that I recognized the subject of the enunciation in the signifier 'ne,' which grammarians call the expletive, a term that already prefigures the incredible opinion of those, and they are to be found among the best, who regard its form as being a matter of mere chance. May the weight that I give it persuade them to think again, before it becomes obvious that they have missed the point (*avant qu'il ne soit avéré qu'ils n'y comprennent rien*)—take out that *ne* and my enunciation loses its attack, *Je* eliding into the impersonal [translation modified: *Je m'élidant dans l'impersonal*]. But I fear that in this way they will come to curse me (*je crains ainsi qu'ils n'en viennent à me honnir*)—slide over that *n'* and its absence, reducing the alleged fear of a declaration of my repugnance to a timid assertion, reduces the emphasis of my enunciation by situating me in the statement" (E 298/28–39, EF 800).

the subject of the enunciation would be completely absorbed into the subject of the statement. In this way, the subject would appear to itself and to the other as a mere object, and would no longer be present as a personally speaking subject.[9]

THE SUBVERSION OF THE SUBJECT

We now understand that the subject of the unconscious is present in a particularly fleeting way in the subject of the statement—and present as a signifier. Of course, this does not give a complete answer to the question of the status of this subject. Lacan further develops this problematic by way of three examples: the super-ego (*Über-ich*), the lapsus (and the *Witz*), and the forgetting of proper names.[10] We will deal first with the super-ego.

Due to the moral education we have all enjoyed to a greater or less extent, we spontaneously experience certain things as permissible or forbidden. This experience goes back to an essentially intersubjective event; that we consider certain things

---

9. According to Lacan, this *ne explétif* functions in a sentence in a way identical to the shifter "I." We said that this shifter, of itself, has no meaning. However, Lacan's own exposition suggests that this is less evident with regard to the *ne explétif*, which seems to give us substantive information concerning the subject of the unconscious.

10. "It follows that the place of the 'inter-said' (*inter-dit*), which is the 'intra-said' (*intra-dit*) of a between-two-subjects, is the very place in which the transparency of the classical subject is divided and passes through the effects of 'fading' [English in the original] that specify the Freudian subject by its occultation by an ever purer signifier: that these effects lead us to the frontiers at which slips of the tongue and witticisms, in their collusion, become confused, even where elision is so much the more allusive in tracking down presence to its lair, that one is surprised that the *Dasein* hunt hasn't done better at it" (E 299/12–20, EF 800–801).

forbidden, and precisely what we see as forbidden (*inter-dit*), is the fruit of what has taken place between two or more persons (*intra-dit*). Clinical experience teaches us, however, that we are not always conscious of the commandments and prohibitions that give our existence form and content. Psychoanalysis even finds the prohibition in those places where the subject is no longer transparent to itself in a knowledge of itself. Something can fall under a prohibition without it being clear to me why it does so, or the prohibition can appear in a camouflaged form. For example, Lacan (1954–55) writes about a Moroccan patient who resided in France for many years, and who suffered from writer's cramp. In the course of the analysis, this symptom was linked with the Islamic commandment that a thief is to have his hands cut off. During the patient's youth his father had in fact been accused of theft, and although the patient had resided in France for many years and no longer had any particular bond with Islamic culture, it was this law that determined his symptom. Even more, this law seems to have been inscribed in its sheer literality in the body of the patient.

Lacan connects this with what he calls the "fading" of the subject.[11] "Fading" refers primarily to the progressive weakening of a sound or to the progressive disappearance of a color, but Lacan uses it to indicate the disappearance of the self-conscious subject. Indeed, the example of the Moroccan patient implies that this subject disappears underneath or behind what Lacan calls a "pure" signifier ("its occultation by an ever purer signifier"). The notion of a "pure" signifier refers to the operation of the order of signifiers independent of its possible meaning effects; the Islamic law that a thief is to have his hands cut

---

11. Lacan borrows this term from Ernest Jones, for whom it refers to (anxiety over) the disappearance of desire.

off is literally inscribed in the body of the patient in its sheer materiality. The self-conscious subject is powerless here, for the subject seems to be completely in the grip of an order that does not take any account of its concerns, feelings, or intentions. It is as if the subject is driven from its central place by the autonomous system of signifiers, and in that sense disappears.

The effects of fading, Lacan continues, inevitably lead us to slips of the tongue (and the *Witz*) and the forgetting of proper names,[12] which are in a sense even more pregnant illustrations of this fading. We will discuss slips of the tongue first. Suppose that a philosophy lecturer, for example, were to say in the course of one of her lectures that she does not think much of the *hysterical* (instead of "historical") philosophy of Hegel. Here the subject is overtaken by her own statement, as it were, or more precisely, overtaken by a signifier that intrudes autonomously upon her statement independent of her conscious intentions. In other words, the self-conscious subject disappears for a moment, and in the place it just occupied, a signifier appears. Of course, it is clear that almost immediately that this happens, the conscious subject reclaims its rights. It will try to restore its control without delay by seeking an explanation for the slip of the tongue, for example, so as to reintegrate it into the life of consciousness. And yet for all its efforts, the subject is thrust from its place by a signifier for that fleeting moment in which it is surprised by its own slip of the tongue.

---

12. In fact, Lacan introduces a sort of hierarchy in the examples he gives of the "fading" of the subject. This is why he says, "[T]he effects of 'fading' . . . specify the Freudian subject by its occultation by *an ever purer signifier* . . ." (E 299/14–16, E 800; my emphasis). The examples are accordingly ordered by the degree to which they illustrate the operation of the pure signifier—which is to say, the signifier as distinct from its possible meanings.

According to Lacan, however, the most penetrating example of what is at stake here is the forgetting of proper names.[13] In this regard, one might think of the example of Freud (1901) being unable to bring to mind the name of Signorelli when he was in the basilica of Orvieto in Italy. Via a complex network of associations, Freud was able to connect his forgetting this name with his preoccupation with death and sexuality. The most important thing here, however, is this: where the signifier "Signorelli" should have appeared, there yawns only an emptiness. The signifier has been completely detached from its possible meaning-effects, as it were; it is present only in its absence. But precisely in this way—that is to say, detached from its possible meanings and in its materiality (which is in this case minimal)—the signifier can function as the starting point for the various chains of association that the analysis has the task of exposing. In its absence, the signifier "Signorelli" calls forth other signifiers that appear to be decisive for the manner in which Freud's existence has been formed.[14] Nowhere is the whereabouts of the lair to which we must track the subject more apparent than in this last example:[15] it is the order of pure signifiers, which autonomously determines and gives form to our existence. We can only won-

---

13. Thus in the quotation we are paraphrasing here (see n. 10), Lacan speaks about an "elision." This term refers to the forgetting of proper names as Freud deals with it in his *The Psychopathology of Everyday Life* (1901).

14. The clinical importance of Lacan's observations in this regard is clear. In the analysis every fixation upon meaning has to be avoided, for such a fixation only leads to a reinforcement of the ego. We will return to consider this point in more detail later.

15. ". . . even where elision [of the signifier, e.g., Signorelli] is so much the more allusive in tracking down presence to its lair . . ." (E 299/18–19, EF 801).

der, Lacan concludes, that the philosophers in their hunt for the *Dasein* have not made more use of this psychoanalytic insight.

We set out from the problem of how we are to understand the subject of the unconscious according to Lacan. We now know that this subject is the subject as intrinsically bound and subordinated to the clearly autonomous operation of the signifier. The subject of the unconscious is only a function of the signifier that determines it, and this is the subversion of the subject that Lacan wants to address.[16]

THE SUBJECT AS DISCONTINUITY IN THE REAL

The signifier introduces a momentary break into discourse ("the function of the cut").[17] The subject of the unconscious shows

---

16. Later it will appear that with this, everything has by no means been said about Lacan's subversion of the subject. In fact the latter—for reasons still be set out—finds its culmination in the castration complex.

17. "Lest the hunt be in vain for us analysts, we must bring everything back to the function of the cut in discourse, the strongest being that which acts as a bar between the signifier and the signified. There the subject that interests us is surprised, since by binding himself in signification he is placed under the sign of the pre-conscious. By which we would arrive at the paradox of conceiving that the discourse in an analytic session is valuable only insofar as it stumbles or is interrupted; if the session itself were not instituted as a cut in a false discourse, or rather, to the extent that the discourse succeeds in emptying itself as speech, in being no more than Mallarmé's worn coinage that is passed from hand to hand 'in silence.' This cut in the signifying chain alone verifies the structure of the subject as discontinuity in the real. If linguistics enables us to see the signifier as the determinant of the signified, analysis reveals the truth of this relation by making the 'holes' in meaning the determinants of its discourse [translation modified: *à faire des trous du sens les déterminants de son discours*]" (E 299/21–36, EF 801).

itself where a signifier interrupts the normal course of discourse and thought, and brings it to a halt;[18] it thus appears where it punches holes in the conscious subject's world of meaning. The slip of the tongue is a striking example of this. Where speech stumbles and the subject loses its grip on itself, the signifiers that fundamentally determine its existence appear. The analyst's hunt for the subject of the unconscious ("Lest the hunt be in vain for us analysts") can only be successful if she directs her attention primarily to these momentary breaks in the speech of her analysands.[19] Analytic speech derives its significance from precisely these moments,[20] in that the priority of signifier over signified is there made clear in an exemplary way. For there the (self-conscious) subject is confronted with its impotence in the face of a signifier (an order of signifiers) over which it has no hold. However much we might believe that our existence takes its form from the meanings to which we are attached, and from the feelings we regard as valuable, our destiny is ultimately determined by a system of signifiers into which we are subsumed. Between signifier and signified there yawns an unbridgeable gap ("a bar between the signifier and the signified"), and for Lacan, that gap is formally identical with the gap Freud discovers be-

---

18. This also what Lacan means when he writes, in a passage we have already quoted earlier (Chapter 1, n. 1), that "the unconscious has been a chain of signifiers that . . . insists on interfering in the breaks offered it by the effective discourse and the cogitation that it informs" (E 297/34–37, EF 799). The unconscious shows itself where it breaks open conscious discourse and the thinking that informs it (e.g., the slip of the tongue), and where the self-conscious subject is surprised by a signifier.

19. ". . . by making 'holes' in the meaning the determinants of its [the analysand's] discourse" (E 299/35–36, EF 801).

20. "[T]he discourse in an analytic session is valuable only insofar as it stumbles or is interrupted . . ." (E 299/27–28, EF 801).

tween the unconscious and the (pre-) conscious.[21] Accordingly, psychoanalysis is primarily concerned with the signifier, and not meaning.

In this context, Lacan refers to the notion of "empty speech,"[22] which he earlier developed at length in "The Function and Field of Speech in Psychoanalysis" (1956, esp. pp. 40–56). One does not need much clinical experience to be familiar with the analysand who talks in endless detail about what has happened to him in the preceding days, about his many difficulties at work, or about the marital problems of his brother or sister. At the same time he gives a running commentary on himself and on his presumed character traits. In this situation, the analyst can easily get the impression that nothing is happening in the analysis—she feels she is the powerless witness of a objectifying and commentating speech that achieves little or nothing. Lacan calls this discourse "false" (*un faux discours*) or "empty," since precisely in being objectifying and commentating, it is an attempt to take our distance from what really moves us. Lacan compares this "empty speech" with a coin on which the image has been worn away, but which nonetheless continues to be passed from hand to hand as valid payment.[23] This last point is

---

21. "There the subject that interests us [the subject of the unconscious] is surprised, since by binding himself in signification he is placed under the sign of the pre-conscious" (E 299/24–26, EF 801).

22. ". . . if the session itself were not instituted as a cut in a false discourse, or rather, to the extent that the discourse succeeds in emptying itself as speech . . ." (E 299/28–30, EF 801).

23. ". . . in being no more than Mallarmé's worn coinage that is passed from hand to hand 'in silence'" (E 299/30–32, EF 801). For our commentary we make use of the passage in "The Function and Field of Speech in Psychoanalysis" in which Lacan further works out this comparison (1956; E 43, EF 251).

of great significance: even when the image on the coin has been obliterated, the coin continues to make up part of the symbolic—it continues to function in a system of exchange that is based on mutual recognition. In an analogous way, "empty" speech is above all *speech*. Even speech that is "empty" participates in the symbolic order of the Other, and precisely for this reason, now and again a signifier is able to break through and interrupt the endless commentary.

We can illustrate this with the following example from Freud's analysis of Dora (1905, p. 47). At a certain moment Dora says to Freud, "Mrs. K. only loves my father because he is a man of means (*ein vermögender Mann*)." One can easily imagine that Dora made this statement in the context of an objectifying discussion of the relationship between her father and Mrs. K., in which she vented her indignation about it, or expressed the judgment that her father was really too good for Mrs. K. According to Lacan, all these views belong to the level of lived meanings, and thus of the pre-conscious. Nevertheless, the analyst—in this case, Freud—cannot limit his listening to this level. In German the signifier "of means" (*vermögend*) does not simply refer to the father's finances; it also refers to sexual potency. In other words, without Dora really intending it, one can hear in the signifier *vermögend* another associative chain—one truly meaningful for the neurotic problems that afflict her. The statement "because he is a man of means" turns out to actually conceal its opposite: "My father is sexually impotent." In a certain sense, the signifier *vermögend* disowns Dora as a conscious subject, without her immediately realizing this. It is the task of the analyst to draw her attention to it, and so point out the break this signifier introduces into her stream of reflections. The analyst, according to Lacan, has to have an eye out less for the meaning of the analysand's discourse than for the materiality of the signifiers, which can interfere with the intended meaning. Her task consists primarily in underlining these moments of potential rupture. In this way the analysand is put in a position to strike out on new associative paths, and so to address the very signifiers that fundamentally determine his existence.[24]

Lacan goes on to say that these breaches in the syntagmatic series of signifiers ("This cut in the signifying chain . . .") teach us to recognize the subject as a discontinuity in the real.[25] At first sight this definition seems quite paradoxical. The subject of the unconscious, as we have said following Lacan, shows itself where holes are punched in the meaningful world of the self-conscious subject, and where a discontinuity thus occurs. We know, however, that the real escapes (or precedes) every bestowal of meaning. How, then, can the subject of the unconscious be characterized as a "discontinuity in the real"?

As we know, the signifier introduces difference—and thus negativity—into the real, which is of itself pure continuity, and

---

24. The end of the analytic session must also, according to Lacan, be reinterpreted from this perspective. The clause "if the session itself were not instituted as a cut" in the passage we are commenting upon here (see n. 17) seems to allude to this. Indeed, throughout his entire career Lacan opposed a merely mechanical conception of the end of the analytic session. In the traditional setting, the analyst pre-sets a determinate length for every session—for example forty-five minutes—and routinely adheres to this duration, irrespective of what happens in the session. In this way, according to Lacan, the conclusion of the session has no significance for the actual analytic work. It is simply a problem of the chronometer. For Lacan, on the contrary, the end of the session must also be given an interpretative significance. Like interpretation in the strict sense, the end of the session "scans" the meaningful moments in the speech of the analysand. This implies both that an analytic session cannot have its length set beforehand, and that its duration varies.

25. "This cut in the signifying chain alone verifies the structure of the subject as discontinuity in the real" (E 299 32–33, EF 801).

it is on the basis of this difference that a meaningful order can come about. Lacan further claims that the subject is intrinsically dependent upon this signifier, by which it is fundamentally determined. And finally, we know that because and insofar as it is the subject of the signifier, this subject never coincides with itself; every determination is insufficient to say precisely what the subject "is." The subject is therefore a discontinuity in the real, into which it introduces negativity because and insofar as it is the subject of the signifier.

The difference we discussed above between the subject of the enunciation and the subject of the statement, however, implies that the former is constantly determined in the latter. In the statement, the subject of the enunciation appears in an identifiable form both to itself and to the other. It thereby gains a content in which it can believe, such that its basic indeterminacy—the negativity that fundamentally characterizes it—is withdrawn from view. It projects a positivity to which it attaches itself, and in this way misrecognizes its essential dependence upon the order of signifiers and its own associated indeterminacy.[26] Where this identity is again broken open by the

---

26. Obviously, the dynamic we are dealing with in this section on the subjects of the enunciation and the statement can only be understood in the light of the third fundamental category of Lacanian thought: the imaginary. (We will discuss this category in more detail in relation to the second version of the graph.)

A brief reference to Sartre might introduce more clarity here. Sartre describes the subject (*pour-soi*) as capable of "nihilation": the *pour-soi* always escapes itself, and never coincides with any of its supposed properties. Whatever I say about myself, whatever identity I measure out for myself, I will never coincide with it. Thus, according to Sartre, one can say that the past offers certain possibilities for the present and the future, but not that these possibilities determine me in a necessary fashion or that I can derive my identity from them. For these possibilities only count as such, insofar as I posit them

movement of signifiers ("holes in the meaning") the subject appears as what it is: a discontinuity in the real.

WO ES WAR, SOLL ICH WERDEN[27]

According to Lacan, what we have said so far about the status of the subject of the unconscious should enable an original reinterpretation of Freud's famous dictum concerning the aim of analysis: *Wo Es war, soll Ich werden*. Freud formulates this idea in his 1933 text *New Introductory Lectures on Psycho-Analysis* (p. 80). There the ego has a sort of mediating function between the de-

---

in a completely autonomous and active manner. My future remains, strictly speaking, completely open. The *pour-soi* is in this sense the permanent and active denial of any identity by which it would obtain a stable and determinable content (for example, on the basis of what has occurred in the past). In this way the *pour-soi* introduces a negativity into the sheer identity and positivity of the real (*en-soi*) that simply coincides with itself. As soon as the subject receives a determinate content with which it can identify, such that it can say, "I am that," it unavoidably threatens to disappear into the indifferent identity of the *en-soi*. For Sartre, in other words, every identity and positivity ultimately refers to the fullness of the *en-soi*, which does not know negativity. For the relation between Lacan and Sartre vis-à-vis the status of subjectivity, see Van Haute 1990, pp. 93–129.

27. "It was along this line of approach that Freud was able to carry out the imperative, which he brought to a level of sublimity worthy of the pre-Socratics in the formulation, '*Wo es war, soll Ich werden*'. . . . To take one step at a time in Freud's grammar: 'there where it was . . .' (*là où ce fut* . . .), which means what? If it were only that which had been (in an aoristic, indefinite form), how can I come there in order to make myself be there, to state it now? But the French says: '*Là où c'était* . . .' Let us make use of the benefit that French gives us of a distinct imperfect. There where it was just now, there where it was for a while, between an extinction that is still glowing and a birth that is retarded, 'I' can come into being and disappear from what I say" (E 299/37, 300/11, EF 801).

mands of the Id, which refer back to the repressed and the activity of the drives, and the super-ego, which represents the demands of culture. In order to be able to take upon itself this mediating function, the ego must pass through a whole course of development. It has to be sufficiently strong to resist the demands of the Id, and it has to transform itself into a moral and ethical knowledge representing reality and culture in the psyche. Freud consequently gives a diachronic reading of his own dictum, referring it to a future that is prepared in the analysis. In a sense, Lacan's reading of this dictum (which he says has the sublime power of a pre-Socratic aphorism, *la gnomique pré-Socratique*) reverses that of Freud. The I (the subject of the statement) occurs at the level of what Heidegger (1962) calls "idle talk" (*das Gerede*; p. 211)—speech that understands everything without ever arriving at a personal statement. "One" adapts oneself to what "one" says and thinks. Thus, without analysis, Dora's mere commentary on the extramarital relationship of her father could never have gone far beyond what was normal in the referential system of her own cultural environment. Insofar as one is a child of one's time and culture, "one" (such as Dora) loses oneself in a generality unanimated by any particularity. The analysand loses herself in *Gerede* (empty speech), but this of course does not prevent the *analysis* from being concerned with the order of signifiers as such. The ego must therefore free itself from superficial *Gerede* in order to reconnect with the signifiers of the unconscious. In other words, Lacan gives a retrospective reading of Freud's dictum, against Freud's prospective reading. The I has not so much to develop itself, in the future-oriented sense we sketched earlier, as to return from *Gerede* or the level of the statement (*énoncé*) to the signifiers that determine its existence.

In order to elucidate his interpretation of Freud's aphorism, Lacan goes back to its grammar—and, more specifically, to various possible translations. As it happens, French offers several tenses in which *Wo Es war, soll Ich werden* can be translated. A first possibility is the pluperfect subjunctive (*ça qui eût été*), which views the time of the action immanently—that is to say, independently of the relation to the speaking subject—after the model of the Greek aorist. In other words, it expresses a sort of "atemporal time," which does not implicate the acting subject and for which the time of myth offers perhaps the best illustration. To be sure, myth recognizes time; it is constructed from events that follow one another. But it deals with a sort of time out of time, or perhaps, rather, a time outside the time of the subject that tells the myth. But for just this reason, the aorist is not suited to adequately translate the Freudian *Wo Es war*, for Freud's aphorism concerns the birth of the subject of the unconscious, in which the subject really *is* implicated in what it says, and translation with the aorist excludes this from the outset.[28]

The imperfect offers another possibility.[29] The imperfect can indeed indicate a distinct and specific moment in time, while at the same time expressing that the subject is implicated in this moment in time. Lacan appeals to this possibility in order to clarify his reading of *Wo Es war* . . . We have already seen that the I of the enunciation has only a fleeting and precarious existence apart from its objectivation in the subject of the statement. It shows itself in the quasi-superfluous *ne explétif*, in a slip of

---

28. "If it were only that which had been (in an aoristic, indefinite form), how can I come there in order to make myself be there, to state it now?" (E 300/4–6, EF 801). Lacan points out here that even the one who speaks in the aorist (". . . to state it now") is not personally implied in this speech (". . . how can I come there in order to make myself be there"). For what is at stake here is, as it were, an a-subjective time.

29. The simple past (*la où ce fut*), according to Lacan, is also unsuitable to express what is involved here.

the tongue, or in a scarcely noticeable slippage of the signifier (one can think of the signifier *vermögend* in Freud's case study of Dora). In the same context, we pointed out that where the I does appear, it almost immediately disappears again. In fact, the conscious subject will almost instantaneously try to reintegrate the slip of the tongue into its conscious life, or it will tirelessly seek a rational explanation of the symptoms that endanger its continuity. The subject of the enunciation consequently seems like a sort of ember, which, even as it burns out and is almost gone (*Là où c'était . . .*), still glows; or again, it is something that, the moment it opens itself up, already falters, withdraws back into itself, and fades from view. Yet it is precisely at this moment that the I of the enunciation comes into existence, in that for that moment I no longer dissolve into the statement—I no longer lose myself in *Gerede,* and in that sense I disappear from it ("'I' can come into being and disappear from what I say").[30] The subject of the unconscious only appears where it has already

---

30. "There where it was just now, there where it was for a while, between an extinction that is still glowing and a birth that is retarded, 'I' can come into being and disappear from what I say ["what I say" refers to the said and thus to the subject of the statement or of the signified]" (E 300/8–11, EF 801). Lacan continues in the same vein when in the next paragraph he writes about the subject of the enunciation that betrays or denounces itself ("An enunciation that denounces itself"), thus implying at the same time that the statement or, more generally, the level of *Gerede* is in default ("a statement that renounces itself"). The appearance of the subject of the unconscious offers a fleeting opportunity ("an opportunity that loses itself") to break through the ignorance with regard to this subject ("ignorance that dissipates itself"). The complete paragraph from which these phrases come runs as follows: "An enunciation that denounces itself, a statement that renounces itself, ignorance that dissipates itself, an opportunity that loses itself, what remains here if not the trace of what *must* be in order to fall from being?" (E 300/12–15, EF 801; emphasis in original).

begun to withdraw itself from being ("fall from being"); it obtrudes like the trace of something, which must exist or possess some reality to show up in this way at all.[31]

Lacan further illustrates this interpretation by way of a well-known dream from Freud's (1911) "Formulierungen über zwei Prinzipien des Psychischen Geschehens" ("Formulations on Two Principles of Mental Functioning," pp. 225–226). Having nursed his late father through a long final illness, one of Freud's analysands repeatedly dreamed of conversing with his father just as he used to, as if he had come back to life. The analysand found it extremely distressing that although his father was actually dead, he did not know it. In accordance with the general principle that buttresses his dream-interpretation, Freud claims that this dream can only be made transparent when we view it as the veiled fulfillment of a repressed wish. The manifest dream must then be read as follows: "What the analysand found distressing was that his father was dead (according to the analysand's wish), while at the same time not knowing it (that his son wished it)." The dream thus realizes, in a deformed fashion, both the analysand's repressed wish that the father would die, and his anxiety that his father would learn of this wish.

Lacan uses this dream as a sort of fable, to further elucidate the status of the subject of the enunciation in its relation to the subject of the statement (E 300/16–33, EF 801–802). He says that the figure of the father in the dream shows us something essential about the way this relationship is to be understood.[32]

---

31. "[W]hat remains here if not the trace of what *must* be in order to fall from being?" (E 300/14–15, EF 801; emphasis in original).

32. "If the figure of the dead father survives only by virtue of the fact that one does not tell him the truth of which he is unaware, what, then, is to be said of the *I* [the subject of the enunciation], on which this survival depends?" (E 300/24–26, EF 802).

Like the father in the dream, the subject does not "know" that it is "dead"; it thinks that it always has been as it appears to itself and others in the statement. Like the father in the dream, the subject does not want to know anything about its "death." It does not want to know that it exists only by the grace of an order that condemns it to an ineradicable indeterminacy. This subject, however, is constantly surprised by the signifier in its own speech—in the performance of the enunciation. The subject of the statement and the subject of the enunciation are therefore not two different subjects; the same subject constantly objectifies itself in the statement, and is overtaken by the signifier in the performance of the enunciation. The subject that presumes to find itself in the statement is constantly overtaken by its own truth—which is to say, by the signifier that gives it its form. As soon as the subject bends back and tries to reintegrate itself in the statement—in a knowledge of itself—this truth is lost.[33] The subject of the enunciation never appears without immediately withdrawing itself, and between truth and knowledge there yawns an unbridgeable gap that is the formal analogue of the gap between the signifier and the signified.[34]

---

33. The subject of the enunciation is "a true survival that is abolished by knowledge of itself" (E 300/31–32, EF 802).

34. We will come back to this later when we deal more extensively with the problematic of desire.

3

From the First to the Second Version of the Graph of Desire

INTRODUCTION

We are now sufficiently armed to subject the second version of Lacan's graph to critical scrutiny. This second version of the graph further specifies the "elementary cell," while also introducing a number of new categories and concepts. The most important new category introduced here is undoubtedly that of the imaginary. At first sight it is perhaps curious that Lacan does not bring up this category for discussion until here, for Lacan thematized the imaginary at length long before he made the symbolic and the real an explicit theme of reflection. In fact, the imaginary is the central and almost exclusive subject of Lacan's work in the thirties and forties,[1] whereas the symbolic and the real, by contrast, were only introduced during the fifties.[2] Through the introduction of these two categories, however, the imaginary takes on a somewhat different meaning and function within the totality of the body of Lacanian thought. Indeed, from the fifties onward Lacan formulates a primacy of the symbolic over the imaginary; the imaginary dimension can only come about on the ground of symbolic relations. This explains why in "Subversion" as well

---

1. See, *inter alia,* Lacan 1948, 1949. For the early texts of Lacan on the imaginary and their relation to his later works, see Ogilvie 1987.

2. Specifically, under the influence of structuralism, and especially the work of Claude Lévi-Strauss. Lévi-Strauss's *Les Structures élémentaires de la parenté* appeared in 1949. In addition, the publication of Kojève's *Introduction to the Reading of Hegel,* also in 1949, must undoubtedly be mentioned. Indeed, it is difficult to understand the category of the real apart from this reference. On this point, see Borch-Jacobsen 1991, Van Haute 1990.

as in the construction of the graph, Lacan explicitly discusses the imaginary only after the symbolic and the real.

Before taking up this thematic, however, we will see how the problematic we linked to the "elementary cell" is inscribed in the second version of the graph.

THE OTHER IN THE SECOND VERSION
OF THE GRAPH OF DESIRE

Where and how is the problematic we dealt with in connection with the "elementary cell" reproduced and specified in the second version of the graph? In order to formulate an answer to this question, we will begin with the second version of the graph without taking into account the imaginary, though we will later have to inscribe the imaginary into it. Of course, from the standpoint of the interpretation this might come across as somewhat violent. Our further exposition will then also have to make it clear that this manner of presentation is in fact justified.

If we leave the imaginary out of account, the second version of the graph looks like this:

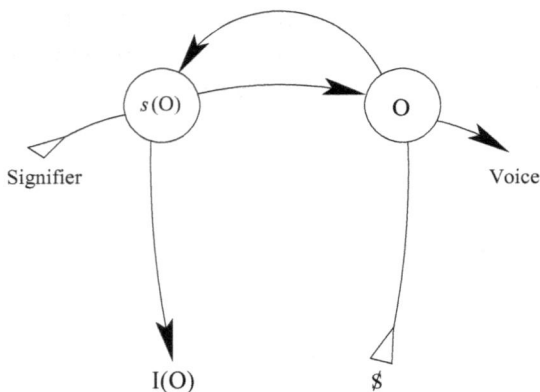

This presentation immediately makes it clear that Lacan no longer sets out from the human being as simply a being of needs, which has yet to enter into language. On the contrary, here the already constituted—and thus split—subject of the signifier ($) immediately functions as the starting point. In the light of our earlier discussion, this should not surprise us. There we pointed out that Lacan thinks of the real body as external to language. The body does not contribute directly to the production of meaning, and it only plays a role in the unconscious insofar as it is subsumed into the order of signifiers. This also means that for Lacan, the body makes no real, positive contribution to the constitution of the subjectivity he is trying to present graphically. Accordingly, the biological body as such can have no place of its own on the graph. Of course, it does not follow from this that the subject in Lacan's graph would not have a body. In fact, $ is from the beginning an essentially bodily subject. The body in question here, however, is the body insofar as it has obtained a determinate meaning from the order of signifiers.

The O at the top right hand corner of the graph refers to the "signifier's treasure,"[3] which imposes a determinate order on the world of needs. It will be remembered that in the "elementary cell" of the graph, the vector $\overrightarrow{S.S'}$ indicated the metonymical concatenation of the signifiers. In a certain sense this vector is contracted into (O), the better to suggest that it is a matter of an *ordered system* of signifiers, and most importantly, that the

---

3. "I will spare you the various stages by giving you at one go the function of the two points of intersection in this simplified graph. . . . O is the locus of the signifier's treasure, which does not mean the code's treasure, for it is not that the univocal correspondence of a sign with something is preserved in it, but that the signifier is constituted only from a synchronic and enumerable collection of elements in which each is sustained only by the principle of its opposition to each of the others" (E 304/8–14, EF 806).

subject which encounters language ($\overrightarrow{\$.I(O)}$) is never confronted solely with an isolated signifier, but always with language as a system ("the signifier is constituted only from a synchronic . . . collection of elements"). A child learning to speak, for example, does not encounter separate words and sounds, but rather a network of them. Even if this network is not clear to the child from the beginning, it is still the case that the words and sounds it picks up are articulated with each other and form a system. If this were not the case they could never be or become meaningful, for this system is not of the order of code, in which a strict correlation exists between the signified and the signifier.[4] We have already seen this—signifiers signify on the basis of their difference, such that a strict correlation between signifier and signified is excluded from the start ("each is sustained only by the principle of its opposition to each of the others").

Here we must note, however, that Lacan talks about a number of signifiers that is in principle enumerable. Now, earlier we used words ("titles," *mer/mère*) to illustrate the various properties of the signifier. Is there, then, a theoretically enumerable number of words? Can new words not be invented without end? Is the word, then, really the chief model that Lacan has in mind when he speaks of signifiers? We must answer these questions in the negative. For Lacan, signifiers are first and foremost the

---

4. Here one might think, for example, of the Morse code system, in which every signal can be coupled with a specific letter. One can also think here of the "language" of bees which can, for example, pass on information as to places where food may be found. For Lacan it is here not a matter of a "language" in the proper sense: "We can say that it is distinguished from language precisely by the fixed correlation of its signs to the reality that they signify" (E 84, EF 297). We should also think here of the mating dances of animals, in which the various elements of the "ritual" have a clear and fixed meaning that can always be followed by an adequate response.

phonemes spoken of by phonology. These phonemes, and the rules they follow, can be determined a priori; it is a matter of the minimal differences in the order of sounds on the basis of which a signifier can signify. This system of phonological differences, however, in no way positively anticipates the possible *meanings* of the signifier. What the signifiers will actually signify is exclusively dependent upon the context in which they are included. The system of language thus only holds open the space by which signifiers can signify. From this specification of the signifier in terms of phonological differences, we also gain a first reading of the fact that Lacan links the order of signifiers with the voice (*signifiant-voix*)[5]—for as phoneme, the signifier has above all a vocal character.

Lacan claims that the synchronic structure of language (O) is more concealed than the diachronic, of which it is nonetheless the foundation.[6] The synchronic structure, however, takes us back to the origin of meaning in the metaphor. The child who says that a dog meows and a cat barks disconnects the sound that imitates the cry (onomatopoeia) from the object (dog, cat), and in this way it breaks through the univocal relation between the sound and the object to make the sign into a signifier. The break between the object and the sign, Lacan continues, imme-

---

5. When we deal further with the structure of desire, we will need to bring this reference to the voice into relation with the so-called "object *a*."

6. "But the synchronic structure is more hidden, and it is this structure that takes us to the source. It is metaphor in so far as the first attribution is constituted in it—the attribution that promulgates 'the dog goes miaow, the cat goes woof-woof,' by which the child, by disconnecting the animal from its cry, suddenly raises the sign to the function of the signifier, and reality to the sophistics of signification, and by contempt for verisimilitude, opens up the diversity of objectifications of the same thing that have to be verified" (E 303/22, 304/3, EF 805).

diately raises reality to the sophistics of meaning; from now on the child can freely signify reality without taking account of what reality announces at first sight or "naturally" ("verisimilitude"). This break is therefore equiprimordial with the process of metaphorization. For in the metaphor, new meanings forever arise from the mere substitution of one signifier by another, independent of any founding reference to a reality that might motivate this substitution.[7]

In the second version of the graph, O refers to the system of phonological differences: the signifier's treasure. The entry into this order presupposes that the subject actively negates the causal link between the object and the sign. In other words, it presupposes a sort of "first metaphor" on the basis of which language as language can function.[8] This "first metaphor" "seals" the break between the object and the sign, as it were; from now on, the production of meaning is exclusively dependent upon the articulation of the signifiers. However, to the extent that these signifiers are determined by their difference and there are thus no positive terms in language, Lacan must also explain how a signifier can ever be coupled with a signified in a more or less stable way. The differential determination of the signifier makes it impossible to found this coupling in the signified. It must, as a result, be realized from within the articulation of the signifiers as such. In order to explain this, Lacan introduces

---

7. This is also how it becomes possible to formulate verifiable scientific hypotheses ("the diversity of objectifications of the same thing that have to be verified"; E 304/2–3, EF 805); the idea that the earth turns around the sun, for example, presupposes that we follow the model of the child above, and no longer take the sensible givens as mere evidences ("by contempt for verisimilitude"; E 304/1–2, EF 805).

8. Later we will relate this "first metaphor" to what Lacan calls the "paternal metaphor."

the notion of the "anchoring point" (*point de capiton*). He situates it on the graph at $s(O)$,[9] which indicates the coagulation (s = signification) of the indeterminate possibilities of meaning in the Other (O).

The notion of the "anchoring point" refers to the point where upholstery (*capitonnage*) is fixed, for example on a chair. By this, Lacan wants to indicate the operation on whose basis "the signifier stops the otherwise endless movement (*glissement*) of the signification."[10] Accordingly, the "anchoring point" concerns the way signifiers are coupled with definite signifieds. Of course, this coupling cannot be realized signifier by signifier, given that signifiers have no one signified proper to them. On the contrary, the coupling comes about retroactively, in the articulated statement as such.[11] Every signifier in the statement anticipates the next one, but the meaning is only clear at the end of the sentence; the meaning of the statement is thus determined from its endpoint, and the signifier retroactively coupled with the signified by the punctuation. In this way, according to Lacan, a definite meaning is fixed ("the punctuation in which the signification is constituted as a finished product"[12]). However, this

---

9. "The second, connoted $s(O)$, is what may be called the punctuation in which the signification is constituted as a finished product" (E 304/15–16, EF 806).

10. ". . . the 'anchoring point' (*point de capiton*), by which the signifier stops the otherwise endless movement (*glissement*) of the signification" (E 303/9–11, EF 805). For the full quotation, see Chapter 1, n. 15.

11. "The diachronic function of this anchoring point is to be found in the sentence, even if the sentence completes its signification only with its last term, each term being anticipated in the construction of the others, and, inversely, sealing their meaning by its retroactive effect" (E 303/18–21, EF 805).

12. "Finished" here stands in contrast with "the otherwise endless movement (*glissement*) of the signification" (E 303/10–11, EF 805) that we spoke about earlier (n. 10).

meaning will be constantly ruptured by the slipping movement of language,[13] and for this reason also, Lacan relates the "anchoring point" to a precarious temporal point ("a moment") rather than to something that endures in a stable manner through time ("a duration"). On the graph, this temporal point stands opposite the system of signifiers, which has to be understood as the place where meaning is generated in the way described.[14]

We can define the relation between the language system and the production of meaning in the following way. The introduction of the signifier implies a break with the real;[15] language erects a screen ("a hollow for concealment") in front of or around the real, which cannot be completely subsumed into language. However, in the production of meanings we constantly try to

---

13. It is not unimportant here to note that the notion of an "anchoring point" was actually introduced in the first version of the graph. What is more, one can say without exaggeration that this first version coincides with the introduction of the "anchoring point." Recall the retrograde movement of the vector $\overrightarrow{\Delta.\$}$: we said that this vector describes the movement in which the subject catches the signifier that condemns it to a split existence. The signifier is like a fish that is caught by the subject (*le poisson qu'il croche*). *Crocher* means "to hook" and also refers to *crochetage*, crochet-work. The vector $\overrightarrow{\Delta.\$}$ thus indicates the isolation or hooking together of a sequence of signifiers, whereby a definite meaning retroactively comes to be. Or, more concretely, a signifier as it were "impresses itself" upon the unstructured presentations, needs, and so on. (Δ), and in its retroactive operation, subsumes them into the order of meaning.

14. "Observe the dyssymetry [sic] of the one, which is a locus (a place, rather than a space), to the other, which is a moment (a rhythm, rather than a duration)" (E 304/17–19, EF 806).

15. "Both [the language system and meaning] participate in this offering to the signifier that is constituted by the hole in the real, the one as a hollow for concealment, the other as a boring-hole to escape from" (E 304/20–22, EF 806).

regain the real and remedy the break with it ("a boring-hole to escape from"). Every act of speaking situates itself in this tense relation between language, which closes off a direct and immediate access to the real, and the production of meaning, in which we try to bridge the gap with the real.

Following Lacan, we earlier illustrated the notion of the "anchoring point" by way of the full stop at the end of a sentence. It almost goes without saying, however, that this is not the only example Lacan has in mind, nor perhaps even the main one. For Lacan primarily wants to explain the psychoanalytic process. Accordingly, we must think of the "anchoring point" primarily in terms of the analysand making a slip of the tongue in the course of a psychoanalytic session, or of Dora calling her father a man of means (*vermögend*). In both cases a signifier of the Other interrupts the endless slipping of meaning. The concatenation of stories and opinions is interrupted for a moment by a signifier that imposes itself upon the subject. In the perspective of this signifier, everything that has been said up to that point in the session (or in a whole series of sessions) appears in a new light. This shows us why Lacan says that the subject even receives the message it emits from the Other.[16] In the analysis, the meaning of the discourse of the analysand is determined retroactively by signifiers that interrupt this discourse at regular intervals ("scansion").[17]

---

16. "[I]t is from the Other that the subject receives even the message that he emits" (E 305/9–10, EF 807).

17. Anticipating the further development of the graph somewhat, we can perhaps already mention here that the signifiers that interrupt the constituted meanings ($s(O)$) have to be situated on the uppermost part of the complete graph, and more specifically at the point ($\$\lozenge D$), which we will discuss later in more detail.

THE SUBJECT AND THE OTHER

O is the Other as the place at or from which meaning is generated. We know that in Lacan, the signified so generated remains open, and in principle indeterminate; the Other in no way positively anticipates the various fixations of meaning that can come about at s(O). Thus there is no relation of presupposition between O and s(O); the meanings can never be simply derived from, or traced back to, a pre-given system of rules.[18]

Lacan contrasts this Other with the source of meaning according to modern game theory. According to Lacan, the possible combinations of rules to which the subject is submitted can be determined a priori in game theory, and depend in no respect on empirical and psychological contingencies. Modern information theory thus believes that meaning is derived from pre-given rules, and Lacan claims that information theory understands language as a code in which signifier and signified are consubstantial. The task of the theory is thus to discover and document the rules by which this code allows information to be exchanged, and in this way, the possible meanings of a signifier can be kept within the limits of what is predictable a priori. Consequently, the production of meaning on this model takes place in a closed circle that runs from O to s(O) and back again; it is in principle possible to trace back any meaning whatsoever to the code, and to the rules that determine its operation.[19] This also means that the subject is in principle master of the message it emits or receives. On the basis of the shared code, the message of a subject

---

18. For the problematic of this section, see Moyaert 1982.

19. Here we only reproduce Lacan's criticism of information theory. We do not go into whether this criticism is justified, as this would lead us too far astray.

can be perfectly reconstructed by a second subject, to whom the message is directed.

For Lacan, of course, this is unacceptable. According to him, the subject is constituted in and through the encounter with an Other in which there is always one signifier too few to definitively determine the signified. The signifier does not stand in the service of a previously given signified, but rather produces it, and signifiers signify only on the basis of their difference from other signifiers. Therefore, there always remains space for new and unexpected possibilities of meaning, which cannot be reduced to a previously given code.[20]

Thus, while the production of meaning does indeed run in a circular movement between O and s(O),[21] for Lacan this is a circle that cannot be closed. In every statement, each signifier anticipates the next ("the assertion . . . refers only to its own

---

20. "For what is omitted in the platitude of modern information theory is the fact that one can speak of code only if it is already the code of the Other, and that is something quite different from what is in question in the message, since it is from this code that the subject is constituted, which means that it is from the Other that the subject receives even the message that he emits. And the notations O and s(O) are justified" (E 305/5–11, EF 807). The place of the code is indeed the Other, in which a strict correlation between signifier and signified can never be realized. Moreover, the message cannot be reduced to the code ("and that is something quite different from what is in question in the message"). The message—what appears as a meaning-effect at s(O)— cannot be perfectly reconstructed from the code, but rather the subject comes into being in the message that it receives from the Other, in the way that we have set out already in connection with the "anchoring point."

21. "The subjection of the subject to the signifier, which occurs in the circuit that goes from s(O) to O and back from O to s(O)[,] is really a circle, even though the assertion that is established in it—for lack of being able to end on anything other than its own scansion, in other words, for lack of an act in which it would find its certainty—refers only to its own anticipation in the composition of the signifier, in itself insignificant" (E 304/23–28, EF 806).

anticipation in the composition of the signifier . . ."), and this anticipatory movement is necessary, but it still does not itself bring about any meaning (". . . its own anticipation in the composition of the signifier, in itself insignificant"). On the contrary, this movement is (provisionally) closed by the punctuation, which determines the moment in which the meaning is retroactively fixed ("the assertion . . . for lack of being able to end on anything other than its own scansion . . ."). In other words, the creation of meaning must be understood in terms of the articulation of the signifiers, and not in terms of a reference to a reality outside of language ("for lack of an act in which it [the assertion] would find its certainty . . .").

However, every statement that comes to be in this way does immediately refer back to the system (O) out of which it is realized, for every statement anticipates other possible statements, and these make a further determination of the meaning of the first statement possible. Thus, for example, in the statement "I think, therefore I am," "I think" stands in opposition to "I experience," "I feel," and so on, which further specify the meaning of this statement.

We can also understand how in this way, what we might call "series of statements" can arise, and together form the "discourse of the Other." This "discourse of the Other" (*discours de l'Autre*) is the historically determined fixation of meaning, whereby signifiers are coupled with signifieds in a more or less stable manner, and reality can appear to us in a certain way as meaningful on the basis of those signifieds. For example, the great religious and ideological systems all belong to this "discourse of the Other," as do the stories our parents and grandparents told us about previous generations of our family. Obviously, the ideas, values, commands, and prohibitions that are expressed in this discourse are often contradictory, and cannot be brought into a simple unity. The discourse of the Other is a complicated network of contradictory stories, commands, and prohibitions, in which we must seek a way to carry on our existence in a meaningful manner.

All of this has the immediate result that the circular movement from O to s(O) and back again always remains open. It cannot be closed; every discourse must recognize its own limitations and incompleteness. For every discourse—every statement—refers to the Other, in which fixations of meaning can only be provisional and the signified will never be definitively determined. The circle of which we spoke is thus rather a spiral, in which after every movement from s(O) to O and back again, the existing limits and boundaries are slightly displaced. Lacan himself suggests the impossibility of closure when he speaks of a "squaring of the circle" (la quadrature du cercle).

We can present this idea in yet another way. The graph describes the way the subject is constituted in and through the confrontation with the order of signifiers.[22] The subject is essentially dependent upon the system of signifiers (O), without which it cannot exist as a subject.[23] It is submitted to the symbolic order from which it must inevitably derive ("to have to count itself in on it"); at the same time, every determination is insufficient to say "who or what" this subject is precisely. Every

---

22. "The subjection of the subject to the signifier, which occurs in the circuit that goes from s(O) to O and back from O to s(O) . . ." (E 304/23–24, EF 806).

23. "Yet such a squaring of the circle is impossible, but only by virtue of the fact that the subject is constituted only by subtracting himself from it and by decompleting it essentially in order, at one and the same time, to have to count itself in on it, and to function in it only as lack [translation modified: s'y compter et n'y faire fonction que de manque]" (E 304/38, 305/2, EF 806–807).

determination of it remains deficient, so that the subject can never coincide with the Other.[24] The subject remains, essentially indeterminable, in the Other, outside of which it cannot exist ("[it has] to count itself in on it, and . . . function in it only as lack").[25]

Not only can the circular movement between O and s(O) not be closed—it is, in addition, founded in itself. The production of meaning does not find its ground in a pre-given reality that is expressed in language. It is, rather, exclusively dependent on the articulation of the signifiers among themselves. Consequently, there is no external criterion that would allow us to definitively decide for one discourse as against others.[26] How, for example, could a definitive judgment ever be expressed about the truth of the stories told about our families, when it is precisely from these stories that our families get their form? Or how could one ever find in reality a conclusive proof for or against the systems of meaning by which we live, such as the great religious and ideological systems, when our perception and experience of reality is determined by them in its smallest de-

---

24. "[T]he subject is constituted only by subtracting himself from it [the circular movement] and by decompleting it essentially in order . . . to have to count itself in on it, and to function in it only as lack" (E 304/39, 305/2, EF 806–807).

25. The existential significance of this abstract idea will be discussed in more detail later on, when we deal with the structure of desire.

26. "Thus it is from somewhere other than the Reality that it concerns that Truth derives its guarantee: it is from Speech. Just as it is from Speech that Truth receives the mark that establishes it in a fictional structure" (E 305/39, 306/2, EF 808). "Let us start out from the conception of the Other as the locus of the signifier. Any statement of authority has no other guarantee than its very enunciation, and it is pointless for it to seek it in another signifier, which could not appear outside this locus in any way. Which is what I mean when I say that no metalanguage can be spoken, or, more aphoristically, that there is no Other of the Other" (E 310/36, 311/2, EF 813).

tails? This also explains why Lacan speaks about the "fictional structure of the truth" (*structure de fiction*). The "discourse of the Other"—for example, the great religious and ideological systems—cannot simply be understood as a reproduction (whether faithful or not) of reality, since this reality can only appear as meaningful on the basis of this discourse. In this sense, the discourse of the Other has an essentially performative character; it institutes itself what it describes. This discourse, therefore, has only itself as its guarantee. Lacan also expresses this idea by claiming that there is "no Other of the Other" or "that there is no metalanguage which can be spoken."

THE OTHER AS "WITNESS"

According to Lacan, language introduces the dimension of the truth into reality. As long as the break between object and sign is not effected, it makes no sense to talk about the "truth"; in a world in which there is no distance between reality and those who live in it, the truth can never be a problem. This presupposes, on the contrary, that a gap is achieved between the object and the sign, by which reality loses its self-evidence. It presupposes, in other words, the realization of the "first metaphor," which we discussed above. The "first metaphor" makes a signifier of the sign, and in this way it introduces not only the dimension of the truth, but also the possibility of lying, which is something more and something other than pretense.[27] Animals are also capable of the lat-

---

27. "Indeed, animals, too, show that they are capable of such behavior when they are being hunted; they manage to put their pursuers off the scent by making a false start. This can go so far as to suggest on the part of the game animal the nobility of honoring the element of display to be found in the hunt.

ter—an animal fleeing before a hunter will sometimes turn back on its tracks and choose another path, in the hope that the hunter will believe that the first track is actually the right one.[28] However, an animal will never trick a hunter into thinking a track is false, only then to escape along this track. Animals, so Lacan writes, may well pretend, but they do not pretend to pretend, for to pretend that one is lying in order to mislead another, one must be in a position to recognize the signifier as a signifier. This presupposes that one can fully distance oneself from the belief in a strict coupling between object and sign, such that one can let the sign say something other than what it suggests at first sight. Lacan goes on to write that just as animals do not leave "false" false trails, neither do they wipe out their tracks, for this would presuppose that the animal realized that the track did not require its living presence to continue to refer to it. More precisely, an animal never makes itself the signified of a signifier attesting to a presence that is past (see also Lacan 1957–58, p. 343).

For lies to work, we must believe in truth. The complex strategies that we sometimes employ to deceive the other can only work when this other is ready in principle to believe what we say; deception is only possible against the background of belief in truth.[29] Consequently, if the signifier introduces the

---

But an animal does not pretend to pretend. He does not make tracks whose deception lies in the fact that they will be taken as false, while being in fact true ones, ones, that is, that indicate his true trail. Nor does an animal cover up its tracks, which would be tantamount to making itself the subject of the signifier" (E 305/24–32, EF 807).

28. "[T]hey [animals] manage to put their pursuers off the scent by making a false start" (E 305/26–27, EF 807).

29. "But it is clear that Speech begins only with the passage from 'pretence' to the order of the signifier, and that the signifier requires another locus—

possibility of lying and deception, then it is only because and in the degree that it is intrinsically interwoven with a reference to the truth. We already pointed out that the circular movement between s(O) and O can never be closed, because every discourse continues to refer to the Other, in which every fixation of meaning can only be provisional. The reference to the truth that is equiprimordial with speech thus has a complex structure. Every act of speaking refers to an Other that is deemed a guarantee for its truth, but the speech act must thereby recognize that at the same time, it can never coincide with this Other. This Other inevitably transcends every discourse, for it is the place from which every discourse arises, and from which it will again be ruptured;[30] and it is for precisely this reason that it can also invoke the reference to a "witnessing Other" (*l'Autre témoin*), under whose auspices every discourse takes place without ever being able to coincide with it ("the witness Other than any of its partners").

We know that for Lacan, there is no Other of the Other, and that every discourse must recognize its own limitedness and incompleteness. The circular movement of s(O) to O and back again cannot be closed. According to Lacan, if it *were* closed, we would

---

the locus of the Other, the Other witness, the witness Other than any of the partners—for the Speech that it supports to be capable of lying, that is to say, of presenting itself as Truth" (E 305/34–38, EF 807).

30. For this reason Lacan also writes in the quotation we are occupied with here, ". . . that the signifier requires another locus . . . for the Speech that it supports to be capable of lying, that is to say, of presenting itself as Truth" (E 305/35–38, EF 807). The Other "supports" every act of speaking, since it is the place from which every such act comes into being ("the Speech that it supports"); as *locus* of the signifier, it makes the lie possible, because it installs the dimension of the truth ("for the Speech that it supports to be capable of lying, that is to say, of presenting itself as Truth").

end up in psychosis,[31] for psychotic discourse—he seems to be thinking particularly of paranoia here—actually gives a message about the code (*messages de code*) and the code of the message (*codes de message*) at one and the same time. Code and message convert perfectly into each other, so that speech loses all obscurity for itself and the subject simply coincides with the Other as "Witness of the truth" ("the subject of psychosis, the subject who is satisfied with that previous Other").[32] One can think here, for example, of a psychotic patient for whom every letter of the alphabet has a specific meaning. Or one can think of patients who study the syllables of their own name because they suspect that a hidden meaning lies enclosed in them. Both the letters of the alphabet and the syllables comprising the name are here understood as a message about the code (*messages de code*), and conversely, this code also puts them in a position to decipher what they hear, see, or participate in without any ambiguity (*codes de message*). Code and message have here simply become mirror images of each other,[33] or to formulate the same thing in terms of the graph: the circle between s(O) and O is closed.

---

31. "Code messages or message codes will be distinguished in pure forms in the subject of psychosis, the subject who is satisfied with that previous Other" (E 305/12–14, EF 807). We will examine this problematic more extensively later on, when we deal with the psychotic position as such.

32. Or to put the same thing another way: for the psychotic there is in fact an Other of the Other, whose place he or she occupies. For the same reason he or she fails to appreciate the impossibility of a metalanguage.

33. One can understand, therefore, that for Lacan psychosis is in a certain sense the truth of "modern information theory." For psychotic (and more particularly paranoid) language is characterized, in analogy with "modern information theory," by a strict coupling of the signified with the signifier.

4

The Symbolic and the Imaginary

THE IMAGINARY: GENERAL REMARKS

Up until now we have mainly addressed the symbolic and the real in their mutual relations. It is now time to submit the category of the imaginary to critical investigation, and to define its place on the graph. Before inscribing the imaginary in the graph, however, we will first try to set out its general meaning. What does Lacan understand by the imaginary?

Lacan developed this category chiefly in the thirties and forties, specifically in relation to the so-called mirror-stage, which functioned as a paradigm for it.[1] According to Lacan, the

---

1. "At this point the ambiguity of a failure to recognize that is essential to knowing myself (*un méconnaître essentiel au me connaître*) is introduced. For, in this 'rear view' (*rétrovisée*), all that the subject can be certain of is the anticipated image coming to meet him that he catches of himself in his mirror. I shall not return here to the function of my 'mirror stage,' that first strategic point that I developed in opposition to the favor accorded in psychoanalytic theory to the supposedly *autonomous ego*. The academic restoration of this supposedly 'autonomous ego' justified my view that a misunderstanding was involved in any attempt to strengthen the ego in a type of analysis that took as its criterion of 'success' a successful adaptation to society—a phenomenon of mental abdication that was bound up with the aging of the psychoanalytic group in the diaspora of the war, and the reduction of a distinguished practice to a label suitable to the 'American way of life.' In any case, what the subject finds in this altered image of his body is the paradigm of all the forms of resemblance that will bring over on to the world of objects a tinge of hostility, by projecting on them the manifestation of the narcissistic image, which, from the pleasure derived from meeting himself in the mirror, becomes when confronting his fellow man an outlet for his most intimate aggressivity" (E 306/17, 307/9, EF 808–809).

dynamic of the mirror-stage teaches us that the ego comes into being in and through an identification with an image of itself, and because it is with one's own mirror image, Lacan calls this identification "narcissistic." This narcissistic identification[2] puts the infant in a position to grasp itself as a unity at a moment when its motoric coordination and coenesthetic experience of unity are not yet fully realized. Here one can think of the example of the small child in its crib, tentatively feeling for itself. The child does not always immediately find the hand or foot for which it reaches, as if it does not yet know very well what belongs to its own body and what does not. The image anticipates an experience of unity that thus does not yet exist in reality. On the basis of the identification with this image, the infant feels it has a certain degree of control over itself; it is no longer a plaything of confused body experience, as yet without a stable attachment to a recognizable bodily form. For Lacan, this explains the jubilation that accompanies the mirror experience:[3] the child playfully experiments with the relation between the movements of the image with respect to its reflected surroundings, and with the relation of this image to itself and the persons and objects that surround it (Lacan 1949; E 1, EF 93). The equivalence to the image for which the identification strives, however, is doomed to fail. On the basis of the identification, I *am* the image in which I find myself as a totality and a unity. Yet at the same time, this identification brings about a division of the ego. I identify myself with an image that at the same time separates

---

2. Obviously this identification is not only with the mirror image in the strict sense, but also with other children of a similar age, as long as the age difference does not exceed a certain threshold.

3. ". . . from the pleasure (*l'effet jubilatoire*) derived from meeting himself in the mirror . . ." (E 307/7–8, EF 809).

me from myself: I am another. "I" find myself by anticipation in something that I myself am not, and with which I will never be identical.

In this context, let us return to the initial situation of the mirror-stage. In the first moment, the infant does not yet grasp itself as a bodily unity, and seems in a large degree to be the plaything of the sensations and affects that well up from its body but that it can not adequately locate. Here the identification with the mirror image brings comfort. The mirror image offers a sort of matrix, on the basis of which a certain control and mastery over the confused (and confusing) experience of the body becomes possible. This control and this mastery, however, can never be total; for that over which we strive for mastery can at best be only partially visualized, and escapes the image with which I identify myself. The sensations and affects by which I am touched are thus not immediately present in the image, and always remain somewhat incomprehensible. A great deal goes on in the lived body that I cannot really place in the image by which I appear to myself; I always experience myself somewhat differently from the way in which I see myself.[4] Between the imaginary body and the real body of sensation yawns an unbridgeable chasm. Lacan speaks in this context of a "primordial

---

4. Thus in his text "The Mirror Stage as Formative of the Function of the I," Lacan (1949) writes, "But the important point is that this form situates the agency of the ego, before its social determination, in a fictional direction, which will always remain irreducible for the individual alone, or rather, which will only rejoin the coming-into-being (*le devenir*) of the subject asymptotically, whatever the success of the dialectical syntheses by which he must resolve as *I* his discordance with his own reality" (E 2, EF 94).

Later on we will have to bring this difference between self-experience and self-image into relation with the gap between the real body and the symbolic, which we dealt with earlier.

Discord" that characterizes the relation of humanity to nature and to its own body (Lacan 1949; E 4, EF 96).

We called the mirror-stage the paradigm of the imaginary. This also implies that Lacan calls imaginary all relationships in which I identify myself with an other in his or her totality, as well as all situations in which I try to grasp myself in an image of myself. Take, for example, a scientist forever arguing with colleagues who study the same topics or authors as she does. Due to her identification with her colleagues, she feels threatened by them and envies their achievements, for on the basis of her identification, she *is* the other, and the achievements in question really should have been her own. Alternatively, one might consider the case of an analysand who spends his time in analysis giving long descriptions of what his character is really, and of his numerous positive and negative characteristics. An analysand who speaks this way sets up an image of himself with which he identifies, and which he hopes his analyst will want to confirm. But both the scientist and the analysand from our examples will very quickly be confronted with the hopeless character of their project. No one is an exact copy of someone else, and even our analysand will quickly realize that his self-image displays significant hiatuses. Again and again affects will arise (jealousy, aggressivity, etc.) that cannot be reconciled with his self-image; and again and again, he will be surprised by his own speech. In this way he comes into contact with "something" in him that cannot be mastered, and that interferes with the image he believed could be the perfect reflection of his being.[5]

According to Lacan, however, it is proper to the peculiar dynamic of the ego to misrecognize its structural inequivalence

---

5. One can recognize here the problematic of "empty speech," which we dealt with above.

with the image with which it identifies. The ego thinks it encounters itself in the image; it believes in the equivalence between what it is and what it sees (or thinks about itself). For Lacan, every cognition of the self is necessarily accompanied by a misrecognition. The image in which I think I recognize myself has an essentially anticipatory character: it anticipates a unity that does not yet exist and which, for familiar reasons, can never be complete.[6] This also explains why Lacan calls the ego an *imaginary* structure—on the one hand the ego comes to be by means of an identification with an image, while on the other it has an essentially illusory character. The ego believes in the possibility of an equivalence that is structurally impossible.

This last point also allows us to describe some further characteristics of the "imaginary relation." In the first place, imaginary relations are marked by a specific form of *aggressivity*. The ego comes to be in and through an identification with an image: I am the other. For the ego that lives believing in its equivalence with the image, every inequivalence will be unbearable, and will provoke aggressivity. One can imagine, for example, that our aforementioned scientist will react with aggression when she finds out that her colleague-competitor's publication is better received than her own publications on the same subject. This anger might be directed against the colleague concerned—our aggrieved scientist might reproach him for being a conceited show-off, and say that he considers it beneath him to greet her politely, or deliberately fails to footnote her contribution. This makes it immediately

---

6. "At this point the ambiguity of a failure to recognize that is essential to knowing myself (*un méconnaître essential au me connaître*) is introduced. For, in this 'rear view' (*rétrovisée*), all that the subject can be certain of is the anticipated image coming to meet him that he catches of himself in his mirror" (E 306/17–21, EF 808).

clear that in situations such as these, the subject will not only experience her own aggressivity, but will also have the impression of being treated aggressively by others. However, the aggression might just as well be directed against the ego instead, so that she sinks into depression, for example: "If I do not receive the recognition I deserve, then nothing is worth the trouble." In just the same manner, our analysand might react to any remarks of the analyst that endanger his self-image with aggression against himself, his analyst, or the analysis itself. In the worst case, he could break off the analysis or fall prey to despair: "What is the use of analysis when my analyst does not accept what I tell him about myself?" It is clear that in the majority of cases, the aggression is directed against both the image (or whoever incarnates the model with which I identify) and the ego alternately.[7] Since I *am* the other, by virtue of identification, the distinction between the pole against which the aggression is directed and the pole from which it comes will in principle be unstable.

The ambiguity of imaginary aggressivity, however, goes even further than we have just indicated. We suggested that imaginary aggressivity is caused in principle by the inequivalence of the ego and the image from which it borrows its identity. In fact, however, it is aroused just as much by the enslavement of the ego to the imaginary other. The ego owes its identity to the other; in order to be or to become someone, I have to identify with something that comes from without, and thus with something I myself am not and have not brought about. I can only acquire my "own" identity by alienating myself in and through an identification with another. The imaginary genesis of the ego is, in other words, marked by an irresolvable paradox: one's "own" identity is always

---

7. In paranoia, for example, where the patient experiences the aggression as coming exclusively from without, this dialectic is blocked.

and structurally a borrowed identity. This implies that the other appears as an obstacle that has to be destroyed, and that precisely in the degree that my identification with it is successful. Affects such as jealousy and feelings of rivalry are also essentially bound up with the imaginary. One might think, for example, of children who cannot bear that their brother or sister receive anything unless they themselves receive something of similar worth, or of husbands who cannot stand their wives talking to other men. Seeing themselves as the same as the other in the strictest sense, by virtue of imaginary identification, they can only see this other as a usurper.

The ego arises on the basis of an identification with an image, and this ego belongs to the structure of subjectivity itself. The mirror-stage is thus no passing phase; on the contrary, it is codeterminative for how we stand in the world and relate to ourselves and to others. This implies that the possibility of an aggressive derailment belongs, to a greater or lesser extent, to all our relations with others. The other is not only someone like me to whom I am attached—he or she is also always a potential enemy.[8]

Lacan has often been reproached for leaving little or no place for the affect in his metapsychology. The foregoing clearly shows that this criticism must at least be nuanced. Lacan does indeed conceive of the whole field of what we normally understand as affects in terms of imaginary intersubjectivity, but what is at stake when he does so is less a misjudgment or neglect of the affects

---

8. "In any case, what the subject finds in this altered image of his body is the paradigm of all the forms of resemblance that will bring over on to the world of objects a tinge of hostility, by projecting on them the manifestation of the narcissistic image, which, from the pleasure derived from meeting himself in the mirror, becomes when confronting his fellow man an outlet for his most intimate aggressivity" (E 307/4–9, EF 809).

than a resituating of them. We have already mentioned aggressivity, jealousy, and feelings of rivalry; but other affects too can and must be understood primarily in terms of the imaginary. Let us take fear and pity as examples. We feel pity only for those who are like us—those in whom we can recognize ourselves. Fear similarly presupposes an identifiable and recognizable danger;[9] for example, we fear someone because we ascribe motives and intentions to her not entirely alien to our own. Fear and pity thus play a role in relations with the other insofar as I can identify myself with her. They are affects that intervene in relationships with an alter ego that can in principle appear familiar for precisely this reason.

From the beginning, the introduction of the mirror-stage had more than metapsychological significance for Lacan; it was also of eminent strategic importance in his conflict with the ego-psychologists,[10] represented by Kris, Hartmann, and Loewenstein, three psychoanalysts who fled the Nazis to the United States and subsequently carried out the most important part of their theoretical work there. The ego-psychologists set out from the idea

---

9. This is precisely what distinguishes fear from anxiety. For Lacan, anxiety has a fundamentally different status from the affects we discuss here—it occupies an exceptional position. We will return to examine the significance of anxiety in more detail later.

10. "I shall not return here to the function of my 'mirror stage,' that first strategic point that I developed in opposition to the favor accorded in psychoanalytic theory to the supposedly *autonomous ego*. The academic restoration of this supposedly 'autonomous ego' justified my view that a misunderstanding was involved in any attempt to strengthen the ego in a type of analysis that took as its criterion of 'success' a successful adaptation to society—a phenomenon of mental abdication that was bound up with the aging of the psychoanalytic group in the diaspora of the war, and the reduction of a distinguished practice to a label suitable to the 'American way of life'" (E 306/ 21, 307/3, EF 808–809).

that there must be a conflict-free core in the ego, which can act as the "ally" of the analyst. The aim of the analysis, then, consists in reinforcing this conflict-free core, so as to enable it to better control the conflict between the demands of the drives and the demands of reality. According to Lacan, ego-psychology thereby sets itself up as the promoter of a strong and autonomous ego, which we might say "rules" as a "sovereign" over the activity of the drives. This ego is capable of bringing the activity of the drives into concord with what the social context prescribes as fitting, and according to these ego-psychologists, that social context is represented in the analysis by the analyst. One can therefore understand why they describe the aim of the analysis in terms of an identification with the analyst. If the analyst does indeed represent social reality, then it almost goes without saying that the shortest path to adapting the activity of the drives to reality runs through the analyst.

Naturally Lacan cannot accept such an interpretation of the psychoanalytic process. For him, the ego the ego-psychologists want to reinforce, which has to be capable of meeting the demands of the "American way of life," is nothing more than an imaginary construct; the mastery it seems to promise is essentially illusory, and is directed primarily to closing off the dimension of the unconscious that is the concern of analysis.

THE IDEAL EGO AND THE EGO-IDEAL

Introduction

To this point we have addressed the imaginary in isolation from the symbolic, but beginning in the early fifties, Lacan claims that this isolation is untenable; the imaginary cannot be thought of independently of the symbolic. In the thirties and forties, Lacan still conceived of the imaginary as an effect of a functional organic inadequacy bound up with a prematurity specific to human birth. Although animals depend for a time on adults of their species to survive, they otherwise gain control of all their essential bodily capacities soon after birth; humans, by contrast, are, as it were, born "too early." According to Lacan, this can be seen from the deficient motoric coordination of the newly born child, among other things—an uncoordination that is accompanied by the immaturity of the pyramidal system at the moment of birth (Lacan 1949; E 4, EF 96). In the first phase of his thought, Lacan was of the opinion that the mirror-stage is to be understood as the answer to this situation; the identification anticipates a state of mastery and control to which the real body does not yet have access, and which, as we have seen, it will never completely attain.

The introduction and the development of the category of the symbolic, however, forced Lacan to fundamentally rethink the function of the imaginary in general, and of the mirror-stage in particular. The mirror-stage is no longer thought of as a remedy for a *real* flaw, but as an attempt to undo one instituted by the *symbolic*; the mirror-stage compensates for a lack in the symbolic, not a real (biological) one. Yet this shift is perhaps less drastic than it seems at first sight. The symbolic lack does not simply float in a vacuum. On the contrary, in our discussion of the "elementary cell" of the graph we connected it with the impossibility of completely subsuming the real body into the symbolic. The body essentially escapes the symbolic system from which it obtains its meaning, and it thus always preserves a certain alienness that cannot be cancelled. In this perspective, the mirror-stage has to be understood as an attempt to win back a fullness of life necessarily lost through the entry into language.

In the case of both biologically and symbolically determined lack, then, the mirror-stage and the imaginary have to provide an answer to the "primordial discord" between the subject and its body. But while in the first case this discord has a real basis, in the second it is founded in the symbolic.

The Place of the Ideal Ego and the Ego-Ideal on the Second Version of the Graph

We are now sufficiently armed to inscribe the imaginary, in its dependence upon the symbolic, into the second version of the graph:

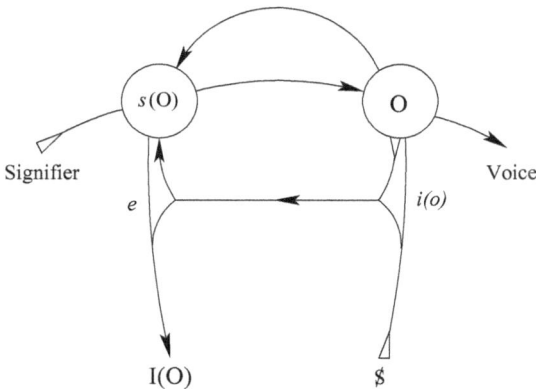

The mirror-stage and the imaginary dimension as we have described them are represented by the vector $\overrightarrow{i(o).e}$, where $i(o)$ stands for the "image of the other," and e for "ego." One notices, however, that the arrow runs from $i(o)$ to e, and not the other way. A first reason for this is the fact that the ego is *formed* by the image with which it identifies; one can compare the bodily pre-subject with Aristotelian "matter," and the image from which this subject borrows its identity with the "form" by which that matter is determined. Lacan adds further that the mirror-stage provides the matrix for the ideal ego, which is an ego that revels in its totalizing perfection and believes it simply coincides with the image, in which it thinks it finds itself. The devastating effects of this ideal ego are easy to see—it believes only in itself, and has lost any possibility of taking distance from itself.

At this point, however, we have to introduce an important nuance. We have already said that from the fifties onward, Lacan interprets the mirror-stage as an answer no longer to a real lack, but rather to a symbolic one. Lacan adds to this that the mirror-stage cannot come about apart from a symbolic ascription. This explains why the vector of the imaginary departs from O, which is to say from the "treasure of signifiers."[11] How are we to understand this concretely?

Consider, for example, a mother who holds her crying child up before the mirror and says, "Look, that's Johnny! Isn't he a big boy!" The movement here starts from O: the image ($i(o)$) is named by the system of signifiers. The symbolic act of ascription ("Look, that's Johnny!") enables the infant to identify with its image. This explains why the vector runs from O via $i(o)$ to e.

We described the signifier as a "principle that actively structures and generates meaning." The expression "Look, that's Johnny! Isn't he a big boy!" establishes a meaning that was not there before; it introduces an order into reality that previously

---

11. "In other words, the pact is everywhere anterior to the violence before perpetuating it, and what I call the symbolic dominates the imaginary . . ." (E 308/20–22, EF 810).

did not exist. It compellingly assigns our crying baby boy a place he could not previously have occupied ("big boy!"). The impact of the signifier is thus difficult to overestimate: the signifier "big boy" establishes a meaning that was not there before, and by which our crying boy is permanently marked.[12] It almost goes without saying that the infant will immediately ascribe great power to the apparent possessor of the key to this principle by which meaning is established.[13]

This example also makes it clear that the Other prefigures what the infant can itself become.[14] The infant is called upon to take its own place in the symbolic system, and it is indispensable that the Other anticipates this possibility. How could the infant ever become someone unless a place has been reserved for it in the Other—in the order of the symbolic? This presupposes that the Other (in the first place the parents) can see in it a "being of (symbolic) possibilities." The crying baby boy from our example therefore does not say to himself, "I'm going to be a big boy." On the contrary, he finds that he already *is* a "big boy," precisely because he is marked by the language of the Other. In other words, he finds that he is that which he already

---

12. Of course, one should not imagine this too naively, as if it would be enough for the mother to say this to the baby boy just once for it to have a great impact. On the contrary, it is evidently a matter here of a process that is extended in time, and by which certain signifiers that are especially invested by the mother can take on a great significance.

13. "The first words spoken (*le dit premier*) stand as a decree, a law, an aphorism, an oracle; they confer their obscure authority upon the real other" (E 306/3–5, EF 808). The first words introduce the subject into an order to which it had no access up until then: the order of the signifier, on the basis of which reality can appear as meaningful.

14. "This is a retroversion effect by which the subject becomes at each stage what he was before and announces himself—he will have been—only in the future perfect tense" (E 306/14–16, EF 808).

was in a previous moment (the moment of anticipated ascription by and in terms of the Other).[15] The tense of the subject is thus, according to Lacan, the "future perfect": "I will have been. In my genesis ('I will') I discover myself as that which I already was for the Other ('have been')."

However, this still does not solve all the problems here. In order that the subject should ever enter into the symbolic, it must be capable of relating to the other other than in a merely imaginary way. The symbolic ascription can only be effective when the other appears to the subject as the representative of an order (of signifiers) that transcends him or her. More specifically, the subject must be capable of attaching itself to the other *qua* Other from which the anticipatory movement goes forth.[16] In any other case, the anticipation will remain purely external to the subject and will have no effect. Obviously, this is not possible by means of an imaginary identification, given that such identification by definition reduces the Other to an equal and fails to recognize any transcendence. At this point in his exposition, Lacan is thus obliged to introduce another sort of identification, one that he says is foundational for the ego-ideal: identification with the "specific trait" (*trait unaire*).

How can I relate to the Other without failing to recognize her alterity and immediately reducing her to an equal? Lacan says that it is possible by means of an identification with a "specific trait" of this Other, where the subject does not identify itself with a total object, but incorporates a specific movement of the hand

---

15. This is also the reason Lacan talks here about a "retroversion effect," in that the subject is, as it were, thrown back upon itself in the movement we are describing here: "I was that (i.e., what I will be) already . . ."

16. Which is to say, the Other as representative of the order (of signifiers) that also transcends her.

or facial expression, for example.[17] We might also think of a child who wants a briefcase just like Daddy's, only smaller. It is clear that these "specific traits" must be understood as signifiers, for here the subject identifies with essentially partial aspects of the object. The child identifies, in other words, not with the other as a whole—as *Gestalt*—but only with a detail that is insignificant in itself. Lacan says that these "specific traits" are "emblems" of the power of the Other ("Take just one signifier as an emblem of this omnipotence . . ."). They are signifiers in which the power of the Other takes on a concrete form, or in which this power is represented in a concrete way.[18] An example can make this clearer.

Let us imagine a student who aspires to a career in a certain academic discipline. A professor who is an authority in this discipline is thus a great model for him—she represents the order in which the student also hopes to have a place. Now, if our student were to behave like the professor in all respects, it would only seem bizarre, ridiculous, or pretentious. The professor in question would then no longer be the representative of an (aca-

---

17. "Take just one signifier as an emblem of this omnipotence, that is to say of this wholly potential power (*ce pouvoir tout en puissance*), this birth of possibility, and you have the specific trait [*trait unaire*: translation modified; see below] which, by filling in the invisible mark that the subject derives from the signifier, alienates this subject in the primary identification that forms the ego-ideal" (E 306/6–10, EF 808). In this regard Lacan speaks about a "specific trait," by analogy with Freud (1921, p. 107). Freud says that the hysteric identifies with an *einziger Zug* of the Other (with a certain trait and not with the Other in his totality). "Specific" (*unaire*) refers to the indefinite article "a" (*un, einziger*)—it is a matter here of one particular trait. *Trait unaire* should therefore be translated as "specific trait." [Sheridan gives "unbroken line," and citations from his translation are hereafter modified accordingly.—Trans.]

18. On the graph of desire, one can perhaps represent this as follows: The subject ($) encounters the Other at O, and at s(O) it pins down certain emblems in which the power of the Other takes on a concrete form.

demic) order to which our student seeks access; on the contrary, the student would simply be treating her as an equal, in a way evidently illegitimate for the rest of the world. The student has to attach himself to his professor, as it were, without immediately reducing her to his exact likeness. He has to enter into a relation in which the Other does not immediately appear as a competitor and a usurper. For Lacan, this is only possible by means of an identification with a "specific trait" of this professor: the way she walks or talks, or even the way she turns the pages of her lecture notes. This identification anchors the student in an order that transcends him, although it does not yet say anything, of course, about the specific manner in which he will himself give form to his own academic career.[19] In other words, this identification establishes an attachment to the Other that does not fail to recognize her alterity, and this is precisely how the Other can (continue to) function as representative of an order that essentially transcends the subject, and to which he seeks access. In contrast to imaginary identification, which simply makes me a rival of the Other, identification with the "specific trait" determines desire without immediately reducing it to a pure duplication of an (imaginary) other. The object to which the identification is oriented consequently functions for the subject as a signifier, and no longer as an imaginary *Gestalt*.[20]

Lacan calls identification with the specific trait the "birth of

---

19. We might also think here of military and civil medals. Of themselves they are often worthless pieces of metal, but they are nevertheless cherished as if they were expensive adornments. This is because they are the tangible mark of the attachment to an ideal (fatherland, freedom, etc.) that transcends us and can give our lives meaning and content.

20. Here Lacan immediately adds, however, that it is a matter of a special sort of signifier—signifiers that have come free, as it were, from the chain of signifiers, in which every determination is only provisional and in which

possibility": the specific trait is a sort of fixed point marking the place from which the subject can become something. It is the place from which the infant can anticipate its own future possibilities in its relation to the Other as such;[21] one thinks, for example, of the little boy who wants a briefcase just like Daddy's, only smaller. Now according to Lacan, this identification with the "specific trait" is constitutive for the ego-ideal—the constellation of "specific traits" of the Other with which the subject has identified itself. Lacan indicates the ego-ideal on the graph with the sigla I(O), because it is constituted in an identification (I) which does not nullify the alterity of its object Other (O), and which therefore concretely anchors the subject in the symbolic.

The identification with the "specific trait" gives a minimal determinacy to the split subject of the signifier. The signifier of the "specific trait," with which the subject identifies itself, "fills in," as it were, the lack of determinacy of the subject (of the unconscious).[22] At the moment that the split subject identifies itself with that signifier, the signifier determines it utterly; the split subject disappears, as it were, under the signifier. Lacan terms this the alienation of the subject.[23]

---

the subject is constantly referred on from one signifier to another. See Lacan 1957–58, p. 294. One also finds there further treatment of the problematic of the "specific trait."

21. ". . . that is to say of this wholly potential power (*ce pouvoir tout en puissance*), this birth of possibility . . ." (E 306/6–7, EF 808).

22. These signifiers are only able to do this because, as we indicated earlier, they have come free from the chain of signifiers. Lacan writes, [C]*e ne sont pas de signifiants mis en jeu dans une chaîne signifiante* ["They are not signifiers put into in play in a signifying chain"] (Lacan 1957–58, p. 294).

23. ". . . the specific trait [translation modified: *trait unaire*] which, by filling in the invisible mark that the subject derives from the signifier, alienates this subject in the primary identification that forms the ego-ideal" (E 306/8–10, EF 808).

Nonetheless, the relation to the Other cannot be reduced to just symbolic identification with the "specific trait."[24] As the subject tries to give itself form in the symbolic, it necessarily encounters the imaginary circuit ($\overrightarrow{i(o).e}$) along its way. The line $\overrightarrow{\$.I(O)}$, which runs via O and s(O), indicates the constitution of the subject in the symbolic on the graph. The movement from S to I(O) is, however, structurally traversed by the vector $i(o).e$, which not only runs in the opposite direction, but is also dominated by completely different tendency. For in the imaginary register, the subject structurally *fails to recognize* the transcendence of its origin; it fails to recognize that it borrows its identity from the Other. It believes, rather, that it is master of itself, and it is blind to its alienation in the symbolic.[25] The ego-ideal thus inevitably stands in a tense relation with the ego and the ideal ego—where the ideal ego appears, the symbolic effectiveness of the ego-ideal is lost or endangered. The graph of desire therefore makes it clear that the dynamic of our existence is sig-

---

24. "It is this image which becomes fixed, the ideal ego, from the point at which the subject stops as ego-ideal. From this point on, the ego is a function of mastery, a play of presence, of bearing (*prestance*), and of constituted rivalry. In the capture to which it is subjected by its imaginary nature, the ego masks its duplicity, that is to say, the consciousness in which it assures itself of an incontestable existence . . . is in no way immanent to it, but, on the contrary, is transcendent, since it is supported by the specific trait [translation modified: *trait unaire*] of the ego ideal . . ." (E 307/10–18, EF 809).

25. "From this point on, the ego is a function of mastery, a play of presence, of bearing (*prestance*), and of constituted rivalry. In the capture to which it is subjected by its imaginary nature, the ego masks its duplicity, that is to say, the consciousness in which it assures itself of an incontestable existence . . . is in no way immanent to it, but, on the contrary, is transcendent, since it is supported by the specific trait [translation modified: *trait unaire*] of the ego ideal . . ." (E 307/11–18, EF 809).

nificantly determined by the irresolvable tension between the ego-ideal and the ideal ego.

The relation to the Other thus is always mediated by numerous imaginary, totalizing identifications,[26] so that the relation between our professor and the student, for example, will also have numerous imaginary aspects. These imaginary identifications, however, are underpinned and borne up by the "specific traits" that form the ideal ego. The symbolic attachment comes logically first. It determines the *direction* the imaginary identifications will take. Or still otherwise, it is precisely because and insofar as there is a symbolic attachment that these imaginary identifications can come into being.[27] The ego takes con-

---

26. "It is this image which becomes fixed, the ideal ego, from the point at which the subject stops as ego ideal" (E 307/10–11, EF 809).

27. Consequently, the symbolic dominates the imaginary. In this context, Lacan also formulates one of his most important objections against Hegelian philosophy. According to Lacan, the conflict between self-consciousnesses, with which the section on self-consciousness in Hegel's *Phenomenology of Spirit* begins, is to be understood by analogy with imaginary aggressivity (E 307/37, 308/25, EF 810). This conflict expresses the original enslavement (*servitude inaugurale*) of humans to their image. On this reading, the Hegelian "desire for recognition" is fundamental to an imaginary identity that comes about by means of an identification with a *Gestalt*. Since this identification makes me the equal of the other, there remains only one way out for desire: the destruction of the other. I desire what the other desires, *because* he desires it, for I *am* the other. The struggle for prestige ("The struggle that establishes it [the dialectic of self-consciousness] is rightly called a struggle of pure prestige . . ."), with which the dialectic of self-consciousness begins, thus receives a psychoanalytic explanation. According to Lacan, what is at stake (*enjeu*) in this struggle is death; the subject puts its life at stake in order to win self-consciousness. This, however, presupposes rules of the game (*règle du jeu*), for a stake only has sense within the context of a symbolic framework to give it meaning. The pre-given system of rules operates precisely to avoid the eventuality that one of the two protagonists in the struggle for recognition fights to the death, and so immediately brings the

crete shape in function of the symbolic identifications of the subject.

The vector of the imaginary thus departs from O and runs via $i(o)$ to e. Here it splits up and runs on towards both $s(O)$ and $I(O)$. We have already dealt with the permanent tension between e and $I(O)$. But why does this vector also run toward $s(O)$? As we know, the dynamic of the mirror stage is situated on the axis $\overrightarrow{i(o).e}$, and refers to the subject as it seeks its identity in an image. Now what Lacan wants to express here is the fact that the production of meaning at $s(O)$ is permanently supported by what takes place on the axis $\overrightarrow{i(o).e}$. The ego constantly crystallizes anew at $s(O)$. It is built up around a more or less stable core of meaning, in which it sees itself—what it is or thinks itself to be—reflected, as in a mirror. That is why Lacan writes that "[T]he ego is only completed by being articulated not as the *I* of discourse, but as a metonymy of its signification" (E 307/ 25–27, EF 809): he means that the ego comes into being as that which is articulated and named in the syntagmatic (metonymical) series, which is to say, in the statement. This immediately implies that the subject as it is objectified in the statement—"the subject *of* the statement"—has simply to be counted as belonging to the domain of the imaginary.

---

dialectic to an end (E 308/19–22, EF 810). According to Lacan, Hegel never saw this primacy of the symbolic over the imaginary, and Lacan therefore concludes, "In other words the pact is everywhere anterior to the violence before perpetuating it, and what I call the symbolic dominates the imaginary . . ." (E 308/19–21, EF 810). For a more detailed commentary on this passage see Van Haute 1990.

5

Language,
the Unconscious,
and Desire

INTRODUCTION

To this point, we have dealt with the problematic of desire only obliquely and implicitly. Lacan explains at the outset, however, that the graph aims to represent the way (unconscious) desire is to be understood in its intrinsic dependence upon the signifier.[1] We now turn to a detailed examination of this intrinsic bond between language and desire, as it appears in the third version of the graph.

We have already situated the mother at point O in the graph. The mother[2] is the first concrete representative—or perhaps, rather, the first incarnation—of that Other on whose basis the imaginary identification with the mirror image comes into being. For reasons that will later become clearer, we will take the relationship with the mother as the starting point for the development of the problematic of desire.

Lacan draws a strict distinction between "need" (*besoin*), demand (*demande*) and desire (*désir*). This distinction goes closely together with the three basic categories of Lacanian thought—the real, the symbolic, and the imaginary, which we have already addressed.[3] We will first attempt to progressively

---

1. "It will serve here to show where desire, in relation to a subject defined in his articulation by the signifier, is situated" (E 303/5–7, EF 805).

2. Obviously, this refers to either the mother or whoever plays her role *de facto*.

3. It would be a mistake, however, to think that these two triads simply overlap each other. Thus demand, insofar as it is marked by a

determine the particular status of desire from its relation to need and to demand, and in this way, it will be possible to unfold the third version of the graph.

BEYOND NEED AND DEMAND: DESIRE

Need (*besoin*) is grounded in a physiological lack, and in principle, there is an adequate object by which it can be satisfied—when I am hungry, I have only to eat for the hunger to disappear. Demand (*demande*), by contrast, pertains fundamentally to linguistically articulated need. It is enacted in the order of language. The subject that articulates the demand is thereby directed to another subject—I ask you for an object that can satisfy my need—and in this sense, demand implies an essentially intersubjective relationship.

Lacan reproaches the psychoanalysts of his day for trying to understand the analytic cure in terms of demand as the linguistic articulation of needs, for in so doing they inevitably raise the problematic of frustration to the truth of human existence and desire. Humans, so these psychoanalysts reason, are beings of needs, and they make demands on their environment in terms of those needs. When their demands are not adequately met, all sorts of neurotic complications result. Now the small child, of course, is entirely dependent upon others for the appropriate satisfaction of its needs, and neurosis is therefore understood as a result of early childhood frustrations (attention that the child

---

misrecognition of lack, belongs to the imaginary; as linguistically articulated need, on the other hand, it refers just as much to the symbolic.

demanded but did not receive, etc.). In this perspective, the aim of the analytic cure is reformulated in terms of relieving these frustrations—by giving the attention and the understanding that one did not receive as a child, and so forth—and learning to deal with them. The latter also implies that analysands must learn to overcome their infantile dependency upon their environment. They must learn to no longer try to obtain in the present, by whatever means, what was denied them in their childhood. Psychoanalysis, Lacan writes, is thereby reduced to a banal educative technique,[4] in which there is no longer a place for desire.

Lacan points out that if we assert that the manner in which early childhood demands are met is determinative for the psychic disturbances that can surface later in life, it is difficult to simultaneously deny that every demand is immediately taken up in the network of signifiers.[5] The dependence of the infant on its surroundings is, as it were, redoubled by its dependence on

---

4. "And this under the pretext that demand, together with the effects of frustration, has submerged everything that reaches them from a practice that has declined into educative banality that cannot be revived even by such a sell-out" (E 309/14–17, EF 811). This passage is situated in the context of a discussion of why philosophers are of the opinion that there is little to be had from Freudian thought. For them the thematization of desire in terms of frustration is of little interest and of little explanatory force. For this reason then they reject psychoanalysis as a whole (E 309/11–17, EF 811).

5. "Yet it is impossible, for those who claim that it is through the welcome accorded to demand that incompatibility is introduced into the needs that are supposed to lie at the origin of the subject, to ignore the fact that there is no demand that does not in some sense pass through the defiles of the signifier" (E 309/26–30, EF 811). The phrase "that incompatibility is introduced into the needs . . ." refers to the psychic disturbances that repeated frustration (due to an inadequate response to the demand of the subject: "the welcome accorded to demand") can bring about.

the universe of language,[6] which can *never* be overcome. We have already pointed out that language institutes a margin over against the biological body, and that needs necessarily receive from the order of signifiers a range that they do not have of themselves, as purely biological needs. The articulation of needs in the order of language and culture leads to their diversification and multiplication, in a way that cannot be understood in terms of biology alone. Thus the need for food is highly diversified, and to a large degree surpasses the level of biological functionality: food is always bound up with rules of politeness, and with all sorts of incontrovertible taboos.[7] All of this cannot be adequately understood in terms of the biological order as such.

Lacan therefore says that the expression of needs in the order of language opens up the dimension of *desire*, which produces a problematic that cannot be comprehended in terms of the frustration and gratification of needs. For example, how can a simple psychology of needs understand and explain the paradoxes of moral philosophy (e.g., how happiness—i.e., the satis-

---

6. "And if the somatic *ananke* of man's powerlessness for some time after birth to move of his own accord, and *a fortiori* to be self-sufficient, ensures that he will be grounded in a psychology of dependence, how can that *ananke* ignore the fact that this dependence is maintained by a world of language, precisely because by and through language needs are diversified and reduced to a point at which their scope appears to be of a quite different order, whether in relation to the subject or to politics? To sum up: to the point that these needs have passed over into the register of desire, with all that this brings in terms of obligations to confront our new experiences with its paradoxes, which have always interested the moralist, with that mark of the infinite that theologians find in it, even with the precariousness of its status, as expressed in its most extreme form by Sartre: desire, a useless passion" (E 309/31, 310/4, EF 811–812).

7. For example, one might think of the prohibition of eating pork and other numerous proscriptions in relation to food in Jewish culture.

faction of desire—can be reconciled with virtue), or the infinity of desire as it has been described by some mystics and theologians? And if we thematize desire in terms of biological need *per se*, how can we ever understand that desire, as Sartre shows, seeks to perpetuate itself on the one hand, while on the other hand it is directed to its own resolution in a state in which the subject would simply coincide with itself? Human desire is thus something more and something other than (linguistically articulated) need, and we did not have to wait for psychoanalysis to realize this. But in that case, what is the specificity of desire according to Lacan, and how does desire arise through language?

Demand thus gives the world of need a range far surpassing the biological. Lacan further relates this to the fact that every demand is essentially an unconditional demand for love,[8] and thus cannot be reduced to the object of the need it articulates.[9] Earlier, we said that demand essentially implies an intersubjective relationship; the demand is directed to an Other, who gives concrete content to the order of signifiers. The infant is in fact confronted not with an abstract Other, but with a concrete and tangible one, who incarnates the order of signifiers in a specific way.[10] We can perhaps best explain this relation by returning to the elementary cell of the graph.

---

8. "It will seem odd, no doubt, that in opening up the immeasurable space that all demand implies, namely, that of being a request for love, I should not leave more play to the question . . ." (E 311/12–14, EF 813). The "question" here being: "What is a Father?" (E 310/19, EF 812), we will come back to treat more fully.

9. In what follows we try to reconstruct a train of thought that Lacan does not as such give in our text, but which we believe is necessary to understand his subsequent argument.

10. This is also why Lacan uses the term *Autre* to designate not only the order of the law and of signifiers as such, but also the subject that gives a concrete content to this order.

It will be remembered that point "Δ" on the graph designates man as a being of needs. In the context that concerns us here, we have to situate at "Δ" the infant as a being of needs, with its natural urge towards affection, warmth, and attachment. This is the child immersed in the world of the elemental, with which it forms a quasi-immediate unity. Here, the child is "pure life," and cannot yet posit the objects that assuage its needs as objects in the proper sense; on the contrary, it takes them as complementary to its own being.[11] The infant, however, inevitably encounters language $(\overrightarrow{S.S'})$ on its way. Or, more concretely, the little child is confronted with the mother, who in reality is the first to occupy the place of the Other and give it a concrete content.[12] The mother is in this sense the first representative of the order of signifiers—an order in which the infant must learn to articulate its needs and its requirement for affection, if it is to be satisfied. The taking up of needs in the world of language is no neutral event, however—linguistic articulation structurally transforms the needs, along with the natural requirement for affection and attachment. From now on, the child demands an object of an Other whose presence is not guaranteed. Language, in other words, breaks through the immediacy of the elemental, to place the infant before an Other that always and unavoidably appears against the background of (possible) absence.

For example, the infant demands the breast of the mother. Obviously this demand is rooted in a state of need—the child is

---

11. It is clear that we must qualify this moment as mythical, as we suggested earlier.

12. Indeed, Lacan writes, "The fact that the Father may be regarded as the original representative of this authority of the Law requires us to specify by what privileged mode of presence he is sustained *beyond the subject who is actually led to occupy the place of the Other, namely the Mother*" (E 311/7–10, EF 813; my emphasis).

hungry and wants to be fed. But above all the child asks that the mother *give* the breast, and that she respond to its appeal. It demands the presence of the mother, and thus her love—the only guarantee of her presence (Borch-Jacobsen 1991, p. 206ff).[13] Lacan terms this demand for love "unconditional" because by definition it goes further than whatever object is necessarily articulated within it.[14] The infant wants to be loved for itself, independent of any economic calculus.[15]

If the demand is to be understood as an unconditional demand for love, then this immediately implies that the object of the demand no longer functions merely as a real object, filling a physiological lack. On the contrary, in the demand the object takes on an eminently symbolic meaning; it is the signifier of the love of the Other. This means that it is essentially a question here of an object that is mediated by language. This object is consequently taken up in the metonymic movement of the order of signifiers, which cannot be closed—there is always one signifier too few to definitively determine the signified, and this means that no object I receive in response to my demands on the Other can ever offer a conclusive guarantee of love.

---

13. Of course, one can ask if Lacan is right to immediately equate the demand for an unconditional presence with a demand for love.

14. We can also recognize this unconditionality in certain forms of love: Will you stay with me no matter what happens? Why didn't you answer my phone calls last night? Didn't you say that you might be home? The lover presumes that his beloved should be at home because he was going to call her—when I call you, you have to be there!

15. This explains why Lacan writes that the demand can only be unconditional "in regard to the Other": ". . . this margin being that which is opened up by demand, *the appeal of which can be unconditional only in regard to the Other . . .*" (E 311/23–25, EF 814; my emphasis). The unconditionality of the demand is intrinsically bound up with the articulation of needs in language. Later we elaborate in more detail on the passage from which this quote comes.

Anyone who wants conclusive proof of the love of the Other inevitably risks ending up in a vicious dynamic. If a pair of lovers each wants absolute assurance of the other's faith and devotion, they can ultimately only find it in common and voluntary death—which immediately ends their love. One can also think of analysands who endlessly keep on asking what they have to do to be happy. These analysands find it impossible to reconcile themselves to the silence of their analyst, which they often experience as aggressive and cruel. In the insistent and often compulsive character of this demand for concrete help, we see the unconditionality that marks the demanding attitude. The refusal of the analyst to enter into this demand signifies for these analysands that the analyst does not love them enough, for example, just like their fathers or mothers before her. They continue to press the point, in the hope of eventually assuring themselves of the love of the analyst. The analyst's task consists in trying to suspend or displace the demand for concrete assistance so that other topics can come up—even if it is only the question of what it is that makes it so difficult for the analysand to give up this demand and free associate. In this way, desire can be given the opportunity to come to the fore.

Lacan points out in this connection that the demand not only opens the infinite, measureless space of love ("the immeasurable space that all demand implies, namely, that of being a request for love"), which cannot be fulfilled by any concrete object—it also closes something off, and withdraws it from view. However much the demand is indeed fundamentally a demand for love, it nonetheless articulates a concrete need, and in so doing it continually threatens to withdraw desire from sight.[16]

---

16. "[It will seem odd that I] should concentrate it on that which is concealed beneath it [translation modified: *ce qui se ferme en deçà*], by the very

Thus the analysand who continually asks for help and advice does not succeed in analyzing her desire as such and for itself. She believes, rather, that the advice of the analyst will enable her to solve her problems once and for all. Her demands are for her no more than they seem *prima facie*—requests for help. It is not at all clear to her that another dimension resonates in the demand. To give another example: the endless whining of a child for sweets (and for more and more of them) is for the child perhaps nothing more than a demand for sweets, and for those surrounding it nothing more than a demand for attention. What neither the child nor those surrounding it realize, however, is that in the whining for sweets may resonate a desire to always have something else, something more—such that no object can assuage that desire. One last example: an analysand says in an introductory session that he wants a solution for his marital problems because he wants to avoid a divorce, but then from a number of other things he says it appears that he is actually already withdrawing from his wife and marriage. In all these cases, precisely because the demand pertains to a concrete object at first sight (help, sweets, the solution to marital problems, etc.), it constantly threatens to obscure the dimension of desire.[17]

---

effect of demand, in order to give desire its proper place. Indeed, it is quite simply, and I will say later in what way, as desire of the Other that man's desire finds form, but it does so in the first instance by representing need only by means of a subjective opacity. I will now explain by what bias this opacity produces, as it were, the substance of desire" (E 311/12–21, EF 813). We leave the idea that "human desire is the desire of the Other" out of consideration for the moment, and return to it later. Presumably, Lacan refers to it here because desire arises through the linguistic articulation (the Other) of the world of needs.

17. Thus Lacan also calls this opacity "the substance of desire" (E 311/20–21, EF 813).

Lacan therefore writes that desire is essentially marked by a subjective opacity: inevitably, what appears first is a concrete demand, for which a concrete solution seems to exist. How can we ever make room for desire here?

DESIRE AND THE LAW: THE DIALECTIC OF DESIRE

Lacan's answer to this problem takes its departure from the relationship between the infant and the first Other—paradigmatically the mother—who gives a concrete content to the symbolic order.[18] At first sight this relation seems to be completely determined by the needs for which the child demands satisfaction. We know that the demand has an unconditional character, which is inseparably bound up with its linguistic nature.[19] In every demand, however, a need is also necessarily formulated—a need that has to be satisfied. But the satisfaction of the need is never really guaranteed, and the infant is inevitably confronted with the inability of the

---

18. "Desire begins to take shape in the margin in which demand becomes separated from need: this margin being that which is opened up by demand, the appeal of which can be unconditional only in regard to the Other, under the form of the possible defect, which need may introduce into it, of having no universal satisfaction (what is called 'anxiety'). A margin which, linear as it may be, reveals its vertigo, on the condition that it is not trampled [translation modified: *pour peu qu'elle ne soit pas recouverte*] by the elephantine feet of the Other's whim. Nevertheless, it is this whim that introduces the phantom of Omnipotence, not of the subject, but of the Other in which this demand is installed (it is time this idiotic cliché was, once and for all, put back in its place), and with this phantom the need for it to be checked by the Law" (E 311/22–32, EF 814).

19. ". . . demand, the appeal of which can be unconditional only in regard to the Other . . ." (E 311/24–25, EF 814).

mother to (immediately) satisfy all its needs.[20] In this way, need introduces a rupture into the relationship between mother and child, and according to Lacan, this rupture is where desire can develop.[21]

What, then, does the mother want? What makes her repeated absences necessary? Or yet again: What does she desire that apparently I cannot give her? To the degree that the little child remains caught in the logic of the unconditional demand for love, it can think of only one solution to this situation—it tries to be or become the object that can fulfill the desire of the mother, and thereby tries to finally assure itself of the mother's love. "If the mother does not give me what I want, then I can always try to coerce her love by presenting myself as the object of her desire." But what is it that the mother actually desires? What must I be or do to obtain the love of the Other? The little child does not possess the key to the desire of the mother; it does

---

20. ". . . this margin being that which is opened up by demand, the appeal of which can be unconditional only in regard to the Other, *under the form of a possible defect, which need may introduce into it, of having no universal satisfaction*" (E 311/23–26, EF 814; my emphasis). There may be another possible reading of this passage: need does not satisfy the universal claims of demand as a demand for love. Need knows only a concrete satisfaction, which as such does not comprehend the dynamic of the demand. This interpretation, however, seems less likely to us given that it points to a structural (and thus necessary) difference between the requirements of the demand and the satisfaction of the need that is formulated in it. Lacan, however, speaks here of "a *possible* defect."

21. Lacan adds to the passage on which we are commenting here that the "possible defect" that need may introduce into the demand of "having no universal satisfaction" is "what is called 'anxiety'" (*ce qu'on appelle angoisse*; E 311/26, EF 814; see n. 18 for full quote). This seems to us to be a reference to "those" (*on*) who see separation anxiety as the prototype of anxiety, a view Lacan rejects. We will return to this later.

not know precisely what she wants. As a result, it makes itself completely dependent upon something over which it has no hold—the object of the mother's desire. For the child, the mother cannot but appear capricious, for despite all its attempts to be what the mother lacks and adapt itself to her, her responses remain unpredictable in the eyes of the infant ("the whim of the Other").[22] She comes and goes as she pleases. Thus, the child is here delivered over to a capricious Other, who seems to decide arbitrarily whether or not she will entertain its demand.[23] As long as the little child remains caught up in the logic of the unconditional demand in this way, and can only understand itself in terms of the (desire of the) mother, there is no place for the development of its own desire. The inevitable rupture between need and demand thus remains without effect.[24]

---

22. Cf. also the following passage from *Les formations de l'inconscient*: *Elle [la loi de la mère] tient simplement, au moins pour le sujet, dans le fait que quelque chose de son* [the child's] *désir est complètement dépendant de quelque chose d'autre, qui, sans doute, s'articule déjà comme tel, qui est bien de l'ordre de la loi, mais cette loi est tout entière dans le sujet qui la supporte, à savoir dans le bon ou le mauvais vouloir de la mère. . . . C'est* [the child] *un assujet parce qu'il s'éprouve et se sent d'abord comme profondément assujetti au caprice de ce dont il dépend . . .* ["It (the law of the mother) holds simply, at least for the subject, in the fact that something of its (the child's) desire is completely dependent on something else, which, no doubt, already articulates itself as such as something of the order of the law, but this law is wholly within the subject that supports it, that is to say, within the good- or the ill-will of the mother. . . . It (the child) is the subject of a subjection (*assujet*) because it senses and feels itself first as profoundly subjected to the whim of that on which it depends . . ."] (Lacan 1957–58, pp. 188–189).

23. This is also the reason Lacan calls this first Other of the demand "real" (E 306/4, EF 805). Indeed, here the Other appears as a power that is not subject to any (symbolic) law.

24. "A margin which, linear as it may be, reveals its vertigo, on the condition that it is not trampled by the elephantine feet of the Other's whim" (E 311/26–28, EF 814).

This also makes it possible to more closely determine the significance of anxiety in Lacan's work, for Lacan associates anxiety with the desire of the Other.[25] Let us see what he means by this.

So long as the child remains locked into the logic of the demand, it also remains powerless before an Other whose desire it wants to fulfill. Now anxiety arises precisely where the infant has the feeling that it could actually *become* the ultimate object of the mother's desire, and that this "project" of being what the mother is lacking might actually succeed. In this regard, one might recall the case of "little Hans" (Freud 1909a). Anxiety first manifests itself when little Hans associates the enigmatic desire of his mother with his own genital sensations. He concludes from this that he himself is the object of his mother's desire. He responds with anxiety to this situation, in which he thinks he is simply nothing other than the object of the desire of his mother and thus threatens to disappear into that desire;[26] for if he were

---

25. "But this prevalence given by the neurotic to demand, which, for an analysis declining into facility, shifted the whole treatment towards the handling of frustration, *conceals its anxiety from the desire of the Other*, anxiety that it is impossible not to recognize when it is covered only by the phobic object . . ." (E 321/12–16, EF 823; my emphasis). We will return to this later in a separate section on the problem of phobia.

26. Thus Lacan writes, immediately after the passage from *Formations de l'inconscient* quoted above (n. 22), *C'est* [the child] *un assujet parce qu'il s'éprouve et se sent d'abord comme profondément assujetti au caprice de ce dont il dépend . . . l'angoisse du petit Hans est essentiellement . . . angoisse d'un assujettissement* ["It (the child) is the subject of a subjection (*assujet*) because it senses and feels itself first as profoundly subjected to the whim of that upon which it depends . . . the anxiety of little Hans is essentially . . . anxiety of subjection"] (Lacan 1957–58, pp. 189–190; my emphasis). The anxiety of little Hans has to do with the fact that he has not separated from his mother, and is only an extension of her. In his relationship with his mother there is no place for his "own" desire. For this whole problematic, see also Lacan 1956–57, p. 199ff.

no more than the object of her desire, any place of his own would be denied him.[27]

The psychoanalytic tradition has always thought that the little child experiences itself as omnipotent. Thus Freud, for example, claims that the ego in the stage of primary narcissism is in a sense its own ideal;[28] it experiences itself as endowed with all perfections. The external world that might correct this image at that moment still has no psychic meaning, according to Freud. In other words, the ego here is self-sufficient. Freud also connects this primary narcissism with the omnipotence of the ideas that to a greater or lesser degree characterize the child's life-world, for example. Lacan calls this theory of the phantasmatic omnipotence of the child an "idiotic cliché," and says that it has to be put in its place once and for all. What we have just said about the real Other puts us in a position to do this. In this perspective, it is in fact not so much that the child experiences itself as omnipotent—rather, the capricious, real Other

---

27. Lacan clarifies this idea by way of a sort of parable about a praying mantis. The female praying mantis literally devours the male during mating. Suppose, Lacan says, that I find myself in the face of a gigantic praying mantis, wearing a mask without knowing what is represented on it (a praying mantis?). Suppose, further, that I cannot see my own reflection in the eye of the insect. I do not know, therefore, what I am for this insect. Consequently, I do not know the desire of the praying mantis, but I do know that the results will be terrible if I am the one she wants—more than enough reason to be anxious. See Lacan, *L'angoisse*, seminar of November 14, 1962 (Lacan 1962–63).

28. By "primary narcissism," Freud understands the stage in the development of the subject in which the ego in the proper sense comes to be. This occurs when the various partial drives, which until then have sought satisfaction in a dispersed manner, are bundled together and take the body as a whole as their object. See Freud 1914, pp. 92–102.

appears omnipotent to the child.[29] This Other not only seems to decide autonomously if it will meet the demand of the child, taking no one else into account; more fundamentally, the infant is delivered over to its desire, and its sheer existence seems to depend on it.

Thus we can also understand why this Other has to be bound by a law governing the relationship between the mother and the infant.[30] A law is necessary to protect the infant from the phantom of the omnipotence of the Other—or from the absolute power of the logic of the unconditional demand, which comes down to the same thing. For without such a law to limit both the claims of the Other and the attempts of the little child to conform to them, the child will be completely delivered over to the Other, and forced to constantly and fruitlessly attempt to adjust itself to the Other in order to gain its love. Only with such a law, then, can the child secure its own place and develop its own desire.

According to Lacan, this means that the law in a sense has its origin in desire.[31] By this Lacan means that desire, if it is to

---

29. "Nevertheless, it is this whim that introduces the phantom of Omnipotence, not of the subject, but of the Other in which this demand is installed (it is time this idiotic cliché was, once and for all, put back in its place) . . ." (E 311/28–31, EF 814).

30. "Nevertheless, it is this whim that introduces the phantom of the Omnipotence . . . and with this phantom the need for it to be checked by the law" (E 311/28–32, EF 814).

31. "But I will stop there and return to the status of the desire that presents itself as autonomous in relation to this mediation of the Law, for the simple reason that it originates in desire, by virtue of the fact that by a strange symmetry it reverses the unconditional nature of the demand for love, in which the subject remains in subjection to the Other, and raises it to the power of absolute condition (in which 'absolute' also implies 'detachment')" (E 311/33–39, EF 814).

come to be at all, demands a law on the basis of which the infant can in some sense free itself from the mother, so that it is no longer obliged to exist exclusively in terms of her wishes and demands. This implies that desire converts the unconditionality of the demand into something absolute. "Absolute" is here to be understood in its etymological meaning: the Latin *absolvere,* which means "to loosen or free." In other words, desire to some degree frees the child from the mother, and the subject is no longer the plaything of the Other.

But what, then, is the *object* of desire? The infant demands something concrete; the demand is a linguistically articulated need. At the same time, however, the little child is confronted with a complete inability on the part of the Other to give an adequate object in response to the child's demand *qua* demand for *love.* For in the demand, the object acquires a symbolic meaning, and it is thereby taken up in the interminable metonymic movement of language. Conversely, the same logic means that the attempts of the child to gain the Other for itself, too, are essentially doomed to fail. The little child demands love, and in order to assure itself of the Other's love, it will inevitably try to meet the demands of the Other in turn. But what precisely does the Other want? Or more correctly, what *object* could be completely adequate to the demands of the Other? For just as much as the objects I receive, the objects I offer the Other have a symbolic meaning; they function as signifiers, which signify only by virtue of their difference from other signifiers. The relation between the infant and the first Other is consequently structured around an irremediable lack installed by the signifier,[32] and it is

---

32. One can recall here the idea we already discussed above: that there is no Other of the Other. In this context this means that there is no Other that could function as the adequate object of desire.

in and through this lack that the subject is able to develop its own desire.

We can now also understand why Lacan speaks about a *dialectic* of desire. The relation between desire and the law indeed has a dialectical character: the order of the law is the order of language, and language introduces a lack out of which desire can arise; on the other hand, the law also arises from desire, which would otherwise remain caught in a total dependence upon the Other. Desire and the law are therefore united by mutual implication, and in this sense are related to each other dialectically.

FURTHER CHARACTERIZATION OF DESIRE: THE TRANSITIONAL OBJECT[33]

To some extent, the infant must detach itself from the Other in order for desire to develop. It must escape the absolute power of the logic of the demand, and transform its unconditionality into something "ab-solute." How are we to imagine this process concretely? In answering this question, Lacan refers to the notion of the transitional object, as developed by the British psychoanalyst Winnicott.[34] Here it is not necessary to set out this important notion *in extenso,* and we will limit ourselves to its essentials.

---

33. See Winnicott 1975.

34. "For the gain obtained over anxiety with regard to need, this detachment is successful in its first, humblest form, that in which it was detected by a certain psychoanalyst in the course of his pediatric practice [Winnicott was trained as a pediatrician], and which is called 'the transitional object,' in other words the bit of 'nappie' or the beloved bit of material that the child never allows to leave his lips or hand" (E 312/1–6, EF 814).

It is often observed that a certain object—a corner of blanket, a bit of material, or a teddy bear—takes on a special significance for the child, especially when it has to go to sleep. The child presses the object to itself, sucks on it, and cannot get to sleep without it. It is an object that can scarcely be distinguished from the child, but at the same time it is also "the first not-me possession" (like the teddy bear). *In concreto* this means that from a libidinous standpoint, this object is somehow situated *between* the objective and subjective orders.

In the first phase of development, according to Winnicott, psychic functioning is characterized by a "primary creativity"; the child hallucinates the object it needs (in this case the breast), and it is the mother's task to offer the breast at precisely that moment. The child can thus believe that reality is its own creation; at this stage it lives in a purely subjective world. The introduction of the reality principle, however, puts an end to this.

In this perspective, the transitional object is an object of a sort that can neither be called subjective nor objective. From the standpoint of the observer, of course, the object involved here is not created by the child; the child, by contrast, does not view the object as coming from the external world. Yet for the child it is not a hallucinatory object either. In some sense, the object exists "between" objectivity and subjectivity—it belongs, so Winnicott claims, to the domain of illusion, and in this domain, the child need not concern itself with whether it belongs to the inner world or the outer one. One might think here of the world of children's play, but for adults, too, the sphere of illusion remains exceptionally important—in art, for example. It would be a huge mistake to read the novels of Cervantes or Dickens in terms of whether or not what they describe corresponds to objective reality.

To some extent, the transitional object thus makes it possible for the infant to detach itself from the mother, with whom it has hitherto tried to live according to the logic of the unconditional demand, and pass over into the larger world of imagination. For Lacan, this implies an overcoming of anxiety; the relation to the Other is no longer governed by the dread of becoming the plaything of its desire.[35] The transitional object allows this escape from the omnipotence of the first Other without thereby abandoning attachment completely. Lacan therefore calls this object an emblem;[36] it is a symbolic sign that replaces the mother as the possible adequate object of my demand for love.

According to Lacan, the appearance of the transitional object is a process of metaphorization. We have already seen that metaphor causes a break with reality; the child who says the dog meows and the cat barks breaks through the univocal relation between the object and the sign. This implies that through the process of metaphorization, direct access to the object is closed off, and the relation to the object is henceforth necessarily mediated by language. In this way meaning can arise, but at the same time something is essentially lost. No matter how much we might try to express it fully, the object can never be totally integrated into the symbolic. Now according to Lacan, the transitional object replaces the mother in the same way as signifiers replace the object. The mother as first Other, with whom we hope to bring about a complementary relation from which every lack

---

35. This is also why Lacan writes, "For the gain obtained over anxiety with regard to need . . ." (E 312/1, EF 814). The expression "with regard to need" apparently refers to the first Other, whose primary task seems to consist in satisfying the needs of the child. The overcoming of anxiety implies that I can detach myself from this Other.

36. "This is no more than an emblem, I say; the representative of representation in the absolute condition is at home in the unconscious, where it causes desire according to the structure of the phantasy that I will now extract from it" (E 312/7–10, EF 814).

would be excluded, is substituted by a transitional object that immediately closes off immediate access to her. From now on the child accepts that the mother is only accessible via substitutes that as such cannot give what is expected from them, that is, the mother herself.[37]

In the passage we are dealing with here, Lacan calls the first Other "the representative of representation." Here Lacan employs Freudian terminology for his own purposes. According to Freud, the drive is represented in the psyche in two different ways: by presentation (*Vorstellungsrepräsentanz*) and by affects (*Affektrepräsentanz*). Now, we know that the world of the affect has to be understood in terms of the imaginary, and as a result does not belong to the unconscious in the proper sense.[38] Accordingly, Lacan reads the expression *Vorstellungsrepräsentanz* ("the representative of the representation") as "the (first) representative of the world of representation (language)," which is to say, the mother. The world of representation is in fact traditionally understood as the order in which reality appears in a meaningful way. Since for Lacan the appearance of reality is exclusively dependent upon the order of language or the order of signifiers, he can equate the (order of) "representation" that Freud talks about with (the order of) the signifier. The "(first) representative or incarnation" of this order is the mother. Lacan goes on to say that once the child has detached itself to some

---

37. It is far from certain whether Winnicott would agree with such an interpretation of the function and significance of the transitional object, for Lacan's interpretation sees the transitional object in the perspective of loss and mourning (for the lost object). This seems to be much less the case with Winnicott.

38. We have already referred to the special status of anxiety in this context.

degree from this "representative of representation" and accepted that it can be accessed only by means of substitutes, it disappears into the unconscious,[39] where it continues to function as the ultimate mainspring of human desire. We now turn to a closer examination of this idea.

THE UNCONSCIOUS IS THE DISCOURSE OF THE OTHER[40]

The unconscious, so Lacan writes in the context we are concerned with here, is the discourse of the Other (*L'inconscient est le discours de l'Autre*). Now Lacan writes that "of" here (*de*) must be read as an objective genitive: "The discourse *about* the Other" (*De alio in oratione*), and in this sense the dictum can be greatly elucidated by the idea that the "representative of representation" continues functioning in the unconscious as the ultimate mainspring of desire.

We have already seen that the relation between the infant and the Other is essentially structured around an irremediable lack installed by the signifier, so that the subject can in prin-

---

39. For this reason Lacan writes, "the representative of representation in the absolute condition . . ." (E 312/7–8, EF 814). For it is a matter of the mother insofar as one can detach oneself from her. This presupposes, as we said above, that the unconditionality of the demand is substituted by something "ab-solute."

40. "This is what I mean by my formula that the unconscious is '*discours de l'Autre*' (discourse of the Other), in which the *de* is to be understood in the sense of the Latin *de* (objective determination): *de Alio in oratione* (completed by: *tua res agitur*). But we must also add that man's desire is the *désir de l'Autre* (the desire of the Other) in which the *de* provides what grammarians call 'the subjective determination,' namely that it is *qua* Other that he desires (which is what provides the true compass of human passion)" (E 312/14–21, EF 814).

ciple give or obtain no adequate answer to the question of what precisely the Other desires (of it). However, this does not stop this problematic from haunting the subject. In fact, according to Lacan, the presentations and fantasies that make up the core of the unconscious refer in numerous ways to our irrevocably lost encounter with the first Other, and the relation we enjoy with it.[41] For example, they attempt to give this loss a concrete form, or to reverse it in the imagination.[42] True, the Other is not an object to which we are directed as to the objects of the demand. It remains, nonetheless, the effective center of gravity to a movement of substitution—a movement that never ends, and that gives life to desire. As a rule, however, this origin of desire remains withdrawn from sight because and insofar as demand inevitably focuses attention on ever new, specific objects.[43]

In the same context, Lacan writes that human desire is the desire of the Other; the subject stands under the mastery of the signifier, which causes the loss that gives life to desire. If we are to understand the peculiar character of human passion, Lacan believes, we must understand this mastery and loss in terms of a break with the biological order and the order of the instincts. Animal instinct implies a sort of "knowledge" of reality, inscribed

---

41. We will deal with this problematic in more detail later, in connection with the status of the phantasy. Its precise significance, however, can only be made completely clear in the chapter on psychopathology (Chapter 8).

42. Therefore Lacan also writes in a passage we have mentioned earlier (see n. 36) that the representative of representation is located in the unconscious, "where it causes desire according to the structure of the phantasy that I will now extract from it" (E 312/8–10, EF 814).

43. "For it is clear that the state of nescience in which man remains in relation to his desire is not so much a nescience of what he demands, which may after all be circumscribed, as a nescience as to where he desires" (E 312/11–13, EF 814).

in the genetic material; instinct belongs to the natural capacities for survival with which the living being is equipped. Instinct thus must be thought of in terms of a minimal coadaptation between the living being and nature. Human desire, by contrast, *cannot* be thought of in terms of adaptation to nature, for it has no object to which it could adapt itself. Human desire is determined by an order that from the beginning excludes the possibility that an adequate object could be found for it. The unconscious goes its own way, taking no account of the interests of the living being and its adaptation to reality,[44] and desire is borne along by signifiers that knead and shape our existence—even against our interests as living beings. Humans thus desire "qua Other" (. . . *c'est en tant qu'Autre qu'il désire*), which is to say because and in the degree that they are marked by the order of signifiers.[45]

---

44. The translation of the Freudian *Trieb* by "instinct" must thus be rejected according to Lacan. The English "drive" is, according to him, a much better translation where it is a matter of the Freudian unconscious. On the basis of a phonetic association with this English translation, Lacan suggests—as a last resort (*recours de désespoir*) should we fail to free the concept of drive from all reference to instinct—that we translate *Trieb* into French with *dérive*; the drive is what slips off or away from the order of biological purposiveness. One can compare this with the English expression "to break adrift." Thus Lacan writes, "At this point, I take up the challenge that is offered to me when what Freud calls *Trieb* is translated as '*instinct*.' 'Drive' would seem to translate the German word quite well in English, but is avoided in the *Standard Edition*. In French, my last resort would be '*dérive*,' if I were unable to give the bastard term '*pulsion*' the necessary forcefulness" (E 301/31–35, EF 803).

45. Thus it also becomes clear why Lacan constantly connects desire with death, and with the Freudian death drive (see E 301/17ff., EF 803); for desire constantly drives us beyond the boundaries of the vital, biological order of the living.

6

The Metapsychological
Significance of
the Phantasy and
of the Object *a*

THE THIRD VERSION OF THE GRAPH OF DESIRE

Desire has no proper object: we have to ask ourselves how the infant is confronted by this fact, and how it comes to be meaningful for it. Here we recall what we said above in relation to the problematic of the demand for love, from which desire arises. The little child, we claimed, ascribes to the first Other a great power, for it seems that this Other possesses the key to all sense and meaning. The child thus supposes that the Other is capable of responding adequately to the question of who or what the child must be to be worthy of its love. The infant expects an oracle from the Other—an oracle that will disclose to it the proper object of the Other's desire. In other words, it expects the mother to tell it what she really wants—to answer the question: *Che vuoi?*

There is another way we can address this same problematic, and so further specify it in terms of the construction of the graph of desire. Much in the relationship between mother and child remains unclear for both parties. For example, the little child will inevitably be confronted with the fact that its mother's desire is not confined to the child; it is not the only one she desires. But then, what else is it that the mother apparently also wants?[1] On the other hand, the mother herself does not have a complete grasp of what drives her either. In other words, in the relationship between the child and the mother (and more gen-

---

1. Of course, the father is also implicitly present in the relationship between mother and child. We will come back to this later.

erally, the parents), the (unconscious) fantasies of the latter also play a role.

It is therefore necessary to postulate another discourse "behind" the conscious discourse, one that escapes both parties. In our current context, this "other" discourse—the discourse of the unconscious—refers primarily to the phantasies of the parents: their repressed wishes and desires. In everything the mother (the parents) say, the child hears the resonance of something else, and it implicitly realizes this something is important to the mother even if it does not know precisely what it is. The child cannot place these suspected parental phantasies, however, and for this reason, they cannot but appear enigmatic. It thus becomes clear that we will have to inscribe a second level on the graph of desire—a level that deals with unconscious desire in the proper sense.[2]

The first confrontation with this unconscious desire occurs in the relationship with the mother, which we situated at O on the graph. To the extent that this unconscious desire appears enigmatic to the infant, this confrontation gives rise to the question, *Che vuoi?*[3]—and the little child expects an answer to this

----

2. The complete structure of this second level of the graph will only become clear in the fourth version. Provisionally, we can only suggest the necessity of this second level, and the manner in which it takes form, in the first instance, in terms of the relation to the mother.

3. This is also why Lacan writes that the subject expects an oracle from the Other: "That is why the question *of* the Other, which comes back to the subject from the place from which he expects an oracular reply . . ." (E 312/ 22–23, EF 815). The infant is first confronted with the problematic of desire and the unconscious (the Other which drives and determines me) in the confrontation with the desire of the Other, from which it expects an oracle. Later we will return to the passage from which this sentence comes.

question of what the mother really wants.[4] No unequivocal and definitive answer to this question is possible, however, for there is no ultimate signifier that determines the object of desire once and for all. The relation between the infant and the first Other is essentially structured around an indissoluble lack. Consequently, the answer to the question "What do you want?" is every time postponed once more. And for precisely this reason, the question rebounds upon the infant in an altered form: "When this Other refuses to give an answer, which I suppose she could give me, what *then* does she want from me? What am I for the Other?"[5]

---

4. This is probably what Lacan is referring to when he writes later in his text, "And this is so even though the Other [i.e. the real Other of the demand] is required (*che vuoi*) to respond to the value of this treasure [i.e., the treasure of the signifiers], that is to say, to reply, from its place in the lower chain certainly [i.e., at O], but also in the signifiers that constitute the upper chain . . ." (E 316/9–12, EF 818). The infant wants to know what the Other actually wants from him. This Other (O), however, is itself also marked by an alterity in itself to which it has no access. Consequently, the answer to this (implicit) demand of the infant is always codetermined by the signifiers that determine the first Other's desire without it realizing it. Accordingly, the answers on the lowest level of the graph are codetermined by the signifiers of the unconscious of the Other, which Lacan will situate on the uppermost level at ($◊D). Lacan further writes—for reasons that will become clear later—that ($◊D) is the algorithm of the drive. This explains why he ends the passage just quoted by saying, ". . . but also in the signifiers that constitute the upper chain, *in terms of drive, in other words*" (my emphasis).

5. "That is why the question *of* the Other, which comes back to the subject from the place from which he expects an oracular reply in some such form as *Che vuoi*?, 'What do you want?,' is the one that best leads him to the path of his own desire—providing he sets out, with the help of the skills of a partner known as a psychoanalyst, to reformulate it, even without knowing it, as 'What does he want of me?'" (E 312/22–27, EF 815).

The subject tries to formulate an answer to this question in phantasy.[6] In this sense, the phantasy is the ultimate attempt of the subject to escape the essentially enigmatic and indeterminate character of desire, and give it a (minimal) determinacy. The metapsychological significance of this phantasy is thus already determined in general terms.

We are now sufficiently armed to present the third version of the graph. Lacan draws this version as follows:

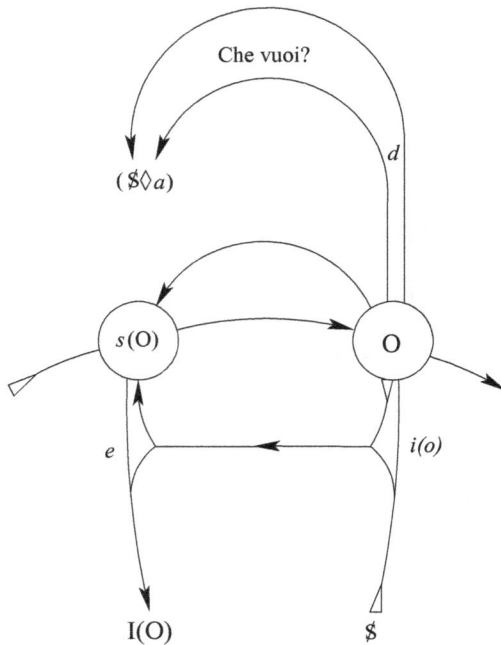

---

6. For example, the phantasy of being present at one's own funeral: What am I for the Other?

The infant is first confronted with the enigma of desire in its relationship with the first Other of the demand (O). Thus an arrow indicating desire (d = desire) also starts out from O. The dynamic of desire is borne by the demand "What do you want (from me?)." Finally, the sigla ($\$\Diamond a$) refers to the phantasy, which is the answer of the subject to the (unconscious) desire of the Other.

This dynamic of desire also lies at the origin of the transference in analysis.[7] On first going into analysis, the subject supposes that the analyst is in a position to tell him what is wrong with him, and what he really desires.[8] The analyst, however, can and will not answer the repeated demands of the analysand to disclose to him the truth of his desire. For the analysand, the question then becomes, even if not explicitly: What does this baffling, silent Other want of me? In this manner, the analysis opens the way to an interrogation of desire, and the interrogation of the desire of the Other-analyst can reactivate the phantasies that comprise the infantile answer to the enigmatic desire of the first Other.

THE SIGNIFICANCE OF THE PHANTASY

Desire transforms the unconditionality of the demand into something "absolute," and this presupposes that the infant can sepa-

---

7. ". . . providing he sets out, with the help of the skills of a partner known as a psychoanalyst, to reformulate it, even without knowing it, as 'What does he want of me?'" (E 312/25–27, EF 814).

8. In his later work Lacan calls this figure of the all-knowing analyst the "subject-supposed-to-know" (*sujet-supposé-savoir*).

rate from the Other.[9] In this way, a space can be made for the imagination and for the constitution of the phantasy. We illustrated this process by way of the appearance of the transitional object, which marks the moment in which the subject first frees itself from the grip of the all-powerful Other. "Coming free," however, does not mean a complete break. The attachment to the first Other continues to exist, but the infant can now formulate its own answer to the loss and lack it experiences in its relation to the Other, and this answer takes the form of the phantasy. The phantasy stages the manner in which the subject relates itself to the incompleteness of the Other, the cause of desire;[10] it "imag(e)-ines" the loss of a *jouissance* that continues to fascinate the subject. In this way, so Lacan thinks, desire and the lack that brings it to life take on a concrete psychical form.

We must complete the structure of the phantasy, so Lacan writes, by linking a moment of *fading* to the condition of an object.[11] What does he mean by this? In the phantasy the split

---

9. This presupposes, as we said above, a recognition of an essential lack in the Other. We will see, further, that this state of affairs is expressed on the graph by the fact that the vector of desire runs via the point indicated by the signifier $S(\emptyset)$ before discharging into the phantasy. The signifier $S(\emptyset)$ indicates the essential lack in the Other. In our current perspective, for example, it points to the recognition of the lack in the Other as the condition for the constitution of the phantasy. This recognition comes to be in and through the metaphor of the Name-of-the-Father. We will come back to this.

10. This is also the reason Lacan goes on to write that ". . . the phantasy [is the] desire of the Other" (E 321/18, EF 824). The phantasy stages the answer of the subject to the inconsistency of the Other, which is to say to the desire of the Other. We will come back to this passage in more detail in our last chapter (Chapter 8).

11. "[A] fairly detailed study is required—a study that can only take place in the analytic experience—that would enable us to complete the structure of the phantasy by linking it essentially, whatever its occasional elisions

subject—the subject of the signifier—relates itself to a special sort of object: the object a. Lacan's formula for the phantasy is thus ($\$\lozenge a$), where $\lozenge$ indicates the relation between the two terms. The object a of the phantasy may not be understood as an object that might fulfill desire—in this sense desire has no object. Lacan, on the contrary, calls the object a the object-*cause* of desire.[12] By this, he wants to suggest that desire is not so much directed at this object as it is provoked by it.

By way of example, we might think of a woman whose desire is aroused when someone looks at her in a certain impertinent way (Fink 1997). Here it is abundantly clear that the phantasy has to do with the relation of the subject to the Other as cause of desire. This phantasy can be described as a scene in which the gaze (of the Other) is connected with the subject (as passive, provocative, etc.); the woman's desire is aroused whenever she comes into a situation in which the conditions of this phantasy are satisfied. Accordingly, the gaze of the Other is here not so much the *telos* of desire, in which it finds satisfaction, but that which *initiates* desire and keeps it going.

As we noted above, Lacan says that the phantasy links the moment of a *fading* of the subject, which is closely tied with its subjection to the order of signifiers, to the condition of an object (in this case, the impertinent gaze of the Other). Now, the signifier condemns the subject to an irremediable indeterminacy, and

---

may be, to the condition of an object (the privilege of which I have done no more than touch upon above in terms of diachrony), the moment of a 'fading' or eclipse of the subject that is closely bound up with the *Spaltung* or splitting that it suffers from its subordination to the signifier" (E 313/7–14, EF 815–816).

12. We will set out this notion of the object a progressively in this and the following sections.

the subject is as it were "dispersed" throughout the signifiers from which its existence takes its form, without being able to find its definitive determination in any one of them. The subject therefore disappears, or "fades" away, under the signifiers without being able to obtain from any of them a definitive identity. At the moment the subject is confronted with this absence of content and with this lack, according to Lacan, it identifies itself with an object that it hopes might eventually give it some minimal content.

A second example, taken from Freud, can further clarify all this. In the notes Freud kept of the analysis of the "Ratman," he records a childhood memory of the latter from the period when he was four or five years old. Freud quotes the Ratman: "We had a very pretty young governess, called Madame Robert. One evening she was lying on the sofa lightly dressed, and reading. I was lying beside her, and begged her to let me creep under her skirts. She told me I might, so long as I said nothing to anyone about it. She had very little on, and I caressed her genitals and belly, which struck me as very strange. After that, I was constantly tormented by a burning curiosity to see the female body."[13] The last sentence makes it clear that the Ratman's desire was underpinned by an event that took place twenty years before his analysis with Freud. The memory of this event thus fulfills the function of a phantasy,[14] for this memory gives to the desire of the Ratman a

---

13. *Nous avions une jeune gouvernante très jolie, Madame Robert. Un soir étendue sur le canapé, légèrement vêtue, elle lisait; allongé à côté d'elle, je lui demande la permission de me glisser sous ses jupes. Elle y consent à condition que je ne dise rien à personne. Elle n'avait presque rien sur elle; je tâte ses parties génitales et son ventre qui me parait curieux. . . . Depuis lors, je n'ai cessé d'être tourmenté par une curiosité brûlante de regarder le corps des femmes* (Freud 1974, cited in Bataille 1987, pp. 36–37) [my translation—Trans.].

14. "On to the phantasy presented in this way, the graph inscribes that desire governs itself . . ." (E 314/6–7, EF 816).

concrete content and direction. It makes of his desire something other than a purely virtual attempt to fill a purely abstract lack.

How, then, are we to understand this phantasy? Freud notes first that contrary to the social etiquette of Vienna around the turn of the century, the Ratman referred to his governess by her family name, "Robert." "Robert" is also a masculine first name, an observation that is in a sense decisive. At the time of the incident the Ratman was four or five years old, and according to Freud was going through the phallic phase of psychosexual development. At this stage the little child would understand sexual difference in terms of the presence or absence of one genital organ: the phallus. Freud claims that at this age, the female genitalia do not yet have any psychic meaning for the child. The genitalia of "Robert" thus seem "strange" (*curieux*) to the Ratman because the phallus is missing from where he expected to find it; in place of the phallus he finds only an emptiness. The term "strange" thus marks a "minus" sign, as it were. The subject relates itself to an object that is missing.[15] The phantasy thus stages the relation of the subject ($) to the incompleteness of the Other as the cause of desire;[16] entry into the order of the signifiers implies the equiprimordial splitting of the subject and creation of a desire that cannot find fulfillment in any object.

How does the subject relate itself to the object? This relationship is indicated in the formula of the phantasy by the sym-

---

15. Later we will set out in more detail the way the objects around which the phantasy is built up (the gaze, the breast, the voice, etc.) have a special status, such that they must be distinguished from the objects of our daily reality; for it is a matter here of *irrecoverable* objects. For just this reason, they are especially suited to incarnate the lack. The object by which desire is provoked (the object a) is an object that is lost for all time.

16. For further commentary on this example from this perspective, see Bataille 1987, pp. 35–40.

bol *a*, which, Lacan claims, one can give very different readings.[17] In the context of the Ratman's phantasy, for example, one could consider the following: the little boy is bound to the object by the searching movement of his hand under the governess's skirts; he is bound to it by his desire to see what he feels, and by his amazement before it. But is it not also striking that both terms of this phantasy are situated in the same place, as it were—under the skirts? Perhaps what is fundamentally at stake here is thus a relation of identification. In the phantasy the Ratman disappears under the skirts of the governess; he situates himself, as it were, completely on the side of the object. The Ratman is in the phantasy nothing more than the object that is missing from the governess, with which he identifies himself.[18]

We termed the object of the phantasy the object-cause of desire, and the phantasy of the Ratman forms a striking illustration of this. It would make little sense to say that the missing object around which this phantasy is constructed is the *aim* of the desire in which it finds its fulfillment. In fact, the object here is no more than a minus sign, and it sets desire in motion pre-

---

17. "This is what is symbolized by the sigla ($\$ \Diamond a$), which I have introduced in the form of an algorithm. . . . For it is created to allow a hundred and one different readings, a multiplicity that is admissible as long as the spoken remains caught in its algebra" (E 313/15–20, EF 816). The *Oxford English Dictionary* defines an algorithm as follows: "A process, or set of rules . . . used esp. in computing [etc.]" (*OED*, 2nd ed., 1989). That the sigla ($\$ \Diamond a$) does not directly correspond to this definition is clear. However, Lacan's somewhat loose use of the term "algorithm" does not detract from the significance of what he writes about it: ($\$ \Diamond a$) expresses the structure of the phantasy. When Lacan also calls the other siglas from which the graph is constructed (e.g. $\$ \Diamond D$), "algorithms," then it is precisely because they are expected to express the structural relationship between the two terms involved.

18. The phantasy, as we said above, "imagines" the loss of an impossible *jouissance* that continues to fascinate the subject.

cisely inasmuch as it is missing; the phallus to which the phantasy of the Ratman refers cannot be recovered.

We can now further elucidate the idea that the phantasy is a scenario in which desire acquires a concrete psychic form. Desire acquires a concrete psychic form in the phantasy because and insofar as it acquires there a *bodily* content; in the phantasy, the lack that gives life to desire is inscribed in the body in a specific manner. "Something" is missing from the body, and that makes the fulfillment of desire impossible. This immediately presents us with a problem, however: the missing object cannot be the object of a demand. Indeed, the constitution of the phantasy presupposes that the infant to some degree escapes the logic of the unconditional demand, in which it believes that the Other can remedy its lack. The phantasy stages the relation of the subject with the essential incompleteness of the Other, and this implies that the unconditionality of demand is transformed into something "ab-solute."

We have already connected this transformation with the appearance of a new sort of object—the transitional object of Winnicott—and in "Subversion" Lacan suggests an analogy,[19] at least in formal terms, between the appearance of this transitional object and the constitution of what he calls the object *a*. Indeed, like the transitional object, the object *a* gives concrete form within the psychic economy to the absoluteness of desire,

---

19. On the basis of the textual material it cannot be determined how Lacan conceives of the relationship between the transitional object of Winnicott and his own object *a*, but a detailed study here of the relation between the two concepts would lead us too far astray. Lacan retains from Winnicott at least the idea that escape from the unconditionality of the demand presupposes the introduction of a new sort of object, in which this process can acquire concrete form (in this connection, see also Chapter 5, n. 37). We will address these ideas in our next section.

in opposition to the unconditionality of the demand. To understand this, however, we must subject this object-cause of desire to closer investigation.

THE SIGNIFICANCE OF THE OBJECT *a*

As we have seen, the object *a* is the object-cause of the desire to which the subject relates in the phantasy. More than this, however, Lacan also defines this object as the object of the *drive*. Indeed, it is clear that in a psychoanalytic perspective, desire is always and necessarily rooted in the body.[20] Thus Freud calls the human being a being of drives, and he describes the drive as a limit-concept between the psychic and the somatic. Consequently, desire must somehow fit in with the drive if it is to acquire concrete bodily form.

According to Freud, the sexual drive is essentially partial. He distinguishes, for example, an oral and an anal drive, which both find their origin in a specific erogenous zone (in this case, the mouth and the anus), and the object of which is not the Other as a total person, but rather a (part) object that is connected in a privileged way with the relevant erogenous zone (in this case, the breast and the feces).[21] These partial drives seek satisfaction

---

20. Of course, in a psychoanalytic perspective, desire has to do not only with the body as such, but with the sexuated body. We will treat this problematic in more detail later.

21. Lacan refers to this when he writes, "Hence the concept of drive, in which he is designated by an organic, oral, anal, etc., mapping that satisfies the requirement of being all the farther away from speaking the more he speaks" (E 314/22–25, EF 816). The meaning of this statement seems to be as follows. The psychoanalytic tradition designates the subject of the unconscious ("in which *he* is designated") in reference to the drive, which is in turn deter-

independently of each other. Moreover, according to Freud there is no genital drive that would direct us, of itself and naturally, to a partner of the opposite sex. Certainly, in the unconscious there is no presentation of "masculinity" or "femininity." What we call "genitality" is thus nothing other than the precarious result of a process of development in which the various partial drives are progressively integrated into a unity. This bundling of the partial drives implies that from now on they seek satisfaction in a total object—an object that Freud says is at least in principle of the opposite sex. The integration of the partial drives remains precarious, however, and can never be complete. The "heaven"(!?) of a totally integrated genitality, Freud teaches, is not open to us as humans.[22]

---

mined in terms of the biological order. In connection with the unconscious, the tradition thus speaks about, for example, anal and oral drives, which express themselves in symptoms, and so on. This formulation has the advantage that it clearly suggests that the subject of the unconscious does not appear as such in language, for this subject answers to other laws and belongs to another order than the subject of consciousness (the order of an organically determined drive). Nevertheless, this subject lets itself be known in symptoms, slips of the tongue, and so on. It "speaks" even if it does not have a linguistic character ("satisfies the requirement of being all the farther away from speaking the more he speaks"). Lacan thus says that in a sense, the traditional opposition between (the subject of) an organically determined drive and the conscious subject anticipates the distinction between the subject of the signified (the subject of the statement) and the unconscious subject of the signifier, which cannot be captured in any one statement.

22. Lacan refers to this problematic when he writes, "For is it not obvious that this feature, this partial feature, rightly emphasized in objects, is applicable not because these objects are part of a total object, the body, but because they represent only partially the function that produces them?" (E 315/8–12, EF 817). The meaning of this passage will be further clarified in the remainder of this section, and also in the section following this one: "The Object *a* and Lacan's Critique of the Psychoanalytic Tradition." See also Van Haute and Geyskens (2002).

The partial drives cannot be thought apart from the various erogenous zones from which they arise,[23] and these erogenous zones have to be understood as privileged sites of the experience of pleasure on the body. Moreover, it is notable that Freud uses the term "erogenous zone" to indicate bodily openings, which not only are crucial for the experience of pleasure, but also play a decisive role in our relations of exchange with the Other. Let us take a few examples.

The oral zone is not only important on account of the pleasurable experiences that can be derived from it (thumb-sucking, for example); it is also the place where we receive nourishment, and it plays a crucial role in verbal communication. No argument is needed to see that, certainly in the first months of life, nourishment holds a central place in the relationship between the infant and the Other. The mother, however, not only offers nourishment to the infant at regular intervals; she also imitates its baby noises, and prohibits it from sticking certain objects in its mouth. In this way, the oral zone is immediately invested with

---

23. "The very delimitation of the 'erogenous zone' that the drive isolates from the metabolism of the function (the act of devouring concerns other organs than the mouth—ask one of Pavlov's dogs) is the result of a cut (*coupure*) expressed in the anatomical mark (*trait*) of a margin or border—lips, 'the enclosure of the teeth,' the rim of the anus, the tip of the penis, the vagina, the slit formed by the eyelids, even the horn-shaped aperture of the ear (I am avoiding embryological details here). Respiratory erogeneity has been little studied, but it is obviously through the spasm that it comes into play. Observe that this mark of the cut is no less obviously present in the object described by analytic theory: the mamilla, feces, the phallus (imaginary object), the urinary flow. (An unthinkable list, if one adds, as I do, the phoneme, the gaze, the voice—the nothing.) For is it not obvious that this feature, this partial feature, rightly emphasized in objects, is applicable not because these objects are part of a total object, the body, but because they represent only partially the function that produces them?" (E 314/35, 315/12, EF 817).

numerous meanings that can continue to have an effect on our subsequent lives.

Something similar is true of the anal zone. This zone is not only a source of pleasure for the infant; it is also a place where an important part of the communication with the Other is concentrated, at least during certain periods of the child's development. The problematic of toilet training, and everything that goes along with it, forms a striking illustration of this. The refusal of the little child to sit on its potty cannot be reduced to biological patterns alone—it expresses the growing independence of the child, and its desire to be more than a mere complement to the Other. In the confrontation with the commands and prohibitions that are involved in toilet training, the anal zone is the stage of a struggle for independence that can permanently determine relations with the Other.

The drive, Lacan writes, isolates the erogenous zones from the functions of the biological metabolism.[24] By this, he means

---

24. Lacan refers in this connection to Pavlov's dogs, in order to suggest that the determination of the erogenous zones cannot simply be thought in terms of biological functionality ("the act of devouring concerns other organs than the mouth—ask one of Pavlov's dogs"; E 314/36–37, EF 817). Pavlov's dogs salivated when they heard a signal bell, even if they were not hungry. According to Lacan, this shows us that more organs are involved in oral activity than simply the mouth (for example, hearing). Consequently, the privileging of the mouth as an erogenous zone cannot be explained exclusively in terms of the biological order; rather it presupposes a sort of excision or isolation, which is brought about by the signifier (". . . the 'erogenous zone' that the drive isolates from the metabolism of the function . . ."; E 314/35–36, EF 817). To some extent, this already makes it clear why Lacan writes that the drive isolates the erogenous zone from the metabolism of the function (the totality of organs that are involved in salivation) on the one hand, while identifying the drive with the "treasure of signifiers" on the other. We will return to this.

that the importance of the erogenous zones cannot be determined primarily in terms of biological regularities; they do not derive their psychic importance from biological function. Instead, the various erogenous zones obtain their meaning from the signifiers of the Other. They are, as it were, "cut out" of the body ("the effect of a cut") by a relation to the Other that is primarily linguistically structured. However, here Lacan immediately adds that the signifier is thus affixed to the anatomical structure of the body itself,[25] so that there is apparently a kind of structural homology between the body and the order of signifiers. It is precisely this homology that makes it possible for the signifier to inscribe itself in the body, and conversely, for the body to be taken up in the order of signifiers and thereby in the economy of the unconscious. What does this entail?

Lacan repeatedly points out that biological sexuality cannot be thought apart from an experience of loss (Lacan 1964, pp. 197–198 and *passim*; see also Conté 1992, p. 93). Sexuality ensures the virtual immortality of the species, but it also implies the mortality and the finitude of the individual that has to maintain the species. According to Lacan, this finitude is "materialized," so to speak, in the experience of the loss of certain objects: the breast[26] and the feces, for example, but also the gaze and the voice. These are objects lost at places where the body alternately opens and shuts (mouth, anus, eyelids, etc.).[27] It is

---

25. ". . . is the result of a cut (*coupure*) which *finds favor* [translation modified: *trouve faveur*] in the anatomical mark (*trait*) of a margin or border . . ." (E 314/37–38, EF 817; my emphasis).

26. One has to keep in mind here that according to the psychoanalytic tradition, the child at first considers the breast a part of its own body.

27. This is why Lacan writes that it is here a matter of an "anatomical mark (*trait*) of a margin or border . . ." (E 314/38, EF 817). Thus the contracting muscles outline a kind of border that marks an opening. Only a clearly

as if these objects mark the essential incompleteness of the bodily individual, and so remind it of its mortality.[28]

One notices the analogy with what we said above concerning the relationship between the subject and the signifier; just as something is irrevocably lost on the level of the bodily openings, so too the subject is continuously lost between two signifiers.[29] For every time the subject thinks it has found determination in a signifier, it is referred on to another signifier, on which the meaning of the first depends.[30] The phantasy is the place where the connection ($\Diamond$) comes into being between this subject that loses itself in the order of signifiers ($\$$) and the object that can give this experience of loss a concrete form on the level of the body. It fol-

---

outlined opening can alternately open and close itself. Lacan mentions, besides the oral zone, the anus, and the eyelids, as well as *inter alia* the opening of the penis, the vagina, the ear, and even the respiratory system, and the objects that are linked with these bodily openings.

28. It goes without saying, however, that the loss of these objects can only be important for the subject insofar as it is also interested in its own completeness. This implies the intervention of the mirror-stage and the imaginary. In our conclusion, we will return to the essential connection between the imaginary, the symbolic, and the real as it announces itself here. In particular, this seems to foreshadow the insights Lacan will later formulate in his theory of the Borromean knots.

29. We said above that the subject does not show itself without withdrawing. We can also express this idea as follows: the subject only "opens" itself ("only gives itself to be known") at the moment that it is already closing itself again ("disappears"). In this motion of opening and closing, something is irrevocably lost. In an analogous way, the body can be understood as a continuous motion of opening and closing, in which something is irrevocably lost. The object a is the enduring memorial to this loss.

30. This is also the reason Lacan later writes in his text that ". . . a signifier is that which represents the subject for another signifier" (E 316/30–31, EF 819). A signifier can only represent (in both senses of the word) the subject in reference to another signifier, and thus in a manner that is always provisional and partial.

lows from this that the object *a* of the drive is not itself a signifier,[31] but rather is what concretely (bodily) inscribes the lack in the psychic economy. It stages in the order of the body the loss that entry into language inevitably brings.[32]

We can further clarify this last point by way of an example from everyday experience. If someone asks me why I love my wife—or, if you like, why I don't leave her—then I can name a whole shopping list of characteristics that I appreciate in her: I can say that I find her beautiful, intelligent, sweet, understanding, a good mother, and so forth. However, these characteristics are like signifiers, none of which can ultimately explain why I love her and stay with her. In fact, as long as I confine myself to tallying up her articulable characteristics, my wife is simply comparable with other women. I find my wife beautiful, but there are women more beautiful; I find her sweet and understanding, but there are women even more so. Why then would I not exchange my wife at the first opportunity for another who possesses the same characteristics but in a higher degree of perfection? And besides, is it not true that however we try to motivate our feelings for this or that Other, we implicitly feel that we shall never succeed? In fact, what interests me in this specific Other, and what causes my desire for him or her (and *not* for another), cannot be said in signifiers (characteristics)—it is situated beyond the order of signifiers.[33] This

---

31. For the object *a*, by definition, falls outside the world that is structured by the signifiers.

32. Once again, however, this dynamic cannot be thought apart from a constituting reference to the mirror stage. We will return to this.

33. Here it is also clear that the Lacanian theory of the differential signifier that always leaves a remainder only acquires meaning in the analysis of concrete, clinical phenomena. Lacan has never wanted to develop a theory of language apart from the phenomena that psychoanalysis seeks to understand.

"remainder," which I cannot express but which at the same time greatly interests me and arouses my desire, announces itself in a certain gaze or tremor of a voice, which unsettles me without my being able to say why. Consequently, when we claim that the object *a* gives a concrete bodily content to the lack, this also means that it functions as a sort of hyphen between the subject and an indissoluble core of alienness in the (always incarnated) Other.

Of course, for all this we do not assume any the less that our desire is exclusively aroused by the unusual human qualities and character traits of the Other. The Other appears then as an image, which fascinates me on account of its special characteristics, and which I believe or hope can satisfy my desire. In more technical terms we can express this as follows: the Other appears as an imaginary *Gestalt* that captivates me and holds me in its grip, in accord with the dynamic that we already earlier described in relation to the mirror-stage.[34] Desire thus acquires the reassuring appearance of rationality and even necessity. We gladly believe that our desire is caused by the intrinsic qualities of the Other as a person, for we assume that our desire does not direct itself to just anything, and that by its nature it leads to something that is intrinsically meaningful.

Nevertheless Lacan's notion of the object *a* implies that desire is aroused by an object quite irrelevant to the relationship with the Other as a person whose characteristics are worthy of love. According to Lacan, desire is indeed caused by a

---

34. Hence, also, the continual attempts to say why I love the Other. For we continue to hope that we will be able to formulate an answer to this question, such that the crack in the mirror will close up and my desire will be completely "explained."

certain (e.g., provocative) gaze, tone of voice,[35] or some other insignificant detail that functions relatively independent of the determinable characteristics of this or that concrete Other. Imaginary captivation, however, makes us continue to believe that the movement of our desire is determined by the intrinsic qualities of the object.[36]

The object *a* can only fulfill its role when it is of an order other than the object of the demand. The object of the demand is an object I can actually give or obtain,[37] and its absence consequently has a merely factical character; in principle, it can always be recovered. The object of the demand thus does not respect the essential and irremediable character of the negativity that is introduced by language. By contrast, the object *a* must give concrete form to the lack without immediately destroying it, or what comes down to the same thing, without reducing it to a lack that could in principle be remedied.[38]

A few examples can make things much clearer here. According to Lacan, the series of objects *a* includes the voice and the gaze as well as the traditional group of the part objects

---

35. Consider, for example, the problematic of sadomasochism.

36. This is the reason Lacan writes, "It is to this object that cannot be grasped in the mirror that the specular image lends its clothes" (E 316/1–2, EF 818). The mirror image—or perhaps better, the other as fascinating *Gestalt*—conceals ever again the object that causes desire. Just as clothing covers our shameful nakedness, so the fascinating *Gestalt* of the other covers the "almost nothing" that is the object *a*.

37. In the light of the example we just gave, we could also say, "a characteristic (beauty, intelligence, etc.) that we may or may not possess."

38. This is why Lacan writes that "this mark of the cut is no less obviously present in the object described by analytic theory [than in the erogenous zones with which they are linked]" (E 315/5–6, EF 817). These objects give, as it were, a tangible character to the irrevocable loss that goes together with the incision of the signifier in the body.

(breast, feces, etc.). Lacan has addressed at length the meaning and function of the gaze in particular—it is, for him, the object *a* par excellence.[39] Now in a sense, the gaze is a very popular subject of conversation; we talk of a loving look, an aggressive or a seductive look, and so on; or we say that we feel ourselves being looked at provocatively. The analysis of these examples makes it very clear that we have to distinguish between the eye and the gaze, and when we feel ourselves being looked at, we refer not to the eye of the other, but the gaze. Even though there seems to be an evident link between the two, it is nevertheless impossible to identify the eye and the gaze with each other, for there is something ungraspable about the gaze.

As I walk along the street, I get the feeling that someone is staring at me; I look around and see several people walking behind me. But whose gaze was it that fell on me? Was it the gaze of one of those walking behind me, or that of someone unseen observing me from a window? In situations like this, it seems impossible to locate the gaze—it occurs, as it were, "somewhere" between me and an observer who need not necessarily be known to me—and neither do I know what this gaze wants from me. Is the gazer just staring aimlessly at the people in the street, or is it someone who is interested in me for some reason or other? All this remains unclear to me, and if I nevertheless try to cap-

---

39. This cannot be understood apart from the historical context in which Lacanian psychoanalysis arose. Thus we find in the work of Sartre, and in the late work of Merleau-Ponty, extended phenomenological analyses of the gaze of which Lacan made abundant use. In what follows we do not want to give a summary of Lacan's complex treatment of the gaze as object *a*. We shall, on the contrary, restrict ourselves to what is necessary to make clear the special status of the gaze. See Bernet (in press).

ture the gaze that pursues me directly, I will end up staring my fellow pedestrians right in the eye.

The eye, on the other hand, has a visibility of a different sort than the gaze of the Other, which always escapes us. In contrast to the gaze, it is actually an identifiable object like the table I write on, which I can point to in the external world. None of this means, however, that the gaze does not have a great impact upon me. When I am walking at night through a rather unsavory district of a big city, I can be petrified if I feel that anyone's gaze is following me too intently. We might also think here of a hysterical subject who spends hours trying to decide precisely what to wear: Does this dress show enough of my body, or too much? Do I have too much make-up on, or not enough? This hysteric is under the spell of the gaze of the Other, which, however, she can never determine precisely, or completely get a hold on. As Lacan writes somewhere, I can never see myself from the place from which the Other looks at me; the gaze is an opaque mirror in which I cannot recognize myself.

The gaze is an object I can get no hold on, and it escapes me again and again.[40] Yet the gaze is not nothing—and we have the

---

40. In this respect the gaze resembles the voice. Indeed, for Lacan, the voice is just as much an exemplary instance of the object *a* as is the gaze. The voice can be understood as an object that detaches itself from the body, and that I can never recover in the same form. For example, when I hear my own voice on the radio, I have difficulty recognizing it as my own. On the one hand, the voice "sticks" to my body, as it were; it is *my* singular and irreplaceable voice; on the other hand, it is an object that is irrevocably lost and that cannot be recuperated. The reference to the voice in the lowest part of the graph ("signifier-voice") is thus probably ambiguous. It points on the one hand to the phonological character of the signifiers with which the infant is confronted (see the section in Chapter 3, "The Other in the Second Version of the Graph of Desire," pp. 62–69), while on the other, it probably also has to do with the desire of the mother (O), which finds a concrete "materialization" in the voice as object *a*.

great and sometimes destructive impact the gaze of the Other can have on us to prove it. The gaze is a fleeting object, and does not let itself be captured in the phenomenal world, which is structured by the imaginary and by the symbolic. The objects of the phenomenal world are objects of demand, which can be articulated in signifiers—we can identify them in a more or less stable manner. This is not the case with the gaze. To the extent that the gaze is both present in the phenomenal world, and yet not simply taken up in it, it is a permanent disruption of that world. This is also what Lacan means when he says that the object *a*—in this case, the gaze—has no specular image;[41] for only objectifiable (objectified) and identifiable objects appear in the mirror.[42]

We now also understand why and how the object *a* can give concrete form to the absoluteness of desire. The object *a* is in fact a *dis-incarnation*, as it were, of the lack; it gives it a minimal bodily content (incarnation), but at the same time remains beyond our grasp in the phenomenal world, which it permanently disrupts (dis-incarnation). In contrast to the object of the demand, the object *a* is thus a lasting reminder of the essential and indissoluble character of the lack. The object *a*, we could also say, does give a determination to the void that is introduced by the signifier—but this determination does not destroy this void. On the contrary, it makes of it a "determinate void."[43]

---

41. "These objects have one common feature in my elaboration of them—they have no specular image, or, in other words, alterity" (E 315/13–14, EF 818).

42. Consequently, not only the gaze of the Other, but my own gaze, too, escapes my grasp. For I cannot see myself except by a detour through my reflection, in which I appear to myself as an objectified image—that is to say, as the eye.

43. We borrow this terminology from the late work of Merleau-Ponty. See Merleau-Ponty 1968, *passim*. For the relation between Lacan and Merleau-Ponty with respect to the problem of the object *a*, see *inter alia* Baas 1996, pp. 13–14.

In the phantasy, the loss—that loss to which the subject is essentially condemned on the basis of its inscription in the order of the signifiers—acquires a concrete bodily form. In and through the identification with the object *a*, the subject can "grasp itself," so to speak, in the moment in which it disappears or "slips away"; for the object *a* is a "dis-incarnation" of this disappearance. The phantasy, in this sense, shows the subject in the order of the body as what it is—ultimately indeterminable.

THE OBJECT *a* AND LACAN'S CRITIQUE OF THE PSYCHOANALYTIC TRADITION

Of course, all this does not prevent the neurotic patient from continuing to interpret the object of the phantasy as the object of a demand, and in fact, the neurotic does believe that the lost object can be recovered. Here we might think of the example of analysands that repeatedly demand a conclusive explanation for their suffering. We might also think of analysands who say repeatedly that their parents denied or deprived them of something in one way or another (love, understanding, the possibility of studying a certain subject), and so made their life unbearable or caused it to fail. Or again, there are analysands who sacrifice their lives in order to make their mother or father happy—nothing is too much to keep their parents content—and the failure of this project sometimes goes together with a leaden feeling of guilt, which makes their lives impossible. These analysands somehow make themselves the object that can bring the desire of the Other to fulfillment. A last example: an analysand dreams again and again that she has a penis, and all the while she is locked into a deadly struggle with men, who "should not believe that everything is permitted to them just because they have one." In her phantasy she interprets the male organ as an object that she could also have possessed;[44] it is a great injustice to her that she has been deprived of this organ, to which she ascribes great power. In other words, she understands her neurotic suffering in terms of an object that has been taken from her, and which she untiringly claims back.

All these examples share the fact that the object of the desire is interpreted as the articulable object of a demand. It is as if the neurotic shrinks back before the radicality of the lack; she cannot accept that the loss of the object cannot be remedied, or, more precisely, she cannot bear the ultimate indeterminacy and indeterminability of the desire of the Other. She defends herself with the object of the phantasy by reinterpreting the object of the phantasy according to the logic of the unconditional demand. In this way, the lack continues to exist, but it acquires a purely factical character. The neurotic can only accept the lack to the extent that she can also believe that it can in principle be remedied.[45]

According to Lacan, this last point means that the neurotic understands her suffering in terms of frustration—she has been

---

44. A more complete treatment of this example would require a more detailed exposition of Lacan's theory of the phallus. In particular, we should note that Lacan almost never mentions the phallus in the list of the objects *a*; for the phallus is the signifier of the *lack* of the Other. However, this does not prevent the phallus from functioning in an analogous way to the object *a* in our current example (as in the Ratman example we dealt with earlier). This is confirmed by the fact that Lacan does include the imaginary phallus in the list of objects *a* in "Subversion" (E 315/6–7, EF 817). We will return later to examine more closely the status of the phallus in its relation to the object *a*.

45. As we will see later, this is what distinguishes neurosis from psychosis. In a manner of speaking, the lack is as it were *never inscribed* in the psychotic subject; the lack before which the neurotic flees never acquires meaning for the psychotic.

denied or deprived of something that she should have (and could have) had in order to lead a successful life. The neurotic patient elevates this frustration to the status of the truth of her existence and her desire. She hopes that the analysis can help her to remedy this frustration, which is to say, help her find the object that she believes can put an end to her suffering. And as we already know, the neurotic is not alone in this. Earlier we pointed out that psychoanalytic theorists also have often been (and still are) inclined to understand neurosis as the simple result of early childhood frustrations.[46] We now see why Lacan claims that they have made the neurotic phantasy the guiding thread of theory, instead of interpreting it[47]—they are blind to the problematic of desire, against which the neurotic tries to defend himself at any cost.[48]

The demand is sustained by a belief in a possible totalization. The object of the demand is understood not only as an

---

46. Of course, the point is not to deny the importance of any actual early childhood frustrations—it is more that the analysis is not primarily concerned with these frustrations as such, but with the reworking of them in the phantasy. The analysis operates on the level of desire, not on the level of "real" lacks.

47. "Indeed, the neurotic . . . is he who identifies the lack of the Other with his demand. . . . As a result, the demand of the Other assumes the function of an object in his phantasy. . . . But this prevalence given by the neurotic to the demand, which, for an analysis declining into facility, shifted the whole treatment towards the handling of frustration, conceals its anxiety from the desire of the Other . . ." (E 321/4–14, EF 823–824). The various neuroses must therefore be understood as different ways in which to misrecognize the radicality of the lack. We will examine these passages at greater length later.

48. Later we will see that the position of the neurotic patient is more complex than we can show here. True, the neurotic subject defends itself against desire insofar as it cannot accept the lack; at the same time, however, it holds fast to desire, since its dissolution would be the same as the annihilation of the subject.

object that the body lacks in order to be complete, but also as an object that can be *added* to the body in order to finally *make* it complete.[49] The object *a*, by contrast, excludes any totalization from the outset. It is a permanent disruption of the phenomenal world we live in; it undermines every unity that comes about in that world.

Above all, the notion of the object *a* undermines the idea that human development must be understood as a teleological process—that mutual integration of the various partial drives can result in a complementary relation with the genital Other. For theorists enamored of such a view of development, as we saw earlier, the subject must be capable of a "mature, non-incorporative and 'giving' relation" with an Other, of which genital sexuality makes up an integral part (Fairbairn 1986); there must be a way for "pleasure" and "love" to be reconciled with each other so that both partners in the relation appear to each other as an adequate object for their respective desires. Even Freud seems at times to still believe that psychosexual development can be thought of in this manner, as the mutual integration of the various partial drives. The development of the little child must ideally result in the constitution of a genital stage, in which the partial drives are absorbed without remainder[50] into a genital drive that takes one person of the opposite sex as its privileged object. True, Freud underlines that the drives can never be brought completely under the primacy of genitality, but this does

---

49. Recall the example of the analysand who dreamed she had a penis.

50. The integration must be in principle "without remainder," because otherwise the partial (perverse) drives, not having been brought under the primacy of genitality, would still try to find satisfaction from the unconscious. The complementarity between "love" and "pleasure" that characterizes the genital stage would thus be cancelled.

not prevent him from here and there retaining a complete integration of these drives as the asymptotic goal of the development. This implies that in principle, a continuity continues to exist between the various partial drives and their objects on one hand, and a genital object that is the ultimate *telos* of the development of these drives on the other.

This sort of teleology is excluded from the beginning with the object *a*—it cannot and must not be understood in the perspective of a possible unity. According to Lacan, the various objects *a* are not parts of a (lost) whole, but *essentially* partial representations of the function that they must help realize—(genital) sexuality, insofar as it is interpreted as a (non-incorporative, "giving") relation between two complementary subjects who find mutual fulfillment in each other through that relation.[51] What this means *in concreto* is that because and insofar as there is no adequate object of desire, the relations of the subject to

---

51. "For is it not obvious that this feature, this partial feature, rightly emphasized in objects, is applicable not because these objects are part of a total object, the body, but because they represent only partially the function that produces them [namely sexuality understood as 'genital love'?]" (E 315/8–12, EF 817). On the basis of "Subversion," it seems to us that this is how we must read the dictum "There is no sexual relation," formulated by Lacan in his later work. The "sexual relation" of which Lacan emphasizes the impossibility is "genital love," in the sense given it by Fairbairn and his supporters. Naturally this does not mean that people do not have sexual and love relations *de facto*. It means, rather, that these relations are constructed out of a founding reference to partial objects (and the phantasies that are linked with them), which structurally fall short of the ideal of a total integration of "pleasure and love." This is also the ultimate meaning of the idea that desire does not know any fulfillment. Lacan writes, "Thus it becomes apparent that the relation of the object to the body is in no way defined as a partial identification that would have to be totalized in such a relation . . ." (E 301/26–28, EF 803).

the Other will *always* be structured in terms of phantasies that pertain to part objects. Here we might think, for example, of the so-called "oral" phantasies (e.g., "I want you to take care of me/ be a 'good' breast, just as my mother did/was for me when I was younger") or "anal" phantasies (e.g., "I want to control you, just as I once controlled my feces"). Thus, according to Lacan, the "genital love" of which the object-relations theorists dreamt is an empty daydream. Every relation to the Other is in this regard inadequate, for it lives parasitically on phantasies in which the Other is reduced to a part object.

Let us return once more to the problem of the status of "frustration" in psychoanalytic theory. The object at stake in psychoanalysis is not the object of demand, but the object *a*. This implies that it is impossible for frustration to be the central category in terms of which we think the psychoanalytic process; for the object *a* is not an object that the Other has actively denied me and that I can eventually obtain (if necessary via analysis). Instead, the loss of the object *a* is constitutive for subjectivity as such. It is the constant reminder of the fact that subjectivity is rooted in an indissoluble lack, and confrontation with this lack is the actual goal of the analysis.

This confrontation is no abstract, quasi-metaphysical event, but comes about by way of a concrete interrogation of the phantasy, in which the subject is related to the object *a*. It is a matter not of repairing the lack that the object *a* inscribes in the psyche in a bodily fashion, but of the recognition of its irrevocable character—the reduction of the object to an object of demand must cease, so that the essential heterogeneity of the object *a* can be brought to light. Only in this way can room be made for a desire that is something more and something other than sheer, sterile repetition.

Recall the analysand who experienced the notion that she had been deprived of the phallus as a great injustice. In her experience, the lack of a penis condemned her to an inferiority that she at once vehemently contested ("Men should not believe . . ."). From this standpoint she takes every opportunity to protest and resist this situation. For the psychoanalyst it is a question of distinguishing between two levels: on the one hand, the real injustices and discrimination the analysand had suffered in the course of her life; on the other, the level of the phantasy, in which she understood her femininity in terms of the absence of the phallus, and from which her real relations with men took their meaning. Fundamentally, the aim of analysis cannot be to offer comfort for what has gone wrong in the life of the analysand, or to support her directly in her struggle ("Of course men shouldn't think they can get away with anything just because they've got a . . ."). Instead, the analysand must realize that the phallus is not the object of a demand; she must abandon the idea that she has been deprived of the phallus, and that the absence of it condemns her to the inferiority against which she revolts. Only thus can she free herself from her often sterile conflicts with the men in her life, and give creative meaning to the difference between the sexes. The feminist engagement that might result from this, however, is no longer a psychoanalytic problem.

THE PHANTASY, THE OBJECT *a*, AND SUBJECTIVITY: THE ESSENTIALLY BODILY SIGNIFICANCE OF LACK

The subject of the unconscious is an essentially bodily subject. However, the body in which it takes on concrete form is not the body of biology, but the *erogenous* body. This erogenous body has a phantasmatic character, and is determined in terms of the signifiers of the Other that mark the history of the subject.[52] This implies that the phantasy is the place where the being of the subject is decided; the corporal relation of the subject to the Other and the world is determined primarily in terms of the phantasy.[53] This also makes it somewhat clearer why Lacan calls the phantasy the "fabric" or "stuff" (*l'étoffe*) from which the subject of the unconscious is made.[54]

Lacan further claims that the erogenous, phantasmatic body "turns" about a (determinate) void, for this body is determined by the signifier, so that something is always lost. This "something," which defies all integration, is the object *a*. It is the central element around which the phantasy is constructed, and it is in relation to it that the subject of the unconscious can gain its

---

52. This also explains why an arrow runs from (\$◊D) via *d* to (\$◊*a*) in the complete (fourth) version of the graph, which we shall deal with later. For (\$◊D) designates the signifiers of the unconscious, in relation to which the phantasy acquires form. We will come back on the meaning of this sigla later.

53. Here one might think, for example, of what we wrote above about the phantasy of the Ratman, and about the woman whose desire is determined by an impertinent look. This idea will also be made even more concrete in the chapter on pathology (see in particular the section in Chapter 8, "The Phantasy in Hysteria and Obsessional Neurosis pp. 250–257").

54. "[T]he phantasy is really the 'stuff' of the 'I' that is originally repressed, because it can be indicated only in the 'fading' of the enunciation" (E 314/13–16, EF 816). Here Lacan describes the subject of the signifier or of the unconscious as "originally repressed," because it is lost in an original way, that is, it has no consistency on the level of the enunciation (". . . it can be indicated only in the 'fading' of the enunciation") He further writes, "It is what enables them [the objects *a*] to be the 'stuff,' or rather the lining, though not in any sense the reverse, of the very subject that one takes to be the subject of consciousness. For this subject, who thinks he can accede to himself by designating himself in the statement, is no more than such an object" (E 315/14–18, EF 818).

own determinacy. This determinacy, however, is in principle not of the order of the imaginary,[55] for the object *a* has no specular image. It is rather the permanent disruption of every mirror-relation. For just this reason, the subject can in relation to it take on a form that does not cancel out its essential indeterminability in the phenomenal world.[56]

The subject thinks it finds itself in the statement, and believes it can determine itself in the image in which it appears to itself; but Lacan's theory of the phantasy and the object *a* once again makes it clear that the subject can never be completely subsumed into the image, because it is fundamentally not of the order of the image. The subject "is" nothing other than the heterogeneous object with which it identifies itself, and in which its lack takes on a concrete form.[57] In this sense, the subject "is" not of this (phenomenal) world, and in contrast with the

---

55. Naturally, this does not alter the fact that the neurotic patient interprets the object *a* as an object of a demand, and its relationship with it as an imaginary one.

56. As we know, the phenomenal world is essentially structured in terms of the imaginary and the symbolic.

Note that this explanation also shows us why Lacan calls the object *a* the prototype of the way the body takes on significance for the being of the subject. Elsewhere he says, "Thus it becomes apparent that the relation of the object to the body is in no way defined as a partial identification that would have to be totalized in such a relation [recall here what we said earlier concerning the relation between the partial object and the genital object], *since, on the contrary, this object is the prototype of the significance of the body as that which for being* [of the subject] *is at stake*" (E 301/26–30, EF 803; my emphasis).

57. On this point Lacan offers an example. "Ask the writer about the anxiety that he experiences when faced by the blank sheet of paper, and he will tell you who *is* the turd of his phantasy" (E 315/18–20, EF 818). Anyone who writes every now and then knows the anxiety before the blank virginal page: Will I have enough inspiration? Will I find something worth writing about? At work in the background here is the anxiety of being just a piece of

subject of consciousness, it must be thought of as "eccentric" (ex-centric).[58]

All this has consequences for the way we interpret the lack that marks the subject when it enters the order of language. Indeed, the theory of the object *a* and the phantasy makes it clear that we ought not understand this lack as a metaphysical magnitude; *the* lack does not exist. The signifiers that introduce it are not "signifiers in general"—rather, they are intrinsically bound up with specific erogenous zones and part objects. This means, first of all, that the lack is always and essentially experienced, and acquires (a phantasmatic) meaning, on the level of the body; the finitude of the human being to which symbolic lack refers is primarily corporal. In the second place, and more importantly, it implies that the lack is always and necessarily specified in terms of the various erogenous zones, in relation to which the psychic is inscribed. In this sense, the lack is no ab-

---

garbage (literally, the "turd of the Other") in which the Other (in this case, the potential reader) has not the slightest interest. The moment the anxiety comes over me and I am no longer capable of putting pen to paper, I identify in some sense with this "pile of shit" in which no one has any interest. From a more general, philosophical standpoint we could also formulate this idea as follows: No matter what feeling (for example, the feeling of being rejected) we have, in order to acquire any meaning for us, it must attach itself to a concrete bodily experience, which acts as a sort of prototype or original model.

58. The subject of the unconscious therefore ought not be thought of as a kind of homunculus that pulls the strings from behind the stage like a second ego or consciousness. This is what Lacan is probably thinking when he compares the object *a* with the lining (*doublure*) of a piece of fabric (in this case, the fabric of the subject of consciousness)—it is not merely a matter of the reverse (*envers*) of the fabric (see n. 54). By this he seems to want to suggest that the subject of the unconscious is made of another fabric than the subject of consciousness, and that it cannot be understood on the same model—which is to say, as a sort of second consciousness.

stract given: it can be a lack of control (anal phase), for example, or a lack of autonomy, a sense of being at the mercy of the Other (oral phase). When Lacan calls man a "lack-of-being" (*manque-à-être*), therefore, we have to keep in mind that this symbolic lack always has an essentially bodily significance.[59] Lacan's theory of desire is a theory of *embodied* desire.[60]

---

59. Clinically this means that the psychoanalyst in a certain sense listens to the body, which, so to speak, "breathes" through the signifiers of language.

60. This also implies that the well-known criticism of Lacanian psychoanalysis—that it is a sort of "linguistic idealism"—must be significantly nuanced. For precisely as a theory of language, it is equiprimordially a theory of the body and of embodiment.

7

The Truth of
the Unconscious:
S(Ø), the Castration
Complex, and
the Metaphor of
the Name-of-the-Father

THE FINAL VERSION OF THE GRAPH

The graph of desire is approaching completion. Lacan draws the final version as follows:

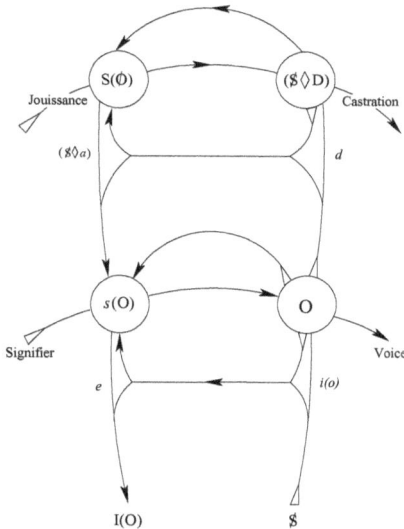

Comparison with the third version of the graph teaches us that Lacan introduces two new siglas here: S(Ø) and ($◊D). From the structure of the graph we immediately see that these two siglas from the upper part of the graph hold a position structurally homologous to the position of the symbols O and s(O) from the lower part. We will first address the meaning and the function of the sigla ($◊D).

(\$◊D) designates the chain of signifiers that determines and gives form to the unconscious desire of a concrete subject.[1] This sigla must as a result be understood as a specification—or better perhaps, a particularization—of O, which designates the "place of the treasure of signifiers" in the lower part of the graph. There we situated the system of signifiers; in other words, O refers to the language system as such, which contains the signifiers that structure the relation to the Other. Certain signifiers from this system will thus have an impact on the subject, continuing to impose their law even when the demand involved has lost its actuality, that is, long after the subject explicitly formulates the demand or is confronted with it.[2]

An example might make this somewhat clearer. A mother constantly asks her child how much she is worth, to which it is encouraged to answer, "Lots and lots of money." The signifiers of this demand can continue to determine the child's desire in any number of ways, even after the mother has ceased to put this question to her child and expect this answer from it. For example, the child might develop a passion for solving mathematical problems, because it wants to know the "right number" (Safouan 1974,

---

1. "But although our completed graph enables us to place the drive as the treasure of the signifiers, its notation as (\$◊D) maintains its structure by linking it with diachrony. It is that which proceeds from the demand when the subject disappears in it. It is obvious enough that demand also disappears, with the single exception that the cut remains, for this cut remains present in that which distinguishes the drive from the organic function it inhabits: namely, its grammatical artifice, so manifest in the reversions of its articulation to both source and object—Freud is unfailingly illuminating on this matter" (E 314/26–34, EF 817). The drive is here linked with diachrony ("linking it with diachrony") because the formula (\$◊D), with which it is designated, also refers to the diachronic (metonymic) concatenation of the signifiers of the unconscious. We will return to this.

2. This is what Lacan means when he talks about the "demand when the subject disappears in it" (E 314/28–29, EF 817).

pp. 104–105, n. 1). In other words, desire is structured by specific signifiers that were originally "chosen" at O. Lacan designates these signifiers with the sigla ($D), and he calls them, by analogy with the system of signifiers as such (O), "the treasure of signifiers." For ($D) designates the system of those particular signifiers that give form to the desire of a concrete subject.

But precisely how much is "lots and lots of money"? The repetition of the signifier "lots" points to the fact that something is omitted here, something that cannot be said. There is no adequate answer possible to the question of just how much money Mommy is worth, and one can easily imagine that it will "never be enough." As we already know, it is a matter here of an impossibility in principle; there is no final signifier that would allow us to formulate an answer. Lacan, we recall, claims that as in every chain of signifiers, meaning on the level of the signifiers of the unconscious is retroactively determined; and if we accept this, we must conclude that where the meaning of "lots and lots of money" might have been determined, there yawns only a void. This void is indicated by the sigla S(Ø): "signifier of a lack in the Other, inherent in its very function as the treasure of the signifiers."[3]

---

3. "What the graph now offers us is situated at the point at which every signifying chain prides itself on looping its signification. If we are to expect such an effect from the unconscious enunciation, it is to be found here in S(Ø), and read as: signifier of a lack in the Other, inherent in its very function as the treasure of the signifier" (E 316/5–9, EF 818). In the place where the production of meaning could have been retroactively closed ("looping its signification"), we find only a void, which is designated by the signifier S(Ø). We already expressed this void above in the formula "There is no Other of the Other." The signifier S(Ø) indicates that there is no ultimate signifier that can guarantee the truth of the discourse. Indeed, Lacan continues, "The lack referred to here [= the lack of which S(Ø) is the signifier] is indeed that which I have already formulated: that there is no Other of the Other. But is this mark made by the Unbeliever of the truth . . ." (E 316/14–16, EF 818).

Now it should come as no surprise that Lacan writes that desire cannot be articulated precisely because and insofar as it *is* articulated (in language).[4] Precisely because desire acquires form from the signifiers of the demand, it is impossible to determine its ultimate object. Because and insofar as I am submitted to the law of language, the ultimate object of desire constantly eludes me.

The full significance of the sigla ($D) can also be explained thus: the subject ($) "fades" away before the signifiers of the demand (D = *demande*); it does not know what the signifiers that insist in it want. Or perhaps better, it does not know what it itself desires through their insistence; for in the place where this problem could have been solved stands the signifier that designates the impossibility of such a solution (S(Ø)).[5]

---

4. "To put it elliptically: it is precisely because desire is articulated that it is not articulable, I mean in the discourse best suited to it, an ethical, not a psychological discourse" (E 302/35–38, EF 804). The last sentence points *inter alia* to the idea that the unconscious is not primarily a matter of feelings, affects, and the like, but of the *law* of the symbolic. For this problematic, and more especially for the further justification of Lacan's reference to ethics here, see Guyomard 1998, Moyaert 1994.

5. Lacan also describes ($D) as the algorithm of the drive (see the passage we cited in n. 1). At first sight this is remarkable, given that the drive seems to refer to the order of the body, while ($D) designates the "treasure of signifiers." The structural homology between body and language that we touched upon earlier can help solve this paradox.

Recall, first, that the body is marked by a continual movement of opening and closing, and in this way it *anticipates* the way the subject of the signifier only shows itself at the moment it disappears; for the subject is what always remains undetermined in the movement of the signifiers. On the other hand, those various erogenous zones where the body alternately opens and closes only acquire a meaning *from* the Other (the signifier). The loss of the objects related to the erogenous zones thus becomes the bodily staging of the loss in the order of language; contrariwise, language itself is anchored in the body (that is to say, receives an essentially bodily meaning). The pulsating movement of the body and of language thus turns out to be the same move-

The introduction of the signifier S(Ø) brings us to the core of Lacanian psychoanalysis, and obliges us to deepen our treatment of the various psychoanalytic themes we have dealt with already. More specifically, Lacan relates this signifier, and the lack it designates, to the Name-of-the-Father[6] and to the phallus as a signifier—which, according to him, holds a position structurally analogous to that of S(Ø). In the same context, the lack is more closely specified as a lack of an (impossible) *jouissance.*[7] The "Name-of-the-Father," the meaning of the phallus, and *jouissance* are central themes of Lacanian psychoanalysis, and we will deal with them further in what follows. Before we do so, however, we will first go a little further into the meaning and place of S(Ø) in Lacanian metapsychology.

---

ment; its apparently different aspects are merely two sides of the same coin, as it were.

Now, this movement is of the order of the *drive* because it is the dynamic force that "drives" the subject forward. Consequently, the drive (the body) and language cannot be thought apart from each other. This explains why Lacan calls the algorithm (\$◊D), which seems to refer exclusively to the order of the signifier, the algorithm of the *drive*. Here, Freud's idea that the drive is a limit-concept between the somatic and the psychic acquires a new and original meaning—we might say that the drive is a limit-concept between the order of the signifier and the order of the body.

The signifier and the body it signifies are thus related like the two sides of a Moebius strip, which cannot be distinguished from each other. In this connection, Lacan suggests that the various vicissitudes of the drive (reversal into the opposite, etc.) have to be understood as kinds of "grammatical artifice" (*artifice grammatical*), which are possible precisely on the basis of the close affinity between the drive and the signifier.

6. "It is already quite enough that at this point [namely, at S(Ø)] I had to situate the dead Father in the Freudian myth" (E 316/21–22, EF 818).

7. Hence *jouissance* figures on the uppermost part of the graph, as does castration—which refers to the impossibility of this *jouissance* (as well as to the signifier that designates this impossibility—the phallus). The status of the subject of the unconscious has to be made concrete in terms of this problematic.

THE SIGNIFICANCE OF S(Ø)

What obliges Lacan to introduce an extra signifier to designate the subject in its indeterminacy? Is it not sufficient to claim that the production of meaning in language can never be closed off, and that the subject escapes any definitive determination? Why must this indeterminacy itself also be articulated in a signifier? One will recall that, according to Lacan, there exists no meaning outside of language. This means that what cannot be expressed in this order does not exist for the subject. In this connection, Lacan writes that we must look upon the system of language—the chain of signifiers—as being complete.[8] By this he means that what cannot be expressed in language cannot be subjectified either, and this implies that the subject can only make its own inability to grasp itself a problem because and insofar as this incomprehensibility is inscribed concretely—that is, with a signifier—in the psyche.

It thus must be possible to inscribe the fundamental indeterminability of the subject in the psychic economy, and the introduction of S(Ø) is the first step towards this.[9] The sigla S(Ø), so Lacan writes, must be understood as a signifier.[10] But what sort

---

8. Lacan writes, "And since the battry [sic] of signifiers, as such, *is by that very fact complete* . . ." (E 316/35, EF 819; my emphasis). We will deal with the whole passage from which this clause is drawn in the following paragraph. For this point, see also Lacan 1960–61, p. 281.

9. Lacan takes the second step—and the decisive one—when he equates this signifier with the phallus a couple of pages further on.

10. "Personally, I will begin with what is articulated in the sigla S(Ø) by being first of all a signifier. My definition of a signifier (there is no other) is as follows: a signifier is that which represents the subject for another signifier. This signifier will therefore be the signifier for which all the other signifiers represent the subject: that is to say, in the absence of this signifier, all the other signifiers represent nothing, since nothing is represented only *for* something

of signifier is at stake here? It is clear from the start that S(∅) cannot be a signifier like any other, for S(∅) is expected to symbolize the lack that is installed *by* the "order of signifiers," and consequently cannot itself simply be part of this order.[11]

Now, we know that this lack has to be thought of as a lack of determinacy in the subject. Lacan's general definition of the signifier thus runs, "A signifier is that which represents the subject for another signifier,"[12] and *every* signifier therefore represents the subject in reference to another signifier. This implies that the subject cannot be identified with any one of the signifiers from which it takes its form. On the contrary, the subject shows itself in the infinite and indeterminate displacement of one signifier by another; in other words, it finds itself always *between* two signifiers. The signifier S(∅) refers to this "between": it is the signifier that symbolizes the message that the subject receives in answer to its question to the Other (*Che vuoi?*), namely that there is no signifier in the Other that can offer an answer to this question, and that the subject is consequently condemned to a desire that will carry it from one signifier to another. This is precisely the reason the O is crossed out; the one signifier in the

---

else. And since the battry [sic] of signifiers, as such, is by that very fact complete, this signifier can only be a line (*trait*) that is drawn from its circle without being able to be counted part of it. It can be symbolized by the inherence of a (–I) in the whole set of signifiers" (E 316/28–38, EF 819).

11. "And since the battry [sic] of signifiers, as such, is by that very fact complete, this signifier can only be a line (*trait*) *that is drawn from its circle without being able to be counted part of it.* It can be symbolized by the inherence of a (–I) in the whole set of signifiers" (E 316/35–38, EF 819; my emphasis). The last sentence of this passage suggests precisely that S(∅) is the signifier that designates that there is always one signifier lacking (–I) in order to close the production of meaning.

12. See n. 10.

Other that would determine the desire of the subject once and for all is lacking (which is represented by the slash).

Given, then, the differential structuration of the signifier, no signifier can represent the subject except for (or in reference to) another. The signifiers do indeed represent the subject, but their differential definition also implies that they defer its determination again and again. This explains why Lacan writes that they all, without exception, ultimately, refer to S(Ø), which articulates precisely this deferral.[13] This signifier therefore forms the horizon against the background of which all other signifiers signify the subject, and on the basis of which the latter relates to its own indeterminability.[14]

---

13. This explains why Lacan writes, "This signifier will therefore be the signifier for which all the other signifiers represent the subject . . ." (E 316/31–32, EF 819).

14. In this context, Lacan (E 318/30, 319/2, EF 821) compares the signifier S(Ø) with the notion of *mana,* which the French anthropologist Claude Lévi-Strauss addresses in his *Introduction to the Work of Marcel Mauss* (Lévi-Strauss 1950, esp. p. xli ff; English translation 1987, pp. 45–66).

Notions such as *mana, hau, wakan,* and so on, frequently occur in the symbolic systems of "primitive" cultures, and according to Lévi-Strauss, they intervene where an inadequacy exists between the order of the signified and the order of the signifier. Lévi-Strauss maintains that the two categories of the signifier and the signified are equiprimordial; once language appears, the whole universe is meaningful.

One cannot infer from the fact that they are equiprimordial, however, that humans are capable of coupling these two orders with each other without remainder. Lévi-Strauss writes, [L]'*homme dispose dès son origine d'une intégralité de signifiant dont il est fort embarrassé pour faire l'allocation à un signifié, donné comme tel sans être pour autant connu* ["(M)an has from the start had at his disposition a signifier-totality which he is at a loss to know how to allocate to a signified, given as such, but no less unknown for being given"] (Lévi-Strauss 1950 p. xlix, 1987 p. 62). Lévi-Strauss thus connects "knowledge" (*sans être pour autant* connu) with an intellectual process, on whose basis aspects of (the order of the) signifier are coupled with aspects of (the

We now also understand why Lacan writes that S(∅) refers to what the subject lacks in order to be able to determine itself exhaustively as *cogito*. For S(∅) designates the point at which the Cartesian *cogito* is confronted with the fact that it always escapes itself in the reflexive movement by which it is characterized.[15] S(∅) designates the point at which the *cogito* has to recognize that not only is it where it thinks; it also thinks where it is not.

Finally, Lacan maintains that the signifier S(∅) is inexpressible (*imprononçable*).[16] Now, we know that Lacan equates the chain of signifiers at point O of the graph with the system of phonological differences; we also know that S(∅) does not make up part of

---

order of the) signified—coupled, that is, in a manner that is imperfect by definition.

Mana, hau, and so on, are thus precisely "floating signifiers," without meaning of their own, which can repair the complementarity between these two orders. They can take on any meaning whatsoever, and are thus capable of filling in the gap between the signifier and the signified—somewhat after the fashion of the French *truc* or *machin* ["thingamabob" or "whatsit"]. Lévi-Strauss further compares these two notions to a "zero-symbol" (*une valeur symbolique zéro*): [C]*'est-à-dire un signe marquant la nécessité d'un contenu symbolique supplémentaire à celui qui charge déjà le signifié, mais pouvant être une valeur quelconque à condition qu'elle fasse encore partie de la réserve disponible . . .*" ["(T)hat is, a sign marking the necessity of a supplementary symbolic content over and above that which the signified already contains, which can be any value at all, provided it is still part of the available reserve . . ."] (Lévi-Strauss 1950 p. l, 1987 p. 64). Thus it is also clear why Lacan will not equate the signifier S(∅) with a "zero-symbol" in the sense of Lévi-Strauss. Signifiers such as *mana*, and so on, have the task of *repairing* the complementarity between the signified and the signifier, while the signifier S(∅) designates the *impossibility* of such a complementarity, and thus cannot simply be part of the order of signifiers (*la réserve disponible . . .*).

15. "This is what the subject lacks in order to think himself exhausted by his *cogito*, namely, that which is unthinkable for him" (E 317/6–7, EF 819).

16. "As such it [the signifier S(∅)] is inexpressible . . ." (E 316/39, EF 819).

this system, since it designates the *effects* of this system on the subject. S(Ø) is consequently *in opposition* to the signifiers at O, and thus is not a "verbal" signifier—it is inexpressible.[17]

This whole theory, however, remains unintelligible unless one sees it as a step in a chain of reasoning designed to introduce the phallus as the signifier of the lack.[18] As we have just seen, Lacan describes the signifier S(Ø) as inexpressible because it falls outside the system of phonological differences, having instead the task of articulating the effects of that system; S(Ø) is thus not a verbal signifier like any other. We also know from previous argument that desire is essentially embodied—the lack from which desire lives must always be understood in terms of its concrete bodily form,[19] for without this bodily anchoring, desire remains merely virtual. Consequently, the signifier that inscribes the fundamental indeterminability of the subject con-

---

17. In "Subversion," Lacan attempts to further clarify the status of S(Ø) by way of an algebraic formula that relies on the theory of imaginary numbers. We accept the judgment of Sokal and Bricmont that these are mathematical fantasies, in which Lacan displays a lack of understanding of number theory; nevertheless, we believe that Lacan's theory of the signifier S(Ø) does not need these mathematical formulas to be clear. For an attempt to nevertheless interpret these formulas, see Lacoue-Labarthe and Nancy 1990—which Sokal and Bricmont describe as "almost as ridiculous as the original" (Sokal and Bricmont 1997, pp. 30–32).

18. In later texts Lacan will distinguish the meaning of S(Ø) and of the phallus from each other. We leave this problematic out of consideration here because it would carry us too far astray. We only note that in Lacan's later work, the signifier S(Ø) designates the absence of a signifier for woman in the symbolic. This signifier then articulates the externality of woman to the order of the signifiers, and therefore to the phallus, which functions in the symbolic as signifier of the sexual difference. See Lacan 1972–73, *passim*; for more commentary on this problematic see André 1986, Verhaeghe 1990.

19. In this connection, see what we wrote above concerning the phantasy and the object *a*.

cretely in the psychic economy must designate the essential link between the body (life) and language. Lacan says that because this signifier cannot itself be of the order of language, a part of the body is chosen to fulfill this role instead. A part of the body functions in a privileged way as signifier of the lack from which desire arises. This part is, according to Lacan, the phallus, which he indeed equates with $S(\emptyset)$.[20]

We can otherwise formulate this same equivalence of $S(\emptyset)$ and the phallus as follows. $S(\emptyset)$ and the phallus need not be understood as two distinct signifiers—in fact, the introduction of $S(\emptyset)$ merely expresses, on the level of the logic of the signifier as such, the *formal necessity* of introducing a new signifier to designate the ultimate indeterminability of the subject. This signifier itself is the phallus.

This argument too, however, will remain very abstract unless we show how the phallus assumes the place of $S(\emptyset)$. This problematic is central to Lacan's theory of the castration complex, and the theory involved is exceptionally important for Lacan. Indeed, that theory constitutes the culmination of the subversion of the subject that Lacan says psychoanalysis

---

20. Lacan writes, "[T]hat is why it [the phallus] is equivalent to the $\sqrt{-1}$ of the signification produced above, of the *jouissance* that it restores by the coefficient of its statement to the function of lack of signifier (-1)" (E 320/3–5, EF 822). The expression "the coefficient of its statement" refers to $\sqrt{-1}$, which is the solution of the algebraic equation in which Lacan wants to grasp the meaning of $S(\emptyset)$ (E 317/5, EF 819). As we said above, we are leaving these mathematical speculations out of consideration. What is important here is to see that Lacan claims that $S(\emptyset)$ and the phallus have the same meaning, and are the signifier that designates the lack in the symbolic. ("that it restores . . . to the function of lack of signifier (-1)"). Later we will address in more detail the connection between the lack in the order of signifiers and (impossible) *jouissance*, a connection that is presupposed in the passage cited.

achieves.[21] Above, we connected this subversion with the idea that the subject of the unconscious is only a function of the signifier(s) by which it is determined, and which condemn it to an irreversible indeterminability. We now know, moreover, that the subject can only relate to this indeterminability because and insofar as the indeterminability itself is inscribed in the unconscious by a particular signifier. That signifier is the phallus; and the meaning and status of the phallus is articulated in and through the castration complex. It is in the castration complex, therefore, that the subversion of the subject thus finds completion.[22]

---

21. Indeed Lacan writes, "In the castration complex we find the major mainspring of the very subversion that I am trying to articulate here by means of its dialectic. For this complex, which was unknown as such until Freud introduced it into the formation of desire, can no longer be ignored in any reflection on the subject" (E 318/3–7, EF 820).

22. Lacan also points out that both (post-Freudian) psychoanalysis and the philosophical tradition have always denied the central role of castration in any theory of subjectivity. According to Lacan, theoreticians of psychoanalysis who try to incorporate psychoanalytical insights into a general psychology (e.g., the ego-psychologists and the French psychoanalyst D. Lagache) have thus sold their scientific credibility in neglecting this core Freudian teaching (E 318/8–18, EF 820).

The situation is little better on the side of philosophy. Lacan claims that the philosophical tradition is dominated by the hope of achieving a closed system of knowledge. Thus in his *Phenomenology of Spirit,* Hegel understands the dialectical development of consciousness as the progressive unfolding of potentialities already implicit in the most elementary figure of consciousness (sense certainty). The figure of absolute knowledge, to which this course of development leads, is consequently a sort of return to this first moment, whereby absolute knowledge actualizes all the potentialities given from the beginning.

Lacan speaks in this regard about a perfectly circular movement—one in which there is no place for a lack that prevents the closing of the circle. Lacan further distinguishes a "dialectical circle" (Hegel and the Hegelians)

THE CASTRATION COMPLEX IN FREUD[23]

Freud (1909a) introduces the problematic of castration in his case study of "little Hans." There he views it as an "infantile sexual theory" (Freud 1908)—an affectively loaded theoretical construct projected by little children in order to get a grip on the problematic of sexual difference. This theory includes the interpretation of sexual difference in terms of whether or not the penis is present; it is not the *difference* between the female and male sex organs that plays the decisive role here, but the presence or absence of the male organ alone.

However, Freud subsequently came to attach more and more universal significance to this "infantile theory." What he first interpreted as a theory, which is not and need not necessarily be present in all little children, he later interprets as a complex, so that it is a matter of an organized whole of affectively loaded presentations that form a particular transitional phase in the psychosexual development of all children. At a certain moment in their psychosexual development—in the course of the phallic phase, Freud claims—*all* children understand sexual difference in terms of the presence or absence of the phallus. One might think, for example, of a little boy who tries to reassure his sister by saying,

---

from a "mathematical circle," and while it is not clear what he means by this, it may be a reference to the work of Lévi-Strauss. For Lévi-Strauss wants to recover the minimal formal (and mathematizable) regularities to which all societies are subject; for him, all concrete social forms should be exhaustively and unambiguously derivable from these regularities. The movement in this case, too, is perfectly circular—indeed, here we can recognize the "modern subject of games theory," which as we already know, Lacan cannot accept (E 318/13–18, EF 820).

23. For a good introduction to the problematic of castration, in psychoanalysis in general and the work of Freud in particular, see Green 1995.

"You can still grow one." Or, conversely, a little girl who silences her brother with the words, "It could still fall off."

These often amusing expressions of the castration complex, however, should not make us forget that as a complex, it is to a large degree unconscious. The presentations that make up its core determine the relationship of the subject to itself (its sexualized body) and the Other in a way that bypasses consciousness.[24] Thus, Freud first discovered it in the analysis of his neurotic patients— or better, perhaps, he believed that clinical practice obliged him to attach a central role to the castration complex in psychosexual development in general, and in neurosis in particular.

In this regard, we cannot emphasize enough that for Freud, the castration complex was first and foremost a phase of development, and not the endpoint of psychosexual evolution. For Freud, the problematic of castration is intrinsically bound up with the oedipal problematic, and at least in principle should be overcome in the final genital (post-pubertal) stage of the development of the libido. In this final stage, the opposition "phallic-castrated," on the basis of which the little child interprets sexual difference, is replaced by the opposition "male-female." The two oppositions cannot be reduced to each other, of course. Thus, the central role of castration in neurosis implies for Freud that castration is not the perspective from which sexual difference as such is to be thought; neurosis is a matter of a fixation on a specific infantile interpretation of sexual difference, not the truth thereof.[25]

---

24. One will remember in this connection the clinical example that we gave earlier, of the woman whose relations with men were formed by the demand "to possess it too."

25. One could also express this problematic in another way: The castration complex is not Freud's theory, but the theory of "little Hans" and of Freud's neurotic patients. In this phase of his work, Freud refers to this "lit-

Clearly, we must understand the development of the castration problematic in Freud as a movement of universalization. What was at first an infantile sexual theory, by which one could follow the vicissitudes of some neurotic patients, was increasingly understood as a necessary phase in psychogenesis; and in the final phase of his intellectual development, Freud seemed to want to go still a step further. In "Analysis Terminable and Interminable" (1937), he writes that psychoanalysis inevitably runs aground on the "rocks of castration";[26] castration, in other words, sets a limit to what is analyzable, and this idea gives the problematic of castration an unprecedented breadth. Indeed, the insight that castration brings us to the limits of what is analyzable implies that it is really the perspective in which sexual difference *as such* is to be thematized. Castration thus takes on a quasi-metaphysical significance.

Lacan's theory of the castration complex and the phallus join up with the last phase of Freud's thought on the subject. Lacan calls the phallus the signifier of lack as such, and the significance and status of the phallus is thus determined in the castration complex. The latter thereby becomes not only the obligatory avenue of access to the symbolic, but also the problematic in whose terms the concrete psychic impact of the symbolic as such must be discussed. Simplifying somewhat, we might also express this as follows: in Freud the castration complex is still the core complex of

---

erally infantile" theory in order to understand neurosis, not in order to think the metaphysical truth of sexual difference. For more on the status of castration in Freud, see Laplanche 1980.

26. More specifically Freud claims that "penis envy" in the woman and resistance to the feminine, passive attitude in the man make up the limits of the analyzable. Both pertain to the relationship to the castration complex (Freud 1937, pp. 250–251).

neurosis; in Lacan, on the contrary, this problematic makes up the core of the truth of our existence as symbolic beings. Let us explore some of the implications of this sweeping radicalization.

THE IMAGINARY PHALLUS

We begin with a return to Freud. In his text on "infantile sexual theories," Freud defines the castration complex as the belief that all people, women included, have a penis, and claims that this belief has a narcissistic motivation. Already in childhood, he writes, the penis is the most important autoerotic sexual object. The great importance that the little boy in particular ascribes to it is apparent from the fact that he is not capable of imagining a person like himself (*eine dem Ich ähnliche Persönlichkeit*) in whom this "essential" part was nevertheless missing.[27]

Lacan tries to further illuminate these Freudian insights in terms of his own theory of the mirror-stage.[28] This theory consists in the claim that the ego arises on the basis of a libidinous investment in the image of the alter ego, with which "I" identify

---

27. "It is precisely in what we must regard as the 'normal' sexual constitution that already in childhood the penis is the leading erotogenic zone and the chief auto-erotic sexual object; and the boy's estimate of its value is logically reflected in his inability to imagine a person like himself who is without this essential constituent" (Freud 1908, pp. 215–216).

28. "The imaginary function is that which Freud formulated to govern the investment of the object as narcissistic object. It was to this point that I returned myself when I showed that the specular image is the channel taken by the transfusion of the body's libido towards the object. But even though part of it remains preserved from this immersion, concentrating within it the most intimate aspect of auto-eroticism, its position at the 'tip' of the form predisposes it to the phantasy of decrepitude in which is completed its exclusion from the specular image and from the prototype that it constitutes for the world of objects" (E 319/31–39, EF 822).

myself. Through this identification, the ego tries to acquire a completeness that it does not possess of itself. We know, however, that this identification is doomed to fail; as we have seen, an unbridgeable chasm gapes between the imaginary body and the real body of sensation. However, it is intrinsic to the very structure and dynamic of the ego to misrecognize its nonequivalence with the image from which it gets its form.

According to Lacan, this misrecognition can only be overcome if the impossibility of totalization is already inscribed in the image with which I identify myself. Indeed, how could we give up our belief in imaginary totalization unless its impossibility is already announced on the level of the specular image itself? The impossibility must be visible in the image, so that the libidinous investment of the specular image can never be total—there is always a remainder that cannot be integrated, and that reminds me of my incompleteness.[29] The unity between the ego and its specular image is thus always strained, because there is something *in the image itself* that, from the beginning, makes that unity impossible or at least problematic.[30]

Lacan goes on to say that the phallus plays a decisive and

29. "It was to this point [i.e., the problem of narcissism] that I returned myself when I showed that the specular image is the channel taken by the transfusion of the body's libido towards the object. But even though part of it [the body] remains preserved from this immersion [which is to say, "insofar as a part of the image cannot simply be integrated . . ."]" (E 319/32–35, EF 822).

30. Here we recognize the line of thought that we already encountered in connection with the introduction of the object *a*. In order that the symbolic can be inscribed in a concrete, bodily way, there must be a sort of structural homology between the symbolic and that upon which it imposes itself (in this case, the imaginary body image). More concretely this means that the imaginary can only be taken up in the dynamic of the symbolic, because and insofar as the essential incompleteness of the subject is already announced in one or other manner on the level of the imaginary.

privileged role in this context[31]—a privilege resulting directly from the primacy of the visual in Lacan's theory of the mirror-stage and of the formation of the ego. For the mirror-stage is characterized by the libidinous investment in the visual *Gestalt*; our relation to this image, according to Lacan, is primarily determined by its visible characteristics. This is the source of the privileged position of the phallus. The phallus is in fact an organ that can be "detached," and this in the double sense of the French *se détacher*:[32] it is an organ that can both "stand out" and also "come off." It is a pregnant *Gestalt*.[33] Moreover, this organ also has an important erotic meaning—it is the locus of pleasurable stimuli that emphasize its importance.[34] Naturally, in girls these pleasurable stimuli arise in the clitoris, but in Lacan's visual logic, that is beside the point. The point is rather that these pleasurable experiences also arise in girls at the place where seemingly—from the viewpoint of what is given visually—there could have been a (male) organ.[35] In other words, according to Lacan the phallus marks for both

---

31. ". . . the paradoxical privilege possessed by the phallus in the dialectic of the unconscious . . ." (E 302/23–24, EF 804). Later we examine in more detail the paragraph from which this passage comes.

32. *Se détacher* means both "to come loose or come off" (for something to detach itself from something else) and "to stand out (e.g., of a figure against a background).

33. Thus in our current passage Lacan talks about "its [the phallus's] position at the 'tip' of the form" (E 319/36–37, EF 822). [Here "at the tip of the form" translates *en pointe dans la forme*. The idea is that the phallus is like a spot or point that sticks out in or from an image; see the previous footnote— Trans.]

34. This is presumably also the reason Lacan, following Freud, writes that this part of the body "concentrat[es] within it the most intimate aspects of auto-eroticism" (E 319/35–36, EF 822).

35. The primacy of the visual in the mirror-stage does not mean that only the visual plays a role there. It means, rather, that in the mirror-stage the visual *Gestalt*, and not the accompanying bodily sensations, functions as the decisive structuring principle.

sexes a crack in the specular image—an organ that might have been there for girls, and for boys, one that might have not—which is thus precluded from complete integration into the image, and makes the subject's every attempt to coincide with it problematic from the outset.[36]

The phallus refers to the penis only insofar as it can be missing from the specular image, and therefore cannot be equated with the real organ. In the real, as Lacan repeatedly writes, nothing is missing; the real is what it is and nothing else. From the standpoint of the real it clearly does not make any sense to say, for example, that something is missing from women that they could have had. This idea only has meaning from the perspective of the imaginary, in which I hope to coincide with my specular image without complications. It is only in relation to the specular image[37] that the real organ can appear as something that endangers the wholeness of the ego. Lacan designates this imaginary problematic of the phallus with the symbol "-φ."

It is not unimportant for us to point out that for Lacan, the imaginary problematic of the phallus does not stand apart from its vocation as the signifier of the lack. The manner in which the phallus appears in the specular image "destines" it to fulfill a special role in the symbolic. Just as, in the symbolic, every

---

36. In this way the imaginary body image constantly threatens to appear as something decrepit, the integration and unity of which is never really assured ("its [this part of the body, i.e., the phallus] position at the 'tip' of the form predisposes it to the phantasy of decrepitude in which is completed its exclusion from the specular image and from the prototype that it constitutes for the world of objects"; E 319/36–39, EF 822). Moreover, the phallus does not really seem to have a sexual significance at this stage. All the emphasis here still lies on the (im)possible wholeness of the image, and not on sexual difference as such.

37. And to whatever fulfills the role of the mirror: the peers I identify with, for example.

presence appears against the background of an absence, so too the phallus necessarily appears against the background of a (possible) absence.[38] This is also, according to Lacan, the reason why precisely this part of the specular image is eminently suited to function as the signifier of lack.[39]

As we have described it so far, the Lacanian problematic of castration fits together seamlessly with Freud's thematization of the same problem. Only from the relation to the mirror and the dynamic of the imaginary can we really understand that the subject—in a second moment—demands the phallus that it does not possess, or when it does possess it, fears to lose it.[40] Castration is thus understood exclusively as frustration:[41] on the basis of an imaginary belief in a possible completion, the subject thinks that it can be or has been deprived of something real, or on the

---

38. This is what Lacan means when he writes that "This choice [i.e., of the phallus as the signifier of lack] is allowed because the phallus, that is, the image of the penis, is negativity in its place in the specular image. It is what predestines the phallus to embody *jouissance* in the dialectic of desire" (E 319/ 24–26, EF 822). In this last clause, Lacan refers to the problematic of *jouissance*, which we will deal with later. The problematic of *jouissance* is a further specification of the lack—in fact, the lack is always a lack of *jouissance*. The phallus points precisely to this lack.

39. We will examine the status of the phallus as signifier in more detail later.

40. The repeated "disappearance" and reappearance of the phallus (periodic erections) can further reinforce the anxiety that the phallus is an organ the possession of which is not guaranteed (especially for boys). This anxiety finds its ultimate justification in the fact that the phallus really is missing in girls. For more on this point see Kristeva 1996, pp. 141–223.

41. In this context, Lacan distinguishes frustration from (symbolic) castration. In frustration, the object is real, the lack that it must fill imaginary. In castration, by contrast, the object is imaginary, and the lack symbolic. On the basis of castration, the originally imaginary object will be able to function as the signifier of the lack instituted by the symbolic. We will develop this point in more detail later.

same level, it assumes that some real object can make up for its lack (and understands the phallus as something that can be recovered in reality).

From the clinical standpoint, this problematic can take on very different forms: the analysand who believes that the absence of the phallus condemns her to an inferiority that at the same time she vehemently contests, for example. In another instance, an analysand dreamed that he and a friend from elementary school were lying in bed, each holding the other's penis and roaring with laughter. In the course of the analysis, it became clear that their fits of laughter expressed his sense of superiority over those who do not possess the vaunted organ. But we can also wonder whether this dream is not also, at a more fundamental level, the veiled expression of a deep-rooted anxiety about possibly *losing* the phallus—the triumph might be short-lived!

As a final example, we can consider Freud's analysis of the "Wolfman." According to Freud, the latter had as a small child been witness to *coitus a tergo* between his parents, and as a result he experienced himself as castrated by his father. Lacan suggests that he must have identified with his mother, and that this identification lay at the origin of his (unconscious) belief that castration was the price for the father's love. According to Freud, what was involved here was an identification in the order of the image. This identification functioned as an "imaginary matrix" from which the Wolfman constantly gave form to and experienced his relationship to himself and to others. It goes without saying, however, that the problematic of the Wolfman cannot be reduced to this imaginary identification. The (imaginary) identification with the mother, on the contrary, conflicted with a (symbolic) identification with the father. After all, the Wolfman is the son of his father, and he is not a woman. In other words, the homosexual captivation by the image of the mother in the primal scene stands opposed to the heterosexual object choice of the Wolfman, and for Freud, the conflict with the homosexual captivation explains the compulsive character of the heterosexual choice, while also elucidating numerous other conflicts that dominate the life of the Wolfman.

To give but one example: when the Wolfman was initiated into Christianity at the age of five or six by his family's Catholic maid, it initially had a liberating effect on him. For the Christian faith brought him into contact with a sort of father other than the one who threatened him with castration. Christian belief also aroused in the Wolfman the consciousness of belonging to a larger community, and taught him to master and sublimate his drives. Belief, in other words, made a social and educable child of the Wolfman. But the devotion of the Wolfman to his belief was not without its conflicts, for God allows his son to die on the cross—and this could not but remind the Wolfman of his "sadistic" father. The content of the Christian faith here is in a sense "drawn in" by the "imaginary matrix" of the primal scene, and his religious devotion and its positive effects, in turn, come under pressure once more (Freud 1918).

In order to fully delineate the significance and importance of the imaginary phallus in the work of Lacan, however, we have to add an important element. According to Lacan, the imaginary phallus plays a decisive and determining role in the relation between the mother and the child[42]—the reader will recall what we said earlier about the relation between the infant and the first real Other of the demand. The infant, we said, tries to posit itself as the object of the mother's desire; it wants to be that which

---

42. Lacan does not address this problematic as such in "Subversion." It seems necessary to deal with it here, however, if we are to grasp "Subversion" properly.

can remedy the lack of the mother. Now in this context, Lacan also writes that the child wants to be the phallus of the mother (Lacan 1956–57, 1957–58, pp. 161–212 and *passim*). How can we understand this seemingly enigmatic statement?

The infant wants to be or to give that which will make up for the lack of the Other. This implies that the relation between the mother and the infant is borne along by the imaginary dynamic of the mirror stage, for only in the imaginary do I believe in the possibility of an adequate answer to the demand for love. We also know that the phallus marks precisely the place in the image where the wholeness of that image itself always appears as problematic, so giving a minimal visibility to the impossibility of imaginary completion. The mother, moreover, does not have the phallus, and the child very soon realizes that her desire, attested to by her repeated absences, must go together with this lack in one way or another. Lacan, then, interprets the efforts of the infant to equate itself with the object of this desire as an attempt to be the missing phallus—for the infant tries to make up for the lack, and the phallus is the visible attestation of that lack in the imaginary.

The child, as we know, must free itself from the grip of the first real Other of demand if it is ever to be able to develop its own desire. From the perspective we have just sketched, this means that the child must abandon its attempts to be the phallus of the mother. It must cease to understand the phallus as an imaginary magnitude, or, what amounts to the same thing, it must cease to experience castration as a frustration. According to Lacan, the separation from the mother in which this transformation comes about presupposes the introduction of the metaphor of the Name-of-the-Father, which seals the break between mother and child and confirms the phallus in its role as the signifier of lack. These two processes—the break with the mother, and the transformation of the phallus into the signifier of lack (the castration complex)—are inseparably bound up with each other, and in the metaphor of the Name-of-the-Father, they find their common ground.[43]

THE FATHER AS SYMBOLIC THIRD[44]

How can the law that separates the child from the mother be psychically inscribed? It is clear that the little child will be confronted from the beginning with the fact that it is not "everything" for the mother; the recurrent absences of the mother cannot but indicate that the desire of the mother is not limited to the child. This creates in the child the confused conjecture that there is a third player in the game, who actually possesses what the little child strives in vain to give to the mother, or what it wants to be for her. This third party—prototypically the father—appears (if unclearly) as someone who is something more and something other than what the child can mean for the mother, and thus confronts the child with its own shortcomings.

---

43. Above we related the separation from the first real Other of demand to the appearance of the transitional object and the object *a*. Our task now is to relate this problematic to the "metaphor of the Name-of-the-Father" as its condition of possibility. Of course, this "metaphor of the Name-of-the-Father" cannot be understood as a process that takes place at a particular moment in time. It expresses rather the structure of a process that comes about on the basis of a complex totality of identifications, intersubjective relationships, and so on.

44. Lacan's remarks on the father and fatherhood are scattered throughout "Subversion." In order to do justice to the systematicity of Lacan's ideas here, we will discuss them all together in light of their underlying common logic. As for the role of the phallus in the relation between the mother (or whoever takes her place) and her child, here too we will have to go somewhat beyond a simple commentary on "Subversion" for the sake of clarity.

The confrontation with the third party, however, is in itself not sufficient to free the child from its imaginary identification with the phallus. On the contrary, the little child can enter
into imaginary identification as much as it ever did, but now with
the father as the supposed possessor of that which completes
the desire of the mother (the imaginary phallus).[45] In this
way the child becomes the rival of the father, whose place it
wants to take over; according to Lacan, the Freudian Oedipus
complex, in which the child struggles with the father for possession of the mother, is the theoretical translation of this situation,[46] and the child can only overcome this rivalry when it is
clear that the father is not the phallus—he can only make legiti-
mate use of it. Fatherhood thus appears as a symbolic function
that is in principle represented by the real father.

This last point is of great importance. The child must abandon
the belief that it can be the phallus of the mother, and this means
that it must gain access to the symbolic law of desire. Now in the
symbolic system, Lacan continues, the father is designated as the
primordial representative of the law.[47] This means that whoever
"separates" the child from the mother—or whoever *de facto* occupies her place—fulfills a *function* that is related in the symbolic
system to the father or fatherhood as such. While this person is
often the biological father, he or she is not *necessarily* so.

The father, and not the mother, is thus the prototypical

---

45. In this context, Lacan draws a distinction between the imaginary
father and the real and symbolic fathers, which we will discuss later.

46. We must understand, however, that in Freud the rivalry over the
mother is central, whereas in Lacan it is the imaginary phallus to which the
child tries to equate itself.

47. "The fact that the father may be regarded as the original representative of this authority of the Law . . ." (E 311/7–8, EF 813).

representative of the law of the symbolic.[48] This point is borne out when Lacan writes further that the identity of the father is in principle uncertain. By contrast to the mother, of whom there can be scarcely any doubt that the child she gives birth to is indeed hers, the identity of the father is at least in principle unknown. *Pater semper incertus est,* declares Roman Law. This implies that fatherhood is structurally always an adoption; one becomes a father by recognizing one's children as one's own. At least in our culture, the father recognizes his children by giving them his name, so that one becomes a father not so much by inseminating the mother as by conferring one's name upon the child. This name takes the place of something that in principle cannot be decided—it closes the wound of an irremediable absence. This means that fatherhood is an eminently symbolic given, for it is essentially the result of a (symbolic) act of attribution, whereby an order arises that was not given previously (in the order of experience/the empirical as such). This, according to Lacan, is the structural reason the law of the symbolic is traditionally identified with the law of the father.

It is important to see here that Lacan is not simply talking about the relation between a man and a woman as such (Van Haute 1995, Verminck 1996). In the first place, Lacan points to a structural difference between being-a-father and being-a-mother. This structural difference has to do with the fact that the father and mother have in principle a different relation to the symbolic: the recognition of the child by the mother is the translation and confirmation of an immediate empirical given (the mother cannot in

---

48. Above we called the mother the "first incarnation" of the Other. We must now make it clear why she can fulfill this role only by an implicit or explicit reference to the father as the "original representative" (E 311/8, EF 813) of the symbolic order.

principle deny to herself that the child has come forth from her); fatherhood, by contrast, seems to suppose a more basic step into the unknown. The attribution of the Name-of-the-Father cannot simply be founded in a reality outside of language, and it is therefore something more and something other than the translation of an empirical certainty. It comes about rather against the background of something that in principle cannot be decided. The Name-of-the-Father institutes a meaning that cannot be directly and immediately derived from the givens of experience.[49]

THE SYMBOLIC FATHER IS THE "DEAD" FATHER: TOTEM AND TABOO

Does all this tell us who or what a father is, however?[50] We have seen that fatherhood is a symbolic function represented by the real father, who confronts the child with the fact that it cannot be "everything" for its mother. In this sense, the father introduces the law of the Other, which makes possible the development of one's own desire. The real father, however, does not introduce this law in his own name; he is not the origin of the

---

49. The possibility of determining the father with certainty through DNA-testing in cases of doubt might not fundamentally change much here. What Lacan is concerned with is the fact that fatherhood is in principle always "a case of doubt," and it is precisely for this reason that DNA-testing can be relevant. Fatherhood can in principle always be contested. This is not the case for motherhood, or at least not in the same way. The structural difference thus continues to exist, even if it seems that it is concealed by the technical possibility of deciding once and for all who is the biological father of a child.

50. "It would be better to read what Freud has to say about its coordinates [i.e., of the Oedipus complex]; for they amount to the question with which he himself set out: 'What is a Father?'" (E 310/17–19, EF 812).

law that he pronounces.[51] This means that the real father himself is also subject to the law he represents.[52] In what, then, does this law find its origin? Or better, who is the father who functions as the original representative of the authority of the law and in whose name the real father speaks?

In order to answer this question, Lacan returns to Freud's (1912–13) famous text "Totem and Taboo," in which Freud explicitly poses the problem of the origin of authority and the law. Freud describes a sort of primal state in which a potent male disposes over all the women, and maintains that the origin of both authority and human history must be understood in these terms. More specifically, he attempts to explain totem religions and the taboos that are part of them in terms of this primal state. He is basically concerned with two taboos here: the incest taboo, and the taboo against killing the totem-animal.[53]

In the first phase of human history, Freud says, the primal father possessed all the women. However, the sexually deprived sons murdered this leader in order to be able to enjoy his privileges themselves. The first result of this was a "war of all against all"—the sons, like the father, each demanded for himself the sole right to all the women. In order to put an end to this war,

---

51. This is impossible because, as we already know, there is no metalanguage that can be spoken. There is no Other of the Other. Lacan thus writes, "And when the Legislator (he who claims to lay down the Law) presents himself to fill the gap [i.e., left by there not being an Other of the Other], he does so as an impostor" (E 311/2–4, EF 813). This Legislator is the "ideal Father." We will return to this phantasmatic figure in more depth in the chapter on psychopathology (Chapter 8).

52. We expressed this idea earlier by saying that the father is not himself the phallus, but the one who can employ it legitimately.

53. Freud 1912–13, pp. 143ff. We do not have enough space here to reproduce Freud's complicated line of argument in detail, and I will limit myself to what is important for our own exposition.

the sons were eventually obliged to accept the "law of the father"; they had to renounce the possession of all the women in order to save the peace. According to Freud, the institution of the incest taboo resulted from this scenario.

It is already striking here that the law of the father is only instituted and accepted after he has disappeared. We would be mistaken, however, to understand the institution of the law in terms of simply pragmatic motives. Freud argues that the sons submit primarily not in order to put an end to the war of all against all, but because they feel guilty. Where does this guilt feeling come from?

The sons hate the father because he stands in the way of the satisfaction of their sexual needs. This hatred, nevertheless, goes hand in hand with feelings of admiration and love—the father was not only an obstacle, but also an example with whom they could identify. After the murder, according to Freud, these feelings of admiration and love gain the upper hand, and the sons' feelings of guilt find their ground in this ambivalent attitude towards the father; they issue from the contradiction between the love for the father and his murder. The sons feel guilty because they have killed the object of their love. The dead father, writes Freud, is much more powerful than the living one ever was. What was forbidden in the primal horde by the father, the sons now forbid themselves, so that on the one hand they set up an inviolable totem animal in place of the father, and on the other, they renounce the possession of all women through the institution of the incest prohibition. The sons, Freud concludes, submit themselves to the leader only after the murder (*nachträglich*), and they do so because they feel guilty.

It is of the greatest importance for our current problem to see that Freud considers the "myth" of the murder of the primal father the historical, phylogenetic basis for the individual's

Oedipus complex; what was played out in the primeval period of human history repeats itself again and again in the life of every one of us. Lacan, on the other hand, sees it *as myth*: this means that the Oedipus complex gives a concrete and contingent content to a structural moment that is articulated in the myth of the primal murder.[54] This structural moment has to do with the installation of a law that makes a total fulfillment of desire impossible, and that is prototypically represented by the father. The Oedipus complex can take on many different forms in different societies, but it will always have to do with the institution of a law that forbids total fulfillment. This law is, according to Lacan, the law of the murdered primal father.

What, then, does Lacan say Freud's myth teaches us about this father whose law is pronounced by the real father? It is noteworthy that the sons in Freud's version of the primal myth submit only after the primal father has disappeared; the father to whom the sons are obedient is a dead father. The sons thus do not submit to an external, physical power. They submit, rather, the moment there is no longer anyone who could enforce the law "in person." The father who stands at the origin of the law is in this sense merely a symbolic reference point—he never appears as a real person, and he is not an incarnate reality. Instead, he exists only as a name—or in more Lacanian terminology, as a signifier.[55]

---

54. It is evident from the following quote that Lacan gives no universal significance to the Oedipus complex as it is set out by Freud: "Yet the Oedipus complex cannot run indefinitely in forms of society that are more and more losing the sense of tragedy" (E 310/34–35, EF 813). However, the disappearance of the Oedipus complex in the classical sense of the word does not mean that there is no longer a necessity for a law to separate the child from the mother, and to declare the impossibility of a completion.

55. ". . . for they [Freud's insights concerning the Oedipus complex and the myth of the primal horde] amount to the question with which he

This implies, according to Lacan, that the authority of the symbolic father has its foundation in nothing other than the enunciation of his name. It has no *fundamentum in re.*

This sits perfectly with the idea that every authoritative statement of the Other as the place of the signifier has only itself (the fact that it is enunciated) as its foundation.[56] In this sense the function of the father, as it emerges from Freud's myth, refers to the impossibility of founding (the law of) the symbolic in the real. The notion that the symbolic father is the "dead" father of Freud's myth of origin consequently concretizes the idea that there can be "no Other of the Other,"[57] and in light of our reading of the graph of desire, this means that the Name-of-the-Father must be situated at $S(\emptyset)$, which expresses the impossibility of a meta-language (E 316/14–24, EF 818).

---

himself set out: 'What is a Father?' 'It is the dead Father,' Freud replies, but no one listens, and, concerning that part of it that Lacan takes up again under the heading 'Name-of-the-Father,' it is regrettable that so unscientific a situation should still deprive him of his normal audience" (E 310/18–23, EF 812). The last sentence refers to the state of psychoanalytic theory at the time Lacan wrote "Subversion." This state—the dominance of ego-psychology—has the result that Lacan is not heard by the public that should actually be his: the psychoanalysts. He also writes, "It is already quite enough that at this point I had to situate the dead Father in the Freudian myth. . . . No doubt the corpse is a signifier, but Moses's tomb is as empty for Freud as that of Christ was for Hegel [the latter being a reference to the problematic of unhappy consciousness in Hegel's *Phenomenology of Spirit*]" (E 316/21–26, EF 818). By this Lacan means to say that the symbolic father is the "dead" father. The symbolic father is the corpse after the murder, and the emptiness that exists only in the form of the guilty feelings of the sons.

56. This explains why Lacan also writes, "Let us set out from the conception of the Other as the locus of the signifier. Any statement of authority has no other guarantee than its very enunciation . . ." (E 310/36–38, EF 813).

57. See the section in Chapter 3, "The Subject and the Other" (pp. 70–75).

We ought not infer from this, however, that Lacan simply takes over Freud's primal myth without further ado. In the first place, Freud thought that the story really occurred just as he had described it. Lacan cannot accept this. The story of the primal horde violently usurping a "first" father is rather, according to Lacan, a mythic expression of the structure of the symbolic that determines us; Lacan terms this interpretation "mythic" because it essentially withdraws something from sight.[58] According to him, Freud in fact underestimates the radicality of the symbolic lack by giving it an imaginary interpretation. We will now look more closely at the implications of Lacan's "mythic" rereading.

Let us recall that the symbolic introduces a lack that makes the fulfillment of desire impossible.[59] Whatever life may have to offer us, we will never feel "That's it!" Our existence plays itself out against the backdrop of a loss that cannot be undone, and this loss, and the dissatisfaction that flows from it, are not therefore the result of social structures that could have been otherwise.[60] On the contrary, they are caused by an Other that makes fulfillment impossible. Lacan writes in this connection

---

58. "Is this *Jouissance*, the lack of which makes the Other insubstantial, mine, then? Experience proves that it is usually forbidden me, not only, as certain fools believe, because of a bad arrangement of society, but rather because of the fault (*faute*) of the Other if he existed: and since the Other does not exist, all that remains to me is to assume the fault upon 'I,' that is to say, to believe in that to which experience leads us all, Freud in the vanguard, namely, to original sin" (E 317/25–32, EF 819–820).

59. In this passage, Lacan calls this fulfillment *jouissance*. We will return to this in more detail later. See the section in Chapter 8, "Introduction: The *Jouissance* of the Other and Pathology" (pp. 219–228).

60. We already know that Freud writes in the same vein that not cultural circumstances, but something in the sexual function itself makes the complete satisfaction of that function impossible. We will come back to this. See Freud 1930, p. 105. Lacan refers to this passage at E 310/9–14, EF 812.

that the Other would be responsible for this state of unfulfillment *if it existed*—while in fact, the Other who represents the
law of the symbolic exists only as a signifier (the Name-of-the-
Father). As a result, it cannot be held responsible for the conditions of our existence. There is, in other words, no one for
us to complain to, no one with whom we can lodge an appeal
against what has been done to us. In this sense, the human
subject stands alone before an Other who does not exist.

Precisely in order to escape this realization, however, the
subject takes the fault upon itself.[61] If the Other cannot be guilty,
because it does not exist, then most likely I have only myself to
blame. Lacan claims that it is simply easier to live with the idea
that everything could have been different—if we had taken another direction in life, if only we had made other choices—than
to look the irrevocability of the conditions of our existence in
the eye. If we must be condemned to a permanent state of loss
and unfulfillment, then better that at least someone be held responsible for it: ourselves if necessary.[62]

This, according to Lacan, is the structural background of
the belief in original sin, of which Freud's myth is a secularized
version.[63] Freud interprets the murder of the father, which every
one of us carries out in the Oedipus complex, as the ontogenetic

---

61. "This *Jouissance* . . . [which] is usually forbidden me . . . because of
the fault (*faute*) of the Other if he existed: and since the Other does not exist,
all that remains to me is to assume the fault upon 'I'" (E 317/25–30, EF 819–
820).

62. This is a typical neurotic position: "Everything that goes wrong is
someone else's fault," or else, "If I had only done everything differently in life,
I would now be reaping a harvest of happiness."

63. "[S]ince the Other does not exist, all that remains to me is to assume the fault upon 'I,' that is to say, to believe in that to which experience

repetition of a primal murder, by which the feeling of guilt for that murder is passed down from one generation to the next. The primal murder is the phylogenetic basis for the feeling of guilt that essentially characterizes sexuality and stands in the way of its complete satisfaction. Clearly, Freud's idea that we phylogenetically inherit guilt for the father's murder is no longer tenable, but Lacan emphasizes that the untenability of the way Freud's ideas are formulated factually ought not stop us trying to explain their structural significance. For Lacan, it appears not so much that Freud was mistaken as that he did not go far enough with his myth of origin—for his psychoanalytic theory of original sin underestimates the radicality of the lack. Freud presents this lack as somehow being "our fault" (something for which humanity is *culpable*, rather than a fatal flaw), as if we could be held responsible for the very structure of the symbolic outside of which, as subjects, we cannot exist. While this notion brings with it a heavy burden, it also has a reassuring character. It is easier to live with a problem for which we can hold someone guilty somehow or other, than one that simply evades our grasp.

---

leads us all, Freud in the vanguard, namely, to original sin" (E 317/29–32, EF 820). Lacan also claims elsewhere in "Subversion" that Freud's myth of the primal father has a theological character. More particularly, where Lacan refers to Freud's idea that something in the sexual function itself stands in the way of its satisfaction (E 310/9–14, EF 812), he immediately adds, "It would be wrong to think that the Freudian myth of the Oedipus complex had put an end to theology on the matter" (E 310/9–14, EF 812). Here Lacan at least implicitly founds the structural insatiability of sexuality, as Freud describes it, in the feelings of guilt that flow from the murder of the primal father. The theological character of this myth consists in its introducing of a sort of hereditary sin that makes satisfaction impossible. Freud himself also considers other factors—structural bisexuality, the problematic of organic repression, and so forth—but Lacan discusses none of them.

THE METAPHOR OF THE NAME-OF-THE-FATHER

Let us return to the problem from which we set out: How can the lack that brings desire to life acquire meaning for the child? Let us first recall what we have learned so far. We have seen that the little child is confronted with the lack by the presence of a third party, prototypically the (real) father, who pronounces the law of the symbolic—the law of the Father. This father, to whose law the child must submit, is a purely symbolic point of reference; it is the Name-of-the-Father,[64] or what amounts to the same thing, it is a pure signifier. The submission to this law means that the child replaces the (imaginary) phallus as representative of the desire of the mother with the Name-of-the-Father.[65] For recognition of the Name-of-the-Father implies that the child accepts that the one who could satisfy the desire of the mother is the "dead" father, who can only appear as a signifier. Or, what amounts to the same thing, the child accepts that desire can only find satisfaction by means of signifiers—and thus that it never

---

64. In this connection, Lacan often plays on the ambiguity of the French *Nom-du-Père* (Name-of-the-Father), which is phonetically identical with *le* Non-*du-Père* (the No-of-the-Father). This "no" relates to the prohibition on equating oneself with the object of the desire of the mother (from the standpoint of the child) and on taking the child as an object that could fulfill desire (from the standpoint of the mother). We will return to this.

65. The recognition of the Name-of-the-Father is equiprimordial with the formation of the ego-ideal. The identification with the "specific trait" institutes a relation with the Other as representative of an order that essentially transcends him. This order is the order of the father, to which we gain access on the basis of the metaphor of the Name-of-the-Father. Lacan does not work this idea out any further in "Subversion." See Lacan 1957–58, pp. 287–301.

finds complete satisfaction.[66] Lacan calls this process of substitution, on the basis of which the Name-of-the-Father comes to stand in the place of the (object of the) desire of the mother, "the paternal metaphor" (*la métaphore paternelle*).

We know that the entry into the order of signifiers presupposes a "first metaphor" that actively negates the causal link between the object and the sign.[67] We can now further specify this "first metaphor" from a psychoanalytic perspective as the metaphor of the Name-of-the-Father; for on the basis of this metaphor, the child abandons the belief that there is an adequate object that corresponds to the desire of the mother. Just as there is no unambiguous coupling between the sign and the object, so too there is no unambiguous coupling between the desire of the mother and the various objects that could satisfy it. In other words, on the basis of the paternal metaphor the child surrenders itself to the movement of signifiers. It gives up hope of ever being able to fully signify or realize desire.

We further connected this "first metaphor" with the appearance of the transitional object, which to some extent separates

---

66. This is also the reason Lacan writes further in "Subversion," "The true function of the Father, which is fundamentally to unite (and not to set in opposition) a desire and the Law, is even more marked than revealed by this" (E 321/31–33, EF 824). This passage belongs to a reference to the "ideal father." This is the phantasy of an almighty father who possesses what is missing from the mother to fulfill her desire. The role of this phantasy in the various neurotic syndromes illustrates, according to Lacan, that the function of the father does not consist in prohibiting desire. For desire is not external to the law, but it is an effect of it. Rather than prohibiting desire, the (real) father must in fact make possible a mediation between the law and desire. The intervention of the real father is directed towards transforming the image of the "ideal father" (and thus of a possible fulfillment of desire) into a reference to a symbolic father.

67. See Chapter 3.

the child from the mother.[68] By way of this metaphor, the child passes over into the larger world of imagination, and no longer gives content to its existence exclusively in terms of the wishes of the first real Other of the demand. In this way it can begin to develop its own desire. We now understand that the "paternal metaphor" forms the structural condition of possibility for this, for the "paternal metaphor" institutes a distance between the child and the first Other. It thus creates the space in which the transitional object can appear.

In this regard, it is of the greatest importance to see that the metaphor of the Name-of-the-Father, as we have described it, also has an eminently normative significance. The father prohibits the mother to the child; the Name-of-the-Father (le Nom-du-Père) is equally the No-of-the-Father (le Non-du-Père). This "no" prohibits the child from taking the mother as a libidinous object, and obliges it to desire in accordance with the law of signifiers. That law also implies that a range of objects is designated that qualify as "permissible" within the symbolic system. In other words, desiring in accordance with the law of the signifier equiprimordially means abandoning the dream of a complete fulfillment, and limiting oneself to objects that are accepted as possible objects of desire within the symbolic system.

We would nevertheless be mistaken to neglect the role of the mother in the "paternal metaphor." We have already said that the confrontation with the symbolic arises in the relation with the mother; in reality, she is the one who first occupies the place of the Other. In our current context, this means that the infant is primarily confronted with the law of the father in the discourse of the mother—in order that the "paternal metaphor" should

---

68. See the section in Chapter 5, "Further Characterization of Desire: The Transitional Object" (pp. 119–123).

come into being, it is of vital importance that the reference to the third party is already present within that discourse. Only when the mother herself recognizes that the infant is not the endpoint of her desire can the little child escape her grip (Aulagnier 1991, Lacan 1957–58, p. 191).

The position of the mother is in this sense much more complex than that of the father. On the one hand she is the first representative of the law of the symbolic:[69] she actively supports the intervention of the father, and without this support the law of the symbolic remains a dead letter—the real father cannot fulfill his role in an adequate manner. On the other hand, the dynamic between the infant and the first real Other of the demand, which we already discussed earlier, implies that the mother also inevitably obscures and conceals this law, and withdraws it from sight.[70]

THE METAPHOR OF THE NAME-OF-THE-FATHER AND SYMBOLIC CASTRATION

The paternal metaphor thus confronts the child with the impossibility of being "everything" for the mother, or what amounts

---

69. Lacan writes in this context, "The fact that the Father may be regarded as the original representative of this authority of the Law requires us to specify by what privileged mode of presence he is sustained beyond the subject who is actually led to occupy the place of the Other, namely, the mother" (E 311/7–10, EF 813). In the order of reality, the mother is the first representative of the law of the Father, and the reference to that law too must accordingly be given in her discourse. We can now also answer the question of the privileged way in which the father is present "beyond" the subject that occupies the place of the Other in reality. "He" is so present as a signifier.

70. See the section in Chapter 5, "Desire and the Law: The Dialectic of Desire" (pp. 112–119).

to the same thing, the child must in and through the paternal metaphor abandon the belief that it can be or give the phallus that would fulfill the mother's desire. According to Lacan, this also means that although the imaginary phallus is at first understood as an object that I can be or give, with the recognition of the Name-of-the-Father it is transformed into the signifier of lack, which role it can then play to the full. Let us see what this might mean.[71]

Recall that the phallus owes its central place in the dynamic of desire to the fact that it only appears in the specular image against the background of a (possible) absence. The infant understands this absence, in the first instance, according to the logic of frustration—on the basis of an imaginary belief in a possible fulfillment, the subject thinks that it has been or can be deprived of something real. In other words, it still assumes that this lack can be made up for by a real object (the phallus, understood as an object that I can recover). The imaginary phallus is thus expected to have a referent in reality, and the infant believes that it can in reality recover it or lose it once again.

Through the intervention of the paternal metaphor, however, the little child abandons its belief in a possible fulfillment. This means that the phallus, for instance, can no longer refer to something I can give or receive in order to fulfill the lack of the Other. The phallus can thus no longer be under-

---

71. "The passage from the (-φ) (small phi) of the phallic image from one side to the other of the equation, from the imaginary to the symbolic, renders it positive in any case, even if it fulfils a lack. Although a support of the (-I), it becomes Φ (capital phi), the symbolic phallus that cannot be negated, the signifier of *jouissance*" (E 320/25–29, EF 823). Lacan here talks about a "passage" precisely in order to suggest a transformation of the imaginary phallus into the signifier of lack.

stood as simply a presentation *of* something; it is rather the presentation of "some-thing" which the little child "knows" or accepts does not, in principle, correspond to anything. The phallus is in this sense a presentation unlike any other; it is a representation whose representational character is annulled, as it were, and thanks to this, the phallus can become the signifier of an impossibility. It becomes the signifier of the impossible fulfillment of desire.[72]

We can now also understand why Lacan writes that the phallus is "positivized" in and through the metaphor of the Name-of-the-Father—or (what amounts to the same thing), the phallus can no longer be "negativized." For the phallus no longer functions as the representation of something that can be lacking or something the possession of which is never really assured.[73] It has rather become the signifier of *jouissance* (the fulfillment of desire) as *impossible*. Lacan designates this symbolic phallus with the symbol Φ.

Lacan calls the process in which the phallus is transformed into the signifier of lack "symbolic castration." In contradistinc-

---

72. We can also express this idea as follows: the (signified) phallus is the unrepresentable final term of desire. The signifier "phallus," then, refers to that phallus (which might be capable of bringing the movement of desire to an end) as impossible.

73. In our opinion, this interpretation is justified if we read what Lacan says here about the phallus as signifier against the background of what he earlier wrote about the role of the phallus in the specular image: "[It] is negativity in its place in the specular image" (E 319/25, EF 822). The idea that the phallus is "negativized" in the specular image refers to the fact that the phallus can be lacking from it. In the context of the mirror-stage, the phallus thus appears as something that is either present or not. If the phallus as signifier can no longer be "negativized" ("cannot be negated"), and as a result is "positivized" ("positive in any case"), it means that the phallus no longer functions as the representation of something that can be lacking or recovered in reality.

tion to imaginary castration, in which the subject believes that it has been deprived of a real object because of an imaginary belief in possible fulfillment, symbolic castration involves the transformation of an imaginary object (the imaginary phallus) into a signifier. This transformation also means the acceptance of lack as the truth of desire. Castration is consequently no longer the rock upon which the analysis runs aground, as Freud still thought; instead, the distinction between imaginary and symbolic castration allows us to theorize the advance beyond imaginary castration, and the acceptance of symbolic castration, as the goal of the analysis. To express the same thing otherwise, the goal of analysis is not adaptation to social reality by means of an identification with the analyst, as the ego-psychologists believed, but the recognition of the Name-of-the-Father.

This last point, however, inevitably implies a sacrifice on the part of the subject,[74] for the subject must abandon the belief in an object that could satisfy desire. This sacrifice and the introduction of the phallus as the signifier of lack are two sides of the same coin.[75]

Note, however, that it is a matter here of a symbolic sacrifice, which has to be strictly distinguished from a real loss of

---

74. "It [the castration complex] is the only indication of that *jouissance* in its infinitude [translation modified: *dans son infinitude*] that brings with it the mark of its prohibition, and, in order to constitute that mark, involves a sacrifice: that which is made in one and the same act with the choice of its symbol, the phallus" (E 319/20–23, EF 822). Lacan here refers again to the problematic of the *jouissance*, which we will discuss later. There we will see that every *jouissance* is limited and finite. An unlimited *jouissance* ("that *jouissance* of its infinitude") is impossible. This impossibility is indicated ("the mark of its prohibition") by the phallus as signifier ("the choice of its symbol").

75. ". . . a sacrifice: that which is made in one and the same act with the choice of its symbol, the phallus" (E 319/22–23, EF 822).

a part of the body.[76] The clinical phenomena that are most commonly associated with the castration complex, and in which bodily integrity as such is threatened, have to do rather with imaginary castration,[77] which is precisely what has to be overcome. In a certain sense, these clinical phenomena actually *conceal* what is fundamentally at stake in castration, rather than typifying it. Symbolic castration, on the other hand, actually implies that I abandon every attempt to make up for the lack of the Other by means of a real object (and thus my own lack as well), and accepting it means the recognition that this lack constitutes the essence of our existence as speaking subjects.

In the course of this chapter it has grown increasingly clear that the metaphor of the Name-of-the-Father forms the keystone of Lacanian psychoanalysis. Earlier we showed that the Lacanian subversion of the subject gets its properly psychoanalytic content from the castration complex, which we said is the culmination of the subversion of the subject. We now know that this complex—and more concretely, the installation of the phallus as signifier of the lack—is itself grounded in the metaphor of

---

76. "We must distinguish, therefore, between the principle of sacrifice, which is symbolic, and the imaginary function that is devoted to that principle of sacrifice, but which, at the same time, masks the fact that it gives it its instrument" (E 319/27–30, EF 822).

77. Lacan refers to this when he writes of "the imaginary function that is devoted to that principle of sacrifice" (E 319/28–29, EF 822). In the imaginary, I devote myself to filling up the lack in the Other, or fear that the Other might demand of me a real sacrifice to make up for his lack. This problematic is overcome in the "paternal metaphor." Lacan immediately adds here that the imaginary function provides the principle of (symbolic) sacrifice with its "instrument" ("it [the imaginary function] gives it its instrument"). As we have shown, he means by this that the object of symbolic castration is the imaginary phallus.

the Name-of-the-Father. This metaphor is thus the ultimate foundation of Lacanian metapsychology.

What is at stake here is more than an abstract philosophical theory—the theory of the metaphor of the Name-of-the-father and the castration complex allows us to cast a strong light upon psychoanalytic psychopathology, and indeed, it is only in Lacan's treatment of psychopathology that we see the true psychoanalytic relevance of the metaphor of the Name-of-the-Father. Psychopathology forms the ultimate touchstone of Lacan's theory of desire.[78] We will deal with this problematic in a separate chapter; before we do so, however, we will investigate further the relation between the primacy of the phallus and the role of sexuality in "Subversion." We will first address the role of sexuality in the unconscious, and then the problem of sexuation and sexual difference.

THE PRIMACY OF THE PHALLUS, SEXUALITY, AND THE UNCONSCIOUS

Freud argues that infantile sexuality is primary in the unconscious; the repressed unconscious presentations always relate in principle to infantile sexuality. This primacy of infantile sexuality not only implies that sexual life originates in the earliest period of childhood; it also suggests that sexuality can no longer be identified solely with adult genital sexuality. According to Freud, adult genital sexuality is in fact the precarious outcome

---

78. To the extent that the castration complex and the Name-of-the-Father are also foundational for the structure of desire, it is little wonder that the problematics of a "subversion of the subject" and a "dialectic of desire" mesh. We will come back to this.

of a process of development that begins in the earliest phase of life, and in this regard, he distinguishes various "stages" that constitute the building blocks from which adult sexual life is formed: the oral, the anal, and the phallic.

It is especially important for our problematic that Freud describes the drives that are associated with these various stages as "partial," and that he emphasizes their intrinsic sexual character. These drives are not directed to the Other as a person; they are directed, rather, to part-objects: the breast, the feces, and so on. Yet according to Freud, these drives are sexual as such and of themselves—that is, apart from any reference to genitality. Thus he sees in thumb-sucking, for example, an act with intrinsically sexual meaning, and while the details of Freud's argument for this controversial thesis need not occupy us here, we should note that he is ultimately obliged to appeal to hypothetical biological data in order to substantiate his claim.

Lacan adopts the Freudian idea that the unconscious is articulated around part-objects; he does not, however, relate these objects to biological development, but rather to the primacy of the symbolic. For him, the various erogenous zones and their respective objects (the objects *a*) are all determined by the symbolic. The erogenous zones, he says, are cut out of the body in terms of the relation to the Other, which is primarily structured by the signifier. At the same time, certain objects receive a privileged meaning as (dis)incarnations of the lack, to which they give a concrete bodily meaning.[79] What does this mean for the sexual status of the unconscious? Can the various part-

---

79. See the section in Chapter 6, "The Phantasy, the Object *a*, and Subjectivity: The Essentially Bodily Significance of Lack" (pp. 158–162).

objects Lacan speaks of (the gaze, the voice, the breast, etc.) still be called sexual, and if so, how?

The various objects *a* give a concrete bodily determination to the lack of which they are (dis)incarnations, and they are therefore not signifiers. They represent the body insofar as it cannot be taken up in the symbolic order.[80] However, this does not mean that the determination of these objects can be thought apart from the relation to the Other, for according to Lacan, there is no meaning outside the symbolic. In relation to the object *a* this implies that it can only fulfill its role in reference to the signifier charged with indicating the impossibility of a total integration in the symbolic, and this signifier is the phallus. We can express the same thing in a different way by saying that the objects *a* give a concrete bodily content to the impossibility of which the phallus is the signifier,[81] which is also the reason Lacan describes the unconscious as essentially sexual: the unconscious

---

80. For this point, see the section in Chapter 6, "The Significance of the Object *a*" (pp. 140–152).

81. From this perspective the following passage becomes intelligible, at least in part: "In its structure as I have defined it, the phantasy contains the (-φ), the imaginary function of castration under a hidden form, reversible from one of its terms to the other" (E 322/23–25, EF 825). The object *a* only receives meaning from a constitutive reference to the phallus; it gives concrete bodily form to the lack of which the phallus is the signifier. The subject relates to this object in the phantasy, which "imagines" the lack in a concrete bodily manner. In the phantasy the sacrifice is thus truly represented in a bodily manner, and that is why Lacan writes that the phantasy constantly refers to the "imaginary function of castration." However, we ought not conclude that the phantasy simply belongs to the imaginary, for it concerns a scenario that is determined by the signifiers of the unconscious, and that is constructed around the object *a,* which as such belongs neither to the imaginary, nor to the symbolic.

is essentially sexual because and insofar as it is characterized by the primacy of the phallus.[82]

With Freud, then, Lacan contends that the unconscious is essentially sexual in nature. However, while Freud has a strong tendency to give a biological foundation to the sexual nature of the partial drives—they are sexual as it were "by nature," apart from any reference to the symbolic order—this is unacceptable for Lacan. The partiality of the drives cannot be understood apart from their fragmentation by the order of signifiers,[83] and the central role of the object *a* in the dynamic of desire and the phantasy can only be made intelligible in reference to this order. At the same time, the sexual and sexuated character of the body and the drives as such is made dependent upon a founding reference to the phallus, and to the metaphor of the Name-of-the-Father that determines the meaning and the function of the phallus. The body only fully acquires a psychic meaning as the source of sexual pleasure in relation to another subject, in terms

---

82. This also further clarifies the following passage that we cited earlier: "What we have here is the principle [namely the fact that the erogenous, unconscious body image is to be understood as a coat of arms] . . . of the paradoxical privilege possessed by the phallus in the dialectic of the unconscious, without the theory produced by the part-object being a sufficient explanation of it" (E 302/22–25, EF 804). The phallus is a part of the body with an emblematic significance; it is as it were "predestined" to function as the signifier of lack. Precisely for this reason, it cannot be reduced to a part-object. The part-objects, on the contrary, only receive their meaning on the basis of their reference to this founding signifier. Perhaps this passage is directed against Melanie Klein and the Kleinians, who consider the phallus to be a part-object just like the others.

83. For example, one might think here of what we said above concerning Pavlov's dogs and the drives (see Chapter 6, n. 24).

of the symbolic order, and therefore in terms of the paternal metaphor and the phallus.[84]

In Freud's psychogenetic perspective, by contrast, the reference to the phallus only comes about at the level of the "phallic stage." True, the previous stages (the oral and the anal) can be resignified retroactively from this phallic stage, but for Freud this does not detract from the fact that they must already of themselves be described as sexual. The phallus, according to Freud (1918), reorganizes in a retroactive (*nachträglich*) fashion the sexual significance of the drives, but is not determinative for their sexual character as it is in Lacan. Moreover, the "phallic phase" is for Freud not the simple summit of psychosexual development; it is a stage that must be overcome, at least in principle. Somewhat provocatively, we can perhaps better sum up this problematic as follows: Lacan replaces the Freudian primacy of sexuality with the primacy of the phallus as signifier.

THE PHALLUS, CASTRATION, AND
THE PROBLEM OF SEXUATION[85]

Of course, the Lacanian primacy of the phallus cannot be without consequences for the problematic of sexuation. The castration and Oedipus complexes are crucial structural moments in

---

84. We will return to this in more detail in our following section, "The Phallus, Castration, and the Problem of Sexuation."

85. For a totally different psychoanalytic approach to sexual difference, in which the primacy of the phallus is rejected, see Zilbach 1998. This text is accompanied by a Lacanian commentary by Hassoun (1998).

Freud, in light of which sexual difference can take on a psychic meaning. The precise significance of the castration complex in Freud remains somewhat unclear, however, and especially in the first period of his work, Freud thought that the infantile primacy of the phallus has to be overcome.

In Lacan, by contrast, this problematic makes up the core and truth of our existence as symbolic beings, and this directly implies that Lacan also tries to understand sexual difference simply in terms of the primacy of the phallus. The respective significations of "being male" and "being female" must therefore be understood in terms of a different relation to the symbolic phallus.[86] In "Subversion," however, Lacan devotes very little attention to this problematic, and it seems that like Freud, he chiefly addresses the castration complex from the standpoint of the little boy. This does not necessarily mean, however, that he does not always assume that the woman has another relationship to the phallus (and thus to the father and the symbolic) than the man. Like Freud, Lacan assumes that the oedipal problematic is negotiated and worked through by the two sexes in different ways, and this difference is connected precisely to the relationship to the phallus, exerting permanent effects on the psychology of both man and woman.[87]

---

86. This last point also suggests that for Lacan, sexual difference can only acquire meaning from the metaphor of the Name-of-the-Father. For the respective meanings of "being male" and "being female" can only be understood in terms of the relation to the phallus, which functions as a signifier on the basis of this metaphor.

87. This may be seen, for example, from the following passage: "And it is this character of the Φ that explains both the particularities of the woman's approach to sexuality, and that which makes the male sex the weak sex in the case of perversion" (E 320/29–31, EF 823). We will address this passage in more detail later.

Lacan's idea of the different meanings of the oedipal problematic for the girl and the boy can perhaps best be summed up[88] as follows: the girl "is, without having it" (*elle est, sans l'avoir*), while the boy "is not, without having it" (*il n'est pas sans l'avoir*; Lacan 1958–59 [Pontalis version], p. 334). It is immediately obvious that these statements only make sense on the assumption that the phallus—even if it is a signifier of an impossible signified—always refers obliquely to the real organ from which the imaginary problematic of castration gets its form.[89] Otherwise it would lose all sexual connotations. The phallus must remain attached to the anatomical reality of sexual difference to be able to play its role as signifier of this difference[90]—in other words, it can only be invoked as an explanatory principle for "the particularities of the woman's approach to sexuality" and as that "which makes the male sex the

---

88. In what follows we limit ourselves to what is strictly necessary for a good grasp of "Subversion."

89. The phallus is thus not a *pure* signifier; it is the signifier of an (impossible) object, and in this sense it does not have a representable presentational content. This does not mean, however, that it is characterized any the less by a minimal reference to the reality of sexual difference, from which it derives its determinacy. If this were not the case, we could not understand how the intervention of the phallus can be decisive for the *sexual* character of the unconscious. Perhaps this is what Lacan refers to when, in a passage we cited above, he talks about the "*paradoxical* privilege of the phallus in the dialectic of the unconscious" (E 302/22–23, EF 804; see n. 32, 82).

90. The idea that the absence of the penis makes the woman the phallus for the (heterosexual) man—that is to say, the object of desire—also presupposes that the signifier "phallus" remains attached to the reality of the sexual difference ("Such is the woman concealed behind her veil: it is the absence of the penis that turns her into the phallus, the object of desire"; E 322/36–37, EF 825). Lacan seems to be saying here that a woman can only appear for the man as that which can fulfill his desire because and insofar as something real is missing from her.

weak sex in the case of perversion"[91] because and insofar as it remains linked to the biological reality of the sexual difference. In this sense, for Lacan as for Freud, "Anatomy is destiny."

Thus Lacan (1957–58) claims, for example, that it is much easier for girls to overcome the rivalry of the imaginary father than it is for boys. Since the little girl knows that she "does not have it," it is for her easier to desist from the struggle. She subsequently receives the phallus symbolically as woman (in coitus) or as mother (in the form of a child). For the boy, by contrast, the reverse is the case. According to Lacan, since he "has it, without being it," it is much more difficult for him not to confuse the symbolic phallus with the imaginary phallus, with which he identifies. If we keep in mind here that the psychoanalytic tradition has always associated the various perversions with a refusal to accept castration,[92] then we also understand why in this regard Lacan calls men "the weaker sex."

This short sketch of a few crucial aspects of the Lacanian Oedipus complex inevitably raises an important problem, specifically, whether Lacan does not implicitly invoke biological reality as an explanatory principle (Borch-Jacobsen 1991, p. 222ff). The "facility" with which the girl accepts (or should accept) the law of the father is always linked with the characteristics of her body. Is not such an appeal to the body remarkable, to say the least,

---

91. "And it is this character of the Φ which explains both the particularities of the woman's approach to sexuality, and that which makes the male sex the weak sex in the case of perversion" (E 320/29–31, EF 823).

92. Thus, for example, Freud explains fetishism in terms of a refusal of the castration of the mother; the fetish then becomes a substitute for her missing phallus. The fetish is chosen according to the last thing the child sees before being confronted with the castration of the mother (hence shoes, furs, and so on). Some forms of homosexuality, according to Freud, can also be made intelligible along these lines. The child that identifies with the mother, as presumed bearer of the phallus, only chooses love objects like itself on this basis.

within a Lacanian perspective?[93] When Lacan himself must ultimately refer to the concrete body in order to explain the different
courses of the Oedipus complex in the boy and in the girl, where
does that leave the primacy of the symbolic?

This problematic should allow us to illuminate somewhat
further the relation between the symbolic and the real (in this case,
the biological body). We pointed out earlier that the phallus both
inscribes the lack in the psyche, and marks the essential relation
between the body (life) and language. Now, the phallus can only
fulfill this function if it continues to refer obliquely to the body,
and therefore the primacy of the symbolic cannot mean that "masculinity" and "femininity" can be thought completely independently of any reference to anatomical constitution.

What are we to make of this? Perhaps the following is the
beginning of an answer. Anatomical constitution as such cannot give us an answer to the question of what it means to be a
"man" or to be a "woman," and we cannot deduce from anatomical constitution itself which of its aspects will count as decisive
for sexual difference.[94] An answer to this question, by contrast,

---

93. Moreover, it is not at all clear why the girl should give in so much
more easily than the boy to this reality, which she should want precisely to
conceal by means of an identification with the imaginary phallus. Lacan's treatment of the female Oedipus complex here is undoubtedly too simplistic. Whatever the case may be, in later texts Lacan himself felt the need to further develop and specify the problematic of sexuation in general and of feminine
sexuality in particular. This problematic would lead us too far astray here.
We refer, therefore, to the literature: see especially Lacan 1972–73, pp. 39–
81 and *passim*; and Verhaeghe 1990.

94. Despite this, Lacan gives the constant impression that the way the
phallus appears in the specular image predestines it to function as the signifier of the lack. This means (or at least could mean) that for Lacan, the symbolic order connects with distinctions that are given in an already inchoate
manner at a pre-linguistic level.

necessarily implies the intervention of the symbolic system; for it is the symbolic system that establishes order by making distinctions, and only the symbolic can therefore make a given anatomical distinction—in this case, the presence or absence of the phallus—decisive in the determination and the psychic meaning of the sexual difference.

We ought not conclude, however, that this intervention of the signifier puts us in a position to answer adequately the question of just what makes us "man" or "woman." Even if masculinity and femininity must be thought in terms of different references to the phallus, these references do not teach us who or what we must be as men or women. Here, in the end, the symbolic system lets us down, for in the symbolic, the signifier that would allow me to determine my identity once and for all is missing. To the question what it is to be a "man" or a "woman," only provisional answers are possible, and the phallus is, according to Lacan, the signifier of this impossibility.[95]

---

95. Of course, we must also connect all of this with what we wrote earlier concerning the "impossibility of a sexual relationship" (so-called "genital love") and the fact that the part-objects are only "partial presentations of the function whereby they are produced." Now the phallus, as we know, is the signifier of the lack, and the unrepresentable final term of desire. In our current context, this means that the phallus is also the signifier of the impossibility of "genital love." On the one hand the various objects a gain their (sexual) meaning from their orientation to the phallus; on the other, the lack signified by the phallus in turn takes on concrete bodily form via the objects a. The objects a in this sense *substitute* for the object, the impossibility of which is articulated by the signifier "phallus"; but they do not remedy its absence. We can thus say that they are partial presentations of an object that *if it existed* would make possible "genital love" in the sense described above.

8

The Impossible *Jouissance*: Elements of a Structural Psychopathology

INTRODUCTION: THE *JOUISSANCE* OF THE OTHER AND PATHOLOGY

The signifier S(Ø) brought us to the heart of Lacanian psychoanalysis. Its characterization obliged us to connect the lack that is introduced by the symbolic with the phallus and the metaphor of the Name-of-the-Father. The discussion of the problematic of castration, which goes hand in hand with this, also made it necessary to further clarify the status of the object *a*, and thus it was possible to elucidate the place Lacan gives to sexuality with regard to the unconscious. Yet have we thereby said everything there is to say here?[1]

It is clear that the symbolic lack that characterizes the subject cannot be thought and understood apart from the body, and it thus became apparent from our exposition of the object *a*, the phantasy, and the phallus that the lack is specified in an essentially embodied way. It would therefore be evidence of an all too intellectualistic approach to determine lack exclusively as a lack

---

1. In this chapter, in accordance with our general point of departure, we address the general principles of structural psychopathology as Lacan develops them in "Subversion." "Subversion" remains rather general in relation to psychopathology, and is often quite allusive as regards the various particular syndromes. In a number of places we will thus be obliged to appeal to other texts from the same period as "Subversion," in order to comprehend the more allusive passages. We will limit ourselves to what is necessary for a good grasp of "Subversion" and the principles that govern Lacanian psychopathology.

of determinacy of the subject. When lack has to be thought essentially and structurally in terms of the body, then it can come as no surprise to find that Lacan further defines it as a lack of jouissance.[2]

The term jouissance has very different meanings in the work of Lacan (Evans 1998), and it would take us too long to address all of them here; but even if we confine ourselves to the manner in which Lacan uses this concept in "Subversion," we are not spared all problems. We find no proper definition of the term jouissance in this text. Our first task, then, is to try to pin it down on the basis of the way it functions in Lacan's argumentation in "Subversion." Given that these arguments run parallel with the construction of the graph of desire, we must also ask ourselves in what way the problematic of jouissance explicitly or implicitly plays a role in that construction. Even if Lacan only introduces the term at the end of his text, the problematic of jouissance is present from the beginning—in the development of the graph of desire.

It will help us track down the meaning of jouissance in "Subversion" to look at the way Lacan introduces the term. Not only does Lacan describe the various forms of pathology as so many defenses against "the jouissance of the Other"; he claims, in addition, that "jouissance is forbidden to him who speaks as

---

2. "But we must insist that jouissance is forbidden to him who speaks as such, although it can only be said between the lines for whoever is subject of the Law, since the Law is grounded in this very prohibition" (E 319/3–5, EF 821). For anyone subject to the law, jouissance cannot be the direct and unambiguous goal of desire. The reference to jouissance continues to be present, but is veiled in symptoms and so forth, and this is what Lacan means when he writes that jouissance can only be said "between the lines." The further discussion of pathology will make this clearer.

such. . . ."[3] From this we can conclude that in our present context, *jouissance* must first be understood as the *"jouissance* of the Other," and that this *jouissance* is forbidden (or made impossible) by the entry into the symbolic[4]—for "speaking" implies that we have entered into the symbolic. Thus the definition of the term *jouissance* almost automatically refers us back to the second version of the graph.

We recall from our examination of the second version of the graph that "the law arises from desire." Desire demands a law, because it would otherwise remain caught up in a complete dependence upon the Other, and in order to develop its own identity and desire, we learned, the child must therefore separate itself from the mother (as first Other). The constitution of subjectivity and of desire thus presupposes that limits are set in the relationship between the mother and the infant, for the infant would otherwise remain at the mercy of the mother, who would then appear as the representative of a unlimited, boundless *jouissance* that carried us beyond the symbolic.[5]

The first real Other of the demand manifests itself to the infant as a power not subject to any law, and this situation is further reinforced by the fact that this Other, as the first incarnation of the symbolic, is inevitably experienced as the origin of all sense and meaning. Thus, for example, it is possible for

---

3. In the next sections we will return to examine this thematic in more depth, and we will also give the necessary references to the text of "Subversion."

4. "But we must insist that *jouissance* is forbidden to him who speaks as such . . . since the Law is grounded in this very prohibition" (E 319/3–5, EF 821).

5. For this point and what follows, see the sections in Chapter 5, "Beyond Need and Demand: Desire" (pp. 104–112), and "Desire and the Law: The Dialectic of Desire" (pp. 112–119).

the infant to believe that the Other knows its thoughts and feelings, for those ideas and feelings cannot be understood independently of the Other's signifiers. Indeed, according to Lacan, the infant literally only learns to identify its feelings and thoughts on the basis of their being named by the Other.[6] The Other thus seems to have access to the sensations and affects that well up from deep within my body, and understands their meaning. The idea can thereby arise that the first Other not only controls what is outside me, but even has control over my body.[7]

The need for a law to separate the mother from the child flows from this; for the child must be able to acquire its own place distinct from the mother, and the claims of the mother upon her child must be tempered. It is imperative that the child learn that the power of the mother is subject to a law, and that she, too, is essentially marked by a lack. All attempts of the little child to set itself up as an object that can fulfill the mother's desire—and so participate in a *jouissance* without limits, a sort of fusional unity—are consequently doomed to fail. They would immediately lead to a destruction of the subject. However, the infant can only give meaning to this impossibility if the mother herself can give a place to the law in her discourse, and in her interaction with the little child.

Thus we saw that the law must both protect us against the threat of an overintrusive Other, and restrain us from striving after a fusional unity with it—a unity in which every distinc-

---

6. For this problematic, see Florence 1997. Florence also gives further references to the psychoanalytic literature.

7. Hence also the importance of the "first lie"; it is precisely the capacity to lie that proves the child has realized that the Other does not know its thoughts, and that it has its own existence, to which the Other does not have immediate access.

tion would be lost and the symbolic system would collapse. The law that does so is the law of the signifier, and it is introduced by the metaphor of the Name-of-the-Father.

Now the entry into the order of signifiers also gives a certain determination and limitation to *jouissance*—for *jouissance* is thereby placed under the mastery of the phallus. This means that on the one hand, *jouissance* is coupled with (the presentation of) specific parts of the body (the erogenous zones), which then function as privileged sites for the experience of pleasure;[8] on the other hand, the presentations and phantasies in which *jouissance* is staged are always explicitly or implicitly attached to sexual difference, and the problematic of sexuation.[9]

The condition of unlimited and boundless *jouissance,* therefore, is that the Name-of-the-Father be absent, and this implies that *jouissance* is not mediated in a stable manner by the signifiers and (phantasmatic) presentations that can protect the subject and give it something to hold onto. If *jouissance* is not so bound, however, the subject will be swamped by it, and unable to keep it at a distance. Lacan suggests further that since the coupling of *jouissance* to presentations and signifiers is also an anchoring of it in privileged bodily zones, the collapse of this order would be experienced as a threat to one's own bodily integrity.[10]

The dream of a total and unlimited *jouissance*, in which the body would be taken up as an undifferentiated entity (i.e., one not symbolically mediated), thus implies the destruction of the

---

8. See the section in Chapter 6, "The Significance of the Object *a*" (pp. 140–152).

9. See the section in Chapter 7, "The Primacy of the Phallus, Sexuality, and the Unconscious" (pp. 207–211).

10. We will examine this problem at greater length in relation to psychosis.

incarnated subject, which exists only by grace of the signifier and the law.[11] For example, we find traces of just such an unmediated *jouissance* in certain forms of automutilation (Verhaeghe 1999). Patients suffering from traumatic automutilation describe a state of increasing tension, which draws them into a maelstrom. The ego disappears into this maelstrom and the body threatens to burst at its seams, and only when the patients mutilate themselves does the tension ebb away. The result is a feeling of great relief: "I am back again." This experience can be described as an undifferentiated bodily *jouissance*; the subject is delivered over to this *jouissance* and threatens to founder in it. In this situation, the cutting seems to act as the equivalent of inscription in the order of signifiers—it is an extreme attempt to introduce into the body a minimal ordering and differentiation, which would allow the *jouissance* to be once more bound to specific presentations. Only thus can a halt be called to the destructive movement of *jouissance*.

It is clear that the term *jouissance*, as we have introduced it here, cannot be understood without the suffix "of the Other," for it refers to a dynamic in which any distinction between the subject and the Other threatens to slip away. The *jouissance* concerned here cannot be "of the subject," then, for in fact, the subject itself disappears into it, to become a mere plaything of the Other—and of course, the subject thus swamped by *jouissance* feels little "pleasure," for it lives in constant dread of fading out of existence completely.[12] Furthermore, in current use the term "pleasure" (*plaisir*) refers to what we spontaneously experience as "pleasurable" or

---

11. If *jouissance* refers beyond the order of the signifier, then in light of what we set out in Chapter 7, we have to add that it also carries us beyond sexuality. We will further specify this problematic in the course of this chapter, primarily in relation to psychosis.

12. "*Jouissance* of the Other" is thus to be distinguished from phallic *jouissance,* in which the subject *can* enjoy without disappearing.

"pleasant," and in this sense too it is clear that Lacanian *jouissance* is of a different order to pleasure, and answers to a different logic— a "logic" that takes precisely no account of what the subject can experience as "pleasant" or "pleasurable."[13]

In the course of our exposition we showed that $S(\emptyset)$ is the signifier around which the graph of desire is constructed, because this signifier refers to something that is originally excluded so that the subject of desire can come into being. We now know that what is excluded is *jouissance*, and that this exclusion further takes on concrete form in the castration complex. This is the reason Lacan locates *jouissance* and castration on the uppermost level of the graph—where the whole dynamic of that founding exclusion and its consequences are mapped out.

Note, however, that just because *jouissance* is "forbidden for him who speaks as such" does not mean it plays no role in the psychic economy. Quite to the contrary, we recall here what we said about the "(first) representative of representation," which continues to function in the unconscious as the ultimate mainspring of desire:[14] for all that the child must separate itself from the mother ("the first representative of representation") to fully exist as a subject, it can also remain under the spell of this first Other in a whole variety of ways. In this regard, we spoke of the "memory" of this first Other who escapes the order of the law as the "center of gravity" of an interminable movement of substitution that brings desire to life;[15] and we can now describe

---

13. We will examine this problematic in more detail later.

14. See the sections in Chapter 5, "Further Characterization of Desire: The Transitional Object" (pp. 119–123) and "The Unconscious Is the Discourse of the Other" (pp. 123–125).

15. This "dream" of an unlimited *jouissance,* as something of which the Other is capable, remains operative in the unconscious. For example, we find traces of it in the belief of some neurotic patients that other people have ac-

this "memory" in terms of an ultimate fusional (but therefore also destructive) possibility. This perspective casts further light on the connection between the problematic of *jouissance* and psychopathology.

On the graph of desire, the letter O represents the place of the first Other of the demand. Accordingly, an arrow representing the movement of desire goes out from O: *Che vuoi?* What do you want (of me)? In our present context, Lacan makes this question more concrete as follows: What am I (in relation to the *jouissance* of the Other)? We can now formulate this question in still other terms: What position can or must I assume in relation to the *jouissance* of the Other? According to Lacan, the various answers the subject can give to this question define respectively the various forms of psychopathology—psychosis, the several forms of neurosis, and the perversions—and these "answers" refer to the various positions that the subject (of the unconscious) can adopt towards the (*jouissance* of) the Other.[16] This implies that the question of (the meaning of) existence must be understood as a question of our relation to *jouissance*; that

---

cess to forms of happiness and *jouissance* that will always remain closed to them: they ascribe to the Other possibilities of *jouissance* and happiness they themselves are essentially deprived of. This is also the reason Lacan describes *jouissance* as forbidden. Now, it is true that the *jouissance* we ascribe to the Other looks like a good to be striven for. This is an illusion, however, for the realization of *jouissance* is internally contradictory with our condition as symbolic beings; achieving it would imply our destruction as subjects of the signifier. However attractive the phantasy of an unlimited *jouissance* might be, the closer we come to this *jouissance*, the more it takes on the form of a nightmare.

16. Since, as we know, the law of the father essentially forbids *jouissance*, the various forms of pathology must also be understood as various ways of relating oneself to this law.

relation determines the answer to the question of who or what we are.[17]

Thus it is also clear why Lacan is not very favorably disposed towards a psychogenetic approach to pathology. In the first place, Lacan is not trying to explain how one *becomes* neurotic or psychotic; instead, he wants to define the positions in relation to *jouissance* that characterize the various forms of pathology. The question of concrete psychogenetic etiology is

---

17. "Indeed, it is too precarious a solution for me even to think of using it as a means of circumventing our problem, namely: 'What am "I"?'" (E 317/17–19, EF 819). We propose that this passage is to be read as we do ("What I am in relation to the *jouissance* of the Other?") because Lacan immediately formulates the following answer to this question ("What am I?"): "'I' am in the place from which a voice is heard clamouring 'the universe is a defect in the purity of Non-Being'. . . . This place is called *jouissance* . . ." (E 317/20–23, EF 819). From the standpoint of *jouissance*, the universe is a "lack or deficiency in the purity of Non-Being"; for the universe is the world in which we carry on our everyday existence, and this world has to pay tribute to the order of the signifier, by which it comes to being. In this sense, there is no "being" (no reality appears) outside of the signifier; what lies beyond the chain of signifiers also lies outside of being. *Jouissance* thus situates itself beyond being (and the signifier), and the "realization" of this *jouissance* is equiprimordial with the disappearance of the subject. *Jouissance* refers, in this perspective, to the purity of "non-being." When I enjoy, the world disappears.

While this *jouissance* is indeed impossible and destructive, however, it nonetheless continues to fascinate me in all manner of ways. When Lacan thus writes that I am at a place called *jouissance*, then he seems to mean that my existence is determined in relation to the (im)possibility of *jouissance*—who or what I become depends on that relation. More concretely, this problematic must be understood in the light of what we said above concerning the "representative of representation," which continues to function in the unconscious as the ultimate mainspring of desire. For all that the child must free itself from the mother in order to exist fully as a subject, it continues to dream of a "happy and successful" relation with her. An unmediated relation with the mother, however, would inevitably entail its destruction as a subject.

thus relegated to a secondary position, subordinate to the question of the *structural* differences between the various syndromes. In what do those structural differences consist, then, according to Lacan? We are now sufficiently armed to specify the problematic of the "*jouissance* of the Other" in its relation to pathology.

THE *JOUISSANCE* OF THE OTHER, THE METAPHOR OF THE NAME-OF-THE-FATHER, AND PSYCHOSIS[18]

As we have seen, the infant must be able to take its distance from the first Other of the demand in order to develop its own desire, and this is accomplished by means of the metaphor of the Name-of-the-Father, which withdraws us from the omnipotence of this first Other. Now where this metaphor cannot be brought into being, the subject will remain defenselessly delivered over to this Other/the mother, and according to Lacan, that is what happens in psychosis; psychosis, as Lacan writes elsewhere, is characterized by a "foreclosure of the Name-of-the-Father" (*forclusion du Nom-du-Père*: Fink 1997, pp. 79–112, Lacan 1955–56, 1957b, Moyaert 1988, Verhaeghe 1994).[19]

But what then is "psychosis"? One often proceeds on the assumption that the term "psychosis" covers a multiplicity of syndromes, which express themselves in very different ways. Against this approach, Lacan's theory of the foreclosure of the

---

18. For reasons set out at the beginning of this chapter, we confine ourselves here to a very general characterization of psychosis in its relation to neurosis. In fact, Lacan does not deal directly with psychosis in "Subversion." For more in-depth treatment of the Lacanian theory of psychosis, we refer the reader to the secondary literature.

19. See especially Lacan 1957b.

Name-of-the-Father tries to offer a general key to the understanding of psychosis, and it is undoubtedly in this that its power and its attractiveness lie. Nevertheless, this strength is perhaps also its weakness, for if we allow that there are diverse psychotic syndromes that cannot simply be reduced to one another, then we might also expect that a theory of psychosis will be able to make sense of these differences in pathology.[20] Lacan's theory of the foreclosure of the Name-of-the-Father, however, does not really allow for this,[21] for it wants to teach us something about psychosis *per se*, and does not seem to concern itself systematically with the possible relevant differentiations *within* the domain of psychosis.[22] Among other things, this is apparent from the way various clinical manifestations that can be understood in terms of the foreclosure of the Name-of-the-Father do not seem equally characteristic of the different psychotic syndromes. Let us give a few illustrations.

---

20. One should keep in mind here that Lacan introduces the "metaphor of the Name-of-the-Father" in a text to which he gave the title "On a Question *Preliminary* to Any Possible Treatment of Psychosis" (my emphasis). It was thus probably not his intention to develop an exhaustive theory of psychosis.

21. This probably also accounts for the continuing attraction of phenomenological psychiatry, which actually does seem to succeed in comprehending the classic psychotic syndromes *in their difference*. In this regard, see *inter alia* the work of the inestimable A. Tatossian (1997).

22. Naturally, this does not mean we should not attempt to further develop Lacan's theoretical insights on this point, particularly with regard to the distinction between paranoia and schizophrenia. Take, for example, De Waelhens's (1978) work on psychosis. Yet it is striking that recent authors such as Fink and Verhaeghe, in their treatment of psychosis, defend the "*forclusion* of the Name-of-the-Father" as the exclusive mechanism for understanding psychosis on the one hand, while on the other they make no further distinction between the various psychotic syndromes. The basic reason for this can most likely be found in the very general character of Lacan's theory. Or must we, as in the Kleinian tradition, think of paranoia and schizophrenia as continuous with each other? In any case, much research remains to be done here.

First, the absence of the metaphor of the Name-of-the-Father can help cast light on the bodily experience of the schizophrenic patient. The schizophrenic patient does not really inhabit her own body. She does, it is true, have a body, but in a certain sense, this body is not her own. The sensations that appear in the body, and the ideas that arise there, do not belong to the subject—they are the thoughts of an anonymous Other that has taken possession of the body. Here the body has lost its significance as a safe refuge in which I can feel at home, and instead it lies open and exposed; objects penetrate it or excise pieces from it. The body of the schizophrenic is in this sense at the mercy of the anonymous *jouissance* of the Other.

Similarly, words graft themselves onto the body of the schizophrenic patient. Thus Freud (1915) tells the story of a schizophrenic woman who declared after an argument with her lover, "My eyes aren't right, they have been turned" (pp. 197–198).[23] Now, the German word *Augenverdreher* (literally "eye-turner") means "deceiver," and the woman's lover is someone who cannot be trusted. Here, however, the expression "eye-turner" has lost its metaphorical dimension; it is reduced to a bodily inscription. We thus see how in schizophrenia, language is powerless to create a distance from reality. The break between language and the object, which characterizes the signifier and on the basis of which reality is taken up in a continuous process of creation of meaning, has not occurred. Language is therefore not detached from the object to which it refers, such that the latter can set itself up as the representative of the entire content of meaning—and the metaphor "eye-turner" thus means that the eye has literally been "turned."

---

23. For more examples and illustrations we refer to the previously cited works.

This problematic of schizophrenic bodily experience is closely bound up with the remarkable relation of the psychotic subject to the difference between the sexes. We know that the body only gets its full meaning (as a source of desire for another subject) from the symbolic order and thus from the paternal metaphor. According to Lacan, the foreclosure of the Name-of-the-Father therefore means that the schizophrenic subject never really chooses a position in relation to the problematic of sexual difference.[24] A clinical example can somewhat clarify what Lacan might mean by this. A patient was under the delusion that she was the emperor of Rome, and when I asked how it was possible that, as a woman, she was the emper*or* (and not the empr*ess*), she simply pulled up her dress. As she did so, she said, "Just look." It is difficult to argue here that she was thereby trying to convince me that I was incorrect. She knew very well that she was a woman. Her action cannot, therefore, be understood as an argument in a discussion (emperor or empress?). From the Lacanian perspective, we could perhaps say rather that her answer expressed a sort of indifference with regard to the problem that I posed; the difference between the sexes (possessing or not possessing the phallus) simply was not a psychically relevant consideration for her—not a problem on which she felt she had to adopt a position.[25]

Thus we see that the psychotic subject cannot get any distance from the first Other, because the metaphor of the Name-

---

24. "[H]e [the schizophrenic] fails to locate himself in relation to the difference between the sexes . . ." (De Waelhens 1978, p. 142).

25. It remains a question whether the meaninglessness of sexual difference, especially when regarded as a general characteristic of psychosis as such, is as generally present as might be expected on the basis of the theory, and as Lacan and his students assume. A thorough treatment of this problematic, however, would lead us too far astray.

of-the-Father has not come into being, and there is thus no gap between the sign and the object by which reality would lose its apparent transparency and self-evident character.[26] We can express the same thing by saying that the psychotic does not recognize the lack in the Other, and thus has no grasp of the constant sliding of meaning under or along the chain of signifiers. The psychotic lives, on the contrary, in a world of fixed and clear meanings, which he encounters, or which even impose themselves upon him, both in words and in reality. Code and message, as we said earlier, mesh perfectly, so that speech loses any opacity for itself, and this underpins the massive certainty that often characterizes the discourse of the psychotic. According to Lacan, the psychotic patient—and more particularly the paranoiac—"knows"; he is located in the place of the witness to which every act of speaking unavoidably refers. We now understand why and how this psychotic position is linked to the fact that the Name-of-the-Father has not acquired its pivotal role in the psyche.[27]

---

26. See the section in Chapter 3, "The Other as 'Witness'" (pp. 75–78).

27. This last point is a striking illustration of the problem we signaled above, that Lacan's theory of psychosis is extremely general in character. The "foreclosure" of the "Name-of-the-Father" explains, for example, both the various characteristics of schizophrenic bodily experience and the certainty of the paranoiac. We could perhaps say that the schizophrenic delusion is also "certain" for the subject, but then the question remains of whether this certainty is characteristic for both in the same manner and to the same degree. Linking the paranoiac's certainty with a fixation at the mirror-stage, as De Waelhens proposes, does not solve all the problems here, for we know that the identification with the mirror-stage presupposes an intervention of the symbolic, and this implies a minimal acceptance of the "Name-of-the-Father"—precisely what has not occurred in psychosis. The strict structural distinction between neurosis and psychosis (foreclosure versus acceptance of the "Name-of-the-Father") thus begins to loosen up, and further refinement (and research) seems necessary.

This last point perhaps also allows us to give an intelligible content to the idea that the psychotic does not really speak (Lacan 1955–56). Speaking implies that we allow ourselves to be towed along by an intention that arises in speech itself, without knowing beforehand where this intention will lead us. In personal speech, every certainty is thus constantly put at risk, and in this sense, to speak is always to seek. Every act of speaking is performed in an irresolvable tension between language, which punches a hole in the real, and the production of meaning, in which we try to bridge the gap with the real.[28]

This tension often seems to be missing in psychosis. Lacan writes in this regard that speech, in the fundamental sense of the word, presupposes the acceptance of the law. In other words: *Jouissance* is forbidden for "anyone who speaks as such."

THE THREE MOMENTS OF THE OEDIPUS COMPLEX

The foreclosure of the Name-of-the-Father gives us a structural criterion for defining the psychotic position. What then of neurosis and perversion? In contrast to psychosis, in which the law is never really inscribed, in neurosis and perversion lack has actually taken on a meaning for the subject. It has acquired meaning, that is to say—but it has not yet been (fully) accepted. We already pointed out that neurosis and perversion must be

---

28. See the section in Chapter 3, "The Other in the Second Version of the Graph of Desire" (pp. 62–69), and more particularly our commentary there on the following passage from "Subversion": "Both participate in this offering to the signifier that is constituted by the hole in the real, the one as a hollow for concealment, the other as a boring-hole to escape from" (E 304/20–22, EF 806).

understood as structurally different positions that the subject (of the unconscious) can adopt towards (the impossible *jouissance* of) the Other. This implies that the acceptance of the law of the father can take various forms, and therefore cannot be understood as an "all or nothing" scenario. Otherwise we could never see, for example, how lack is psychically inscribed in both forms of neurosis and in perversion, while at the same time they are three structurally distinct positions. In other words, we will have to distinguish various "moments" in the institution of the Name-of-the-Father, each of which corresponds to a definite type of pathology.[29] Lacan meets this theoretical requirement in the theory he calls the "three moments of the Oedipus complex."[30]

In the *first moment,* the infant simply identifies itself with the object of the desire of the mother. Lacan calls this the "primitive phallic phase." Here the metaphor of the Name-of-the-Father is in fact active, but only implicitly, as it were;[31] while it is true that the lack in the Other has already gained some psychic effectiveness, it is still not explicitly experienced in relation to a third party. The mother, we could also say, fulfills her role as the first incarnation of the symbolic and of the lack by which it

---

29. In accordance with Lacan's general point of departure, these three "moments" (*trois temps*) must be understood as "logical (and not chronological) moments." They express a structure that can order psychogenesis, but that can in no case be reduced to it.

30. Lacan does not touch directly on this problematic in "Subversion." Nevertheless, it seems that a good grasp of the way Lacan discusses psychopathology in "Subversion" is not possible without dealing with the "three moments of the Oedipus complex." See Lacan 1957–58, pp. 179–212 (*Les trois temps de l'œdipe*).

31. *C'est l'étape phallique primitive, celle où la métaphore paternelle agit en soi . . .* ["It is the primitive phallic stage, in which the paternal metaphor acts in itself . . ."] (Lacan 1957–58, p. 192).

is marked, just as in the more fully fledged scenario; but this lack is still not brought explicitly into relation with the paternal function. The infant, in other words, remains locked in a dual relationship with the mother, and it can continue to placidly identify itself with the object that would make possible the Other's *jouissance*. When we turn to the context of pathology, we see that this level is where the problematic of perversion is played out (Lacan 1957–58, p. 192).[32] The perverse subject recognizes lack, but this recognition is linked with the law of the father either not at all, or only insufficiently.

Only in the *second moment* of the complex is the father explicitly present as the one who has the key to the desire of the mother. In the eyes of the child, the mother is no longer exclusively dependent on the object of desire, but rather on an object that is in the possession of the Other, and this Other now appears as the origin of the law to which mother and child are submitted. The Other, in other words, still takes the form of an "ideal father" who is "all-powerful" and lays down the law in his own name. On this level, then, the father is still not seen entirely as a symbolic instance. We might also express this idea as follows: in the second moment of the Oedipus complex, the infant still believes in the existence of the Other—in the existence of a third without a lack. In terms of his pathology, Lacan couples this second moment of the Oedipus complex with the problematic of neurosis.

According to Lacan, the law only gets its true symbolic content in the *third moment* of the Oedipus complex, and only

---

32. "Only my formulation of the phantasy enables us to reveal that the subject here makes himself the instrument of the Other's *jouissance*" (E 320/ 37–39, EF 823). We will return to examine this passage in more detail later.

then can the imaginary dependence on the Other be overcome. This "third moment" is identical to the creation of the ego-ideal that we discussed earlier, for the identification with the "specific trait" of the ego-ideal makes possible an attachment to the Other that does not misrecognize its essential alterity, and so frees the subject from its mortal rivalry with the father. The latter can thus come to appear as the representative of a law that he has not himself created, and to which he too submits.

We ought not think of these three "moments" of the Oedipus complex as chronologically sequential stages; instead, we must understand them in light of Lacan's structural model of subjectivity and psychopathology. Probably we would do better, therefore, to understand these moments as three "tendencies," each of which is always and inevitably present in the oedipal problematic, so that the core of that problematic consists in the conflictual interplay between them. If this were not the case, then we would have to say, for example, that the neurotic has no ego-ideal (since he did not overcome his imaginary dependence on the Other). The difference between the various forms of pathology, also, must therefore be understood in terms of the varying *weight* of these "moments" of the Oedipus complex, rather than in terms of the simple absence of one or more of them.[33]

Both the neurotic and the perverse subject have been able to free themselves to some extent from the grip of an omnipotent Other; at the same time, however, they both continue to interpret lack in terms of the imaginary, for both—each in its own way—have not given up belief in the existence of the Other. For this reason, Lacan says, the *jouissance* of the Other that swamps the psychotic can remain the threatening horizon within

---

33. It follows from this that the different syndromes we will distinguish in this chapter have to be understood as "ideal-types."

which the pervert and the neurotic carry out their existence. Thus both perversion and the various neuroses have to be understood as at least in part complex defense strategies against the *jouissance* of the Other, which continues to cast its shadow over the existence of the neurotic and the perverse subject. In what follows we will attempt to define briefly these various strategies.

Before taking up this thematic, however, we must first introduce an important refinement of our position. We have already pointed out repeatedly that the entry into the order of the symbolic implies a "sexuation" of *jouissance*; for here the body is brought under the primacy of the phallus and of sexual difference. This entry consequently brings about an essential change in the problematic of *jouissance,* which is subsequently experienced primarily on the level of sexuality.[34] If, therefore, we claim that the various neuroses and perversions are to be understood as defense strategies against *jouissance,* then we must immediately add that in them the problematic of *jouissance* is primarily experienced within the order of sexuality. "Something" in sexuality continues to "remind" the neurotic and the pervert of the limitless *jouissance* in which the subject is destroyed and ruined.

That the threat of a limitless *jouissance* arises precisely in sexuality ought not surprise us; even the simplest phenomenology of sexuality[35] teaches us that it cannot be thought without a dimension of self-loss that strains all imaginary identifications. Our everyday relations are based on the exchange and comparison of recognizable characteristics, but sexuality tends to carry

---

34. As we already explained above, this is not the case in psychosis; in psychosis, the acceptance of the Name-of-the-Father presupposed by the express sexuation of *jouissance* has not yet come about.

35. For a more developed phenomenology of the erotic and of sexuality, see Thoné 1999.

us beyond these characteristics—at a certain point, it no longer matters with whom we are having sex. The personal characteristics of the other are driven into the background and lose their importance, and indeed, one forgets one's "own" person as well. We lose our concern about how we come across or look, and another force takes over from us, as it were, and carries us to a limit where subject and object flow into each other once more, even if only for a moment. In this perspective, it is not surprising that insofar as the problematic of *jouissance* plays a central role in neurosis and perversion, it finds privileged expression in sexuality.

PERVERSION

Lacan's ideas on the perversions (fetishism, sadism, masochism, etc.) build on Freud's later writings dealing with the same subject (esp. Freud 1927, 1940), and at the same time form a significant correction of them. A detailed discussion of the Freudian theory of the perversions would carry us too far astray here, but the main point is that Freud connects them with a refusal of castration. Thus he understands the fetish, for example, as a substitute for the missing phallus of the mother. The little child must sooner or later accept that not all human beings possess a phallus; the fetishist, however, cannot accept this, and creates an "*Ersatz*-phallus" that takes over the role of the maternal phallus (Freud 1927, p. 152). The fetishist thus disavows (*Verleugnung*) a perception that was traumatic for him (the absence of the phallus, p. 153), and therefore, according to Freud, fetishism must be understood in terms of a fundamental conflict between the claims of the drive and those of reality.

In "The Splitting of the Ego in the Process of Defence," Freud (1940) relates the case of a little boy who, between the ages of three and four, was confronted with the female genitals in the course of attempts by an older girl to seduce him (p. 275ff). Freud describes how the boy formed the habit of masturbating in order to discharge the sexual tension that thereby arose. A nursemaid caught him in the act, and threatened to tell his father about it, giving her threats extra force by adding that if she did tell the father, he would take away the boy's male organ. In this regard, Freud claims that the mere perception of the female genitals does not in itself evoke anxiety because the little child does not immediately believe in the castration with which it is thus confronted. The narcissistically motivated unease that can accompany this perception is instead subdued by the belief that "what is missing can still grow." In the case of Freud's patient, then, it is the threat of castration that reawakens the original perception, and the perception confirms the threat. The little boy believes he now knows why the phallus was missing in the little girl, and he can no longer doubt that a similar fate can also befall him. The reality of the threat of castration is from then on beyond any doubt.

Freud writes further that the usual response to the situation just described is to give up the masturbatory satisfaction of the drive—after a more or less long and difficult inner struggle—and accept castration. However, this is not how Freud's patient reacted. Instead of accepting castration, Freud writes, he chose a fetish as a substitute for the missing phallus—because as long as he does not have to admit that women do not have a penis, the threat of castration loses all credibility. He need not be anxious about the possible loss of his own penis, and can continue with his masturbatory activities undisturbed.

What is striking in Freud's observations is that originally, the threatening reference to the father has no effect. The reference to the father does not strike home, it does not "work." In more Lacanian terminology, we might say that Freud's patient refuses to give up his (masturbatory) *jouissance* and submit to the law of the father. According to Lacan, the disavowal that is the core problem of perversion in a Freudian perspective has to do not so much with (a part of) perceived reality, as with the Name-of-the-Father.

Nonetheless, the pervert is not psychotic—the patient from Freud's example does not hallucinate a penis where there is none, as a psychotic might do. Moreover, Freud's fetishistic patient develops a symptom, which shows that he really does take account of the threat of castration. According to Freud, the anxiety about being punished by the father expresses itself in this patient as an anxiety about being eaten up by him. Both opposed reactions to the original conflict—disavowal of sexual difference, and the acceptance of the threat of castration—continue to exist side by side, as the core of a splitting of the ego.[36] In other words, according to Freud (1927), fetishism implies a double and conflictual relation to castration; in it, castration is both disavowed and affirmed at the same time (p. 390ff).

Thus, the disavowal of the Name-of-the-Father that Lacan maintains typifies perversion cannot be equated with the psychotic foreclosure of it. Lacan instead understands perversion as a *remedy* for the inadequate manner in which the law of the father is introduced. On the one hand, the perverse subject disavows the Name-of-the-Father and refuses to give up its *jouissance* in relation to the mother, so that we might say that its *jouissance*

---

36. By "splitting of the ego," Freud understands a psychic process that is characteristic of perversion (and of psychosis), in which two conflicting attitudes to reality exist alongside each other in the heart of the ego. In the one tendency, reality is recognized; in the other, it is rejected and replaced by the creation of desire (as in the fetish). Yet even though both tendencies exist side by side, they exert no influence on each another. See Laplanche and Pontalis 1988, pp. 428–429.

remains "caught" in the "primitive phallic phase." On the other hand, it tries courageously to set limits to this *jouissance,* in order to eventually break free from the first Other. What are we to make of this dual function?

Freud's patient refuses to give up his belief in the maternal phallus and the masturbatory *jouissance* that is bound up with it, and Freud connects this with the traumatic character that the absence of the maternal phallus must have had for him as a child. Lacan, by contrast, connects perversion with the incapacity of the subject to give up his position *as* the phallus of the mother, and this is linked to the fact that the reference to the father is not yet established in an explicit and sufficiently articulated fashion. The perverse subject continues to believe in a *jouissance* without limits. It not only continues to believe in the possibility of the *jouissance* of the Other, but also casts itself as the instrument by which this *jouissance* is possible.[37]

---

37. "Only my formulation of phantasy enables us to reveal that the subject here makes himself the instrument of the Other's *jouissance*" (E 320/ 37–39, EF 823). At the beginning of the paragraph from which this passage comes, Lacan recalls the thesis that the subject relates to the inconsistency of the Other (∅), or what comes down to the same thing, to (the impossibility of) *jouissance,* by means of the object *a.* To the extent that the perverse subject also recognizes the Name-of-the-Father, the object *a* can also fulfill this role in perversion. Perversion teaches us nothing new in this regard about desire ("I will not deal with the question of perversion here, in as much as it accentuates to some extent the function of desire in the man, in so far as he sets up dominance in the privileged place of *jouissance,* the object *a* of the phantasy (*objet petit a*), which he substitutes for the ∅;" E 320/32–35, EF 823).

Lacan further writes that the perverse phantasy is characterized by a "reabsorption of the φ" (*une récupération du* φ; E 320/36, EF 823; typography corrected). This is because the pervert refuses to accept castration, and tries to neutralize the effectiveness of the phallus as signifier of the lack. In this connection we might recall what we said above about the significance of the fetish, which replaces the missing phallus of the mother. Such a recuperation

In a certain sense, this is intuitively clear in the masochistic phantasy, in which the subject unreservedly proffers itself as an instrument for the *jouissance* of the Other.[38] In a somewhat more complicated fashion, however, the same holds for the sadistic phantasy, where the subject equates itself with an Other that does not know any lack and for whom limitless *jouissance* lies within reach.[39] Thus the various characters in Sade's phantasies, for example, are capable of debaucheries the ordinary mortal can only dream of; their stamina, and the sexual possibilities open to them, are quasi-unlimited, and they are permitted to make unlimited use of their victims.[40] Here *jouissance* seems to exceed all bounds.

---

or neutralization of φ, of itself, can scarcely be called original—for in his own way, the neurotic does not want to know anything about castration either. The originality of the perverse position thus lies not in the fact that he misrecognizes castration, but in the fact that he equates himself with the object *a* over which the Other freely disposes in order to make its *jouissance* possible ("Perversion adds a reabsorption of the φ that would scarcely appear original if it did not interest the Other as such in a very particular way. Only my formulation of phantasy enables us to reveal that the subject here makes himself the instrument of the Other's *jouissance*"; E 320/35–39, EF 823).

38. For Lacan's ideas on masochism and sadism one can refer to his scattered remarks on this subject in his seminar on anxiety (Lacan 1962–63). See also Fink 1997.

39. This is what Lacan is referring to when he writes, "To return to phantasy, let us say that the pervert imagines himself to be the Other in order to ensure his *jouissance* . . ." (E 322/13–14, EF 824–825). The expression "to ensure his *jouissance*" refers to the fact that the sadist ensures the *jouissance* of the Other (and thus masks its lack) by ascribing the possibility of unlimited *jouissance* to himself in the phantasy. In what follows this passage, Lacan writes that the neurotic "imagines himself to be a pervert" (E 322/15, EF 825). We will return to the relationship between perversion and neurosis in our next section.

40. For "economic" reasons I leave fetishism out of account in this regard. What we write here concerning masochism and sadism, however, applies *mutatis mutandis* equally to fetishism (and the other perversions). For a

If it is correct that these phantasies are not unconscious in perversion, does this mean that the perverse unconscious is accessible to everyone?[41] If the perverse subject simply lives out his phantasy, must we not conclude from this that in his case one cannot speak of an unconscious in the strict sense? Lacan flatly denies this. For however much the subject might dream of an unlimited *jouissance*, the perverse scenarios are also directed towards setting limits to this desire. Here again, sadism and masochism probably provide the clearest illustrations.

The masochistic subject will do anything for the sake of the *jouissance* of the Other; she abandons herself and her own welfare in order to be its instrument. Yet for Lacan, this is only half the story, and indeed not even the most important half: he writes that the masochistic subject wants primarily (and unknowingly) to make the Other anxious (Lacan 1962–63, session of March 13, 1963). In the masochistic scenario, according to Lacan, the Other is expected to lay down a law. The masochist allows herself to be bound, struck, humiliated, rendered helpless; she is completely at the Other's mercy; she submits utterly. By delivering herself over to the Other in this way, however, the masochist tries to push the Other so far that it becomes too much for him. The Other is as it were forced to enounce a law and to set limits to *jouissance*: "Stop! That's enough." In other words, the masochistic subject endeavors to bring the Other to the point where the *jouissance* becomes intolerable, and he is compelled to call things to a halt, to set some

---

further development of this problematic, and for clinical illustrations, we refer the reader to the literature. See *inter alia* Fink 1997, p. 165ff, Rey-Flaud 1994.

41. "But this does not mean that in the case of the pervert the unconscious is 'open ended.' He, too, after his fashion, defends himself in his desire. For desire is a defence (*défense*), a prohibition (*défense*) against going beyond a certain limit in *jouissance*" (E 322/19–22, EF 825).

limits.[42] By making the Other anxious (through making herself the instrument of the Other's *jouissance*), the masochistic subject succeeds in being subjected to a command.

We thus find in masochism the double attitude to the law that we said was characteristic of perversion. On the one hand, the masochist disavows the law of the father, and makes herself the instrument of the *jouissance* of the Other. At the same time, the masochistic scenario is ultimately directed towards setting a limit on *jouissance* with the help of a law that the masochist herself establishes (or enables to be established). We now understand why Lacan can write in relation to perversion that desire has a defensive character:[43] the desire of the masochistic subject is a defense against the transgression of a limit in the *jouissance* of the Other.[44] It is a final and distorted attempt to at last establish the law of the father.[45]

---

42. In his article "Un cas de masochisme pervers" M. de M'Uzan (1977) describes a very serious case of masochism. He concludes from this case that "pain" is not the ultimate *jouissance* that the masochist strives for. "Pain" is only a means to achieve this *jouissance*. The abuse creates a feeling of invulnerability. It is this feeling of invulnerability from which masochistic *jouissance* is born. De M'Uzan adds, "*A ce moment il ne craint plus rien et c'est le sadique qui dégonfle toujours*" ["At that moment he no longer fears anything, and it is the sadist who always falls flat (*dégonfle*)"] (p. 133). My thanks to T. Geyskens for bringing this text to my attention.

43. Later, however, we will see that every desire—and thus not only the desire of the perverse subject—has a defensive character, and we will see in what sense this is the case.

44. "For desire is a defence (*défense*), a prohibition (*défense*) against going beyond a certain limit in *jouissance*" (E 322/21–22, EF 825).

45. This is also why in later texts Lacan calls perversion *une père-version*. Perversion stages in a distorted fashion a version of the law of the father that either is not established at all, or is so only insufficiently. This also means that, according to Lacan, we must think of perversion as a (partially failed) attempt of the subject to free himself from the desire of the mother.

What applies in the case of the masochist applies equally, *mutatis mutandis*, to the sadistic subject.[46] At first sight one might think that the sadist does not want anything other than to torture and humiliate her victim; she reduces the victim to a mere means to the end of her own *jouissance*. In this sense we might say that the sadist imposes a law upon her victim. But who precisely is imposing a law upon whom here? On the basis of the identification with the victim that seems to essentially characterize the sadistic phantasy, one might just as well claim that the sadist imposes a law upon herself;[47] she puts herself in the place of the Other, and herself enunciates the law that forbids *jouissance*. On the one hand she "subjects" her victim; she thereby makes herself into a subject that knows no lack or limits, so that she does not have to give up her *jouissance*. On the other hand, to the extent that the sadist also identifies with her victim, the sadistic scenario must also be understood, by analogy with the masochistic scenario, as an attempt to finally set limits on this *jouissance*. In this sense, the desire of the sadist also has a defensive character.[48]

---

46. For what follows I have been to a significant degree inspired by the scattered comments of Lacan concerning sadism in his seminar on anxiety, as well as Fink's commentary on these passages. See Fink 1997, p. 190ff.

47. See Cassiers 1988. One can also consider here Ferenczi's famous case study of little Arpad (Ferenczi 1952). Arpad enjoyed killing chickens. He cut open their throats with obvious pleasure and satisfaction. But following that he would himself fall on the floor as if he was dead. He identified with the fate of his victims. Little Arpad is in this sense as much the object as the subject of the law that he enunciates.

48. The same applies in general to fetishism. Thus Fink tells the story of a patient whose fetish—rows of buttons on women's clothing—could serve, by means of a sort of word-bridge, as support for the word of his father, which was necessary to liberate him from the grip of the desire of his mother (the patient was French, and *bouton* referred to both the buttons on clothes as well as to female genitals). See Fink 1997, p. 181ff.

PHOBIA[49]

When psychoanalytic texts treat phobia (anxiety hysteria), they usually do so in the chapter on neurosis. For Lacan too, phobia is a neurosis; he even describes it as "the most radical form of neurosis," because it offers a solution to a problematic relation to the Name-of-the-Father (Lacan 1960–61). For all this, however, phobia nevertheless displays a structural affinity with perversion. Indeed, according to Lacan, it is situated on the boundary between the "primitive phallic phase" (perversion) and the explicit articulation of the function of the father (neurosis). Let us unpack this idea.

Let us first recall how the confrontation with the desire of the first Other initially evokes only anxiety ("conceals its anxiety"; E 321/14, EF 824). As we saw, the infant is at the mercy of the desire of the Other, in which it constantly threatens to disappear as a subject. In order to gain its own place and to develop its own desire, the infant must detach itself from this first Other—and the introduction of the law of the father forms an indispensable condition for this.

According to Lacan, the pronounced weakness or absence of the father (literal or otherwise) can make this process much more difficult. Recall, for example, little Hans's anxiety about his mother (being eaten by his mother, etc.). Lacan says that this anxiety is precipitated by the refusal or incapacity of little Hans's father to provide a reference point that allows the boy to detach

---

49. In "Subversion," Lacan devotes only half a line to phobia ("But this prevalence given by the neurotic to demand, which, for an analysis declining into facility, shifted the whole treatment towards the handling of frustration, conceals its anxiety from the desire of the Other, *anxiety that is impossible not to recognize when it is covered only by the phobic object* . . ."; E 321/12–16, EF 823–824; my emphasis). In what follows, our task will be to make this allusive passage intelligible.

himself from his mother. Thus despite little Hans's insistence, the father repeatedly refuses to illuminate his own role in the birth of Hanna (Hans's sister), for example, preferring to attribute the procreative force exclusively to the mother. As a result, little Hans continues to believe that he is exclusively the product of his mother's desire.

Hans, however, is no psychotic; he can pose the question of what his mother desires. However, the only answer he can come up with to this question is "She desires me," and his anxiety about his mother is the result. The phobic object—in this case, the horse—enables Hans, *in extremis,* to detach himself from his mother and overcome his anxiety about her, and thus fulfill the role of the father. According to Lacan, then, the signifier "horse" is a substitute for the Father, and Hans proceeds to ascribe to this signifier all sorts of characteristics and properties (e.g., anger) that Hans's father precisely did *not* show in reaction to his privileged relationship with his mother.[50]

NEUROSIS: HYSTERIA AND OBSESSIONAL NEUROSIS[51]

Introduction

The psychotic subject, as we know, never really enters into the symbolic. For such a subject, the metaphor of the Name-of-the-Father does not acquire any psychic meaning, and this fact fun-

---

50. For more on Lacan's theory of phobia, and more specifically on the various meanings of the signifier "horse," see Lacan 1956–57, pp. 199–410. See also Fine 1997.

51. For further commentary on the psychoanalytic theory of neurosis in general, and the Lacanian theory in particular, see *inter alia* Corveleyn 1988, Fink 1997, pp. 112–164, Hiel 1990, Nasio 1995, Verhaeghe 1990, 1994. For a more extensive treatment of psychopathology in its relation to the graph of desire, see Lacan 1957–58, pp. 355–510.

damentally distinguishes psychosis from neurosis and perversion. Moreover, we know that according to Lacan the installation of the metaphor of the Name-of-the-Father takes place in three moments, and that psychopathology is defined by structural relations to those moments. Thus the problematic of perversion, for example, situates itself in the first moment—the "primitive phallic phase," in which the position of the father is not yet explicitly articulated—such that the little child remains trapped in a pure dependence on the desire of the mother.

In neurosis, by contrast to perversion, the lack is in fact connected with the function of the father, but this does not mean that the acceptance of the lack is complete. Very generally, we could say that the neurotic subject has indeed undergone castration, but remains stuck in an imaginary interpretation of it. On the one hand, this means that the neurotic subject can continue to believe in the possibility of overcoming the lack that marks it; on the other hand, it also implies that castration is still understood as a violation of the subject's bodily integrity. This goes together with the fact that for the neurotic, the overcoming of the lack for which he strives simultaneously refers to the "*jouissance* of the Other," which he fears more than anything. So seen, the problematic of neurosis circles unceasingly about a lack that the neurotic wants to maintain as much as overcome.

We still have to make this somewhat more specific. Castration and the metaphor of the Name-of-the-Father imply a confrontation with sexual difference—a confrontation that we already pointed out brings about an essential transformation in the problematic of *jouissance*. Subsequent to that encounter, this problematic is experienced primarily within the order of sexuality, where the thematic of sexual difference is most concretely expressed. From this, we can already understand to some degree why sexuality can play such an important role in the gen-esis and dynamics of neurosis, for according to Lacan, neurosis is also fundamentally a matter of our relation to *jouissance*. Be-cause it has only worked incompletely through the castration complex, the neurotic subject continues to wrestle with this problematic, which can turn his life—and not just his strictly sexual life—into a real Calvary.

All this sufficiently indicates that the subjective position of the neurotic differs fundamentally from that of the psychotic subject. But where is the choice between these two positions made? Here we should recall what we wrote concerning the first confrontation with the desire of the Other: the subject is confronted with a desire, but it has not the least idea what that desire wants—*Che vuoi?*—and it responds to this problem with the phantasy. Now the phantasy, Lacan writes, is the desire of the Other, and this means that the phantasy is the place where the position of the subject is determined; the phantasy articulates the position of the subject with respect to the *jouissance* of the Other.[52] If we are to determine the difference between obses-sional neurosis and hysteria, therefore, we must discover the structure of the phantasies that determine the form in which each syndrome manifests itself. Let us first look at obsessional neurosis.

---

52. "But this prevalence given by the neurotic to demand, which, for an analysis declining into facility, shifted the whole treatment towards the handling of frustration, conceals its anxiety from the desire of the Other, anxiety that is impossible not to recognize when it is covered only by the phobic object, but more difficult to understand in the case of the other two neuroses, when one is not in possession of the thread that makes it possible to present the phantasy as desire of the Other" (E 321/12–18, EF 823–824). We have already commented on the first part of this passage (see Chapter 6, n. 47).

The Phantasy in Hysteria
and Obsessional Neurosis

The clinician is familiar with the figure of the analysand who talks unceasingly, explains everything with great assurance, and rejects with some annoyance every intervention of the analyst.[53] Even if this analysand should deign to entertain the analyst's question, it will not stop him from continuing with his original story once he has given a perfunctory reply. When the analyst points out to him a slip of the tongue or a peculiar statement, he is often very surprised that he "could have said that," and is immediately ready with a rationalizing explanation that negates the effect of the slip of the tongue. He might as well say from the outset that any slip of the tongue can have no significance whatsoever; to all intents and purposes such analysands cannot or will not accept that they could have communicated something

---

53. "One then finds its two terms shattered, as it were: the first, in the case of the obsessional, in as much as he denies the desire of the Other in forming his phantasy by accentuating the impossibility of the subject vanishing, the second, in the case of the hysteric, in as much as desire is maintained only through the lack of satisfaction that is introduced into it when he eludes himself as object. These features are confirmed by the fundamental need of the obsessional neurotic to stand in the place of the Other, and by the disbelieving side of the hysterical intrigue" (E 321/18–27, EF 824). The expression "the two terms" refers to the two elements around which the phantasy turns: the subject ($) and the object a. In obsessional neurosis, the subject denies its dependence on the object, and thus confirms its independence from the Other. In hysteria, by contrast, the subject turns itself *into* the object that determines the desire of the Other. In this perspective, all the emphasis in the obsessional problematic lies on the subject-pole. In the hysterical problematic, by contrast, all the emphasis lies on the object-pole. This is why Lacan writes above, "One then finds [in the hysterical and in the obsessional phantasy] its two terms [subject and object] *shattered, as it were.* . . ." Our subsequent exposition will, of course, make this clearer.

other than what they consciously intended. Every reference to a "strange voice within me" is immediately neutralized here—the obsessional neurotic subject does not believe in the existence of the unconscious, and finds it incredible and unacceptable that as a conscious subject, he could disappear or "fade" away beneath the signifier. The obsessional neurotic thus turns himself into a subject that recognizes no lack, and erases the slash through the letter S in the phantasy.[54]

This last point implies that the obsessional neurotic also denies any dependence on an Other that transcends him. Once again a reference to the analytic situation can make clear what this means. In the analysis, the analyst represents a law to which she herself, as analyst, is also subject. An obsessional patient, then, is precisely one who acts as the guarantor for this Other,[55] and in this way neutralizes her. When the session is finished, he does not wait for a sign from the analyst; he himself says, "Our time must be about up." When the analyst dares to formulate a remark or to pose a question, he points out to her that the analyst is expected to be silent and allow the unconscious to come to the fore.

Of course, we do not only find such typically obsessional neurotic manifestations in analysis. It is just as characteristic for the relational (and especially sexual) life of the obsessional neurotic patient. The following example (Fink 1997, p. 123ff) should

---

54. This is why Lacan writes, "[H]e denies the desire of the Other in forming his phantasy by accentuating the impossibility of the subject vanishing . . ." (E 321/20–21, EF 824). Naturally, the expression "the desire of the Other" also refers in our current context to the desire of the analyst—to allow the unconscious to speak.

55. Hence "the fundamental need of the obsessional neurotic to stand in the place of the Other . . ." (E 321/25–26, EF 824).

make this much clearer. A man meets a woman to whom he is greatly attracted, seduces her, and begins a sexual relationship with her. For him, she is the cause of his desire. At the same time he cannot stop himself from planning ahead of time when they will have sex. He then always asks another woman to call him *while* he is making love with his girlfriend, and when the telephone rings, he talks to the person at the other end of the line while continuing his sexual activity. His partner is in this way neutralized, and he can "forget" that he is dependent on her or her desire.[56]

The obsessional neurotic patient from this example avoids his sexual partner becoming a privileged cause of his desire, something that would destroy his autarchic self-sufficiency.[57] Similarly, when orgasm threatens to bring his stream of thought to a momentary halt, the telephone conversation saves him from disappearing—however briefly—as a thinking, conscious subject. Now obviously, the obsessional neurotic subject can achieve the same result in other ways. For example, he can imagine that he is with somebody else during sex, and in this way too he can deny the significance of his concrete partner in the relationship. These examples clearly illustrate that the obsessional neurotic subject not only wants to erase the slash through the letter S; equally, he cannot accept that the object *a* of his phantasy can escape his grasp and thus remind him of his lack. The sexual partner here takes the place of the object-cause of desire, and the obsessional neurotic relates to this object in a manner that

---

56. "[H]e [the obsessional neurotic] denies the desire of the Other . . ." (E 321/20, EF 824).

57. One will recall: "[H]e [the obsessional neurotic] denies the desire of the Other in forming his phantasy by accentuating the impossibility of the subject vanishing . . ." (E 321/20–21, EF 824).

prevents his self-sufficient position from being put in danger from the outset.[58]

Things are very different in the hysterical phantasy.[59] In the obsessional neurotic phantasy, the desire of the Other is neutralized; in the hysterical phantasy, by contrast, only the Other desires. The hysterical subject seems not to occupy its own position as a desiring subject, but rather is exclusively the object of the desire of the Other. Who does not know of men and women who are constantly at the center of all sorts of love affairs, and yet at the same time deny any personal responsibility for them? "It's them who are always falling in love with me," they say, "I'm in no way responsible." At the same time, however, the hysteric refuses to entertain all the advances of these Others. The hysteric is thus the object of the desire of the Other, but at the same time, she persistently refuses to be the object of his (sexual) *jouissance*. This aversion to sexuality in hysteria can take many different forms;[60] it is always a structural component

---

58. The obsessional neurotic problematic manifests itself, of course, in domains other than just sexuality and the love life of the patient. One can think, for example, of the difficulty many obsessional neurotic patients have in successfully completing their studies. They cannot bear not to be in "perfect" command of the examination material, and they stay at home rather than do a good (or even very good) exam that nevertheless is not perfect, and thus confronts them with their limitations.

59. We limit ourselves in what follows to hysteria in women, since this seems to be the theme of Lacan's text. This is also why we use the feminine pronoun in our text. Of course, some of the characteristics of hysteria described here nevertheless pertain as much to the hysterical man as to the hysterical woman.

60. The aversion to sexuality can indeed take the form of an avoidance of all sexual contact—whether or not corresponding to socially acceptable motives—but it need not do so. Even when the hysteric has sexual contact, she will, for example, describe this as an unacceptable violation of her bodily

of hysteria, and Freud even writes that repulsion for the sexual is in itself a sufficient criterion for calling someone "hysterical." If the hysteric does arouse desire (whether consciously or not), then she also makes sure that it remains unsatisfying. She constantly withdraws herself as an object of the Other's *jouissance*.[61] In order to understand all of this, however, we must go somewhat deeper into the clinical manifestations of hysteria.[62] Hysteria is characterized by a relentless striving after perfection, which cannot tolerate any relativization. Things are never "good enough"; the patient cannot leave things as they are. Whatever result she might achieve, she is immediately pricked by doubts, and a feeling of dissatisfaction rears its head, so that again and again she is driven on to achieve a state from which every lack would be banished.

This striving after perfection marks intersubjective relations in particular. The hysterical patient is tormented by the question of who or what she is (as object) for the Other, and therefore doubts as to whether she is sufficiently appreciated by her

---

integrity—a symbol of male domination—that she only submits to for the sake of her partner and in order to make him happy. In the age of "sexual liberation" hysteria can even give rise to forms of hyper-sexuality. One theme, nevertheless, always recurs—the impossibility of integrating sexuality as a pleasurable means of bonding with a man. See *inter alia* Corveleyn 1988, p. 75ff.

61. "[D]esire is maintained [in the phantasy of the hysteric] only through the lack of satisfaction that is introduced [by the hysteric] into it [desire] when he eludes himself as object" (E 321/22–24, EF 824). The hysteric can, of course, withdraw as the object of *jouissance* in very different ways. For the repulsion for sexuality need not necessarily result in total abstinence. Thus the hysteric will, for example, imagine in sexual contact that she is someone else, or that she is somewhere else. The hysteric, so one could say, "offers herself, but does not give herself."

62. In what follows I have drawn much inspiration from the already cited article of Corveleyn 1988.

friends and acquaintances, and whether or not they really enjoy seeing her, drive her to ever-renewed attempts to earn and absolutely secure their appreciation and affection. The least discord is enough for doubt to rear its head once more. Similarly, the hysterical patient is consumed by analogous doubts and dissatisfactions in her professional life. Does she work well enough, and is she sufficiently recognized by her colleagues? She constantly watches for signs of approval and disapproval in her colleagues and superiors, and again and again she seeks forms of affirmation that can take the doubt away, if only for a moment. But all too often this search for an unconditional affection and absolute appreciation leads to the negative certainty that no one appreciates or loves her.[63]

In the sexual relations of the hysteric, this drive for perfection manifests itself as a search for a man who cannot disappoint her. The sexual object of the hysteric is an ideal object, a man without lack—and thus without desire. This explains why the hysteric prefers unattainable men (men who are married or hold a social position that does not allow them to start a relationship), or at least men who at first pay no attention to her. Once the desire for such a man is aroused, she tries to seduce him, almost as if she wants to test the unattainability that makes the Other so attractive.[64] She devotes all her energy to her project, and is constantly on the lookout for the least sign showing that her efforts are not in vain—that eventually she can become the object

---

63. The affinity between hysteria and paranoia, to which Freud once referred in a letter to Fliess, probably finds its origin here. See *inter alia* Vergote 1984.

64. ". . . the disbelieving side of the hysterical intrigue . . ." (E 321/26–27, EF 824). The hysteric does not really believe in the perfection of the man she chooses.

that fulfills the Other's desire. The hysteric, in other words, turns herself into the object the Other lacks in order to be perfect,[65] and dreams of overcoming the inconsistency of the Other and so bringing him into existence.[66]

In hysterical patients' analytical scenarios, too, one observes a dynamic completely analogous to the one we have just described. The hysteric seeks in the analyst a "master," without lack and without desire, who will liberate her from her suffering; she hopes to find in him a completely neutral figure, without desire of his own, who can help her to overcome her problems once and for all. Thus, in contrast to the obsessional neurotic, the hysteric recognizes her dependence upon the Other. She likes nothing more than for the analyst to intervene, and complains bitterly about his silence, which she so often interprets as a lack of interest. She wants to know what she is and what she means for this silent Other.

At the same time, however, she will do everything in her power to dethrone this new master, and is constantly in search of unexpected traces of the desire of the analyst, which she actively tries to provoke. Can't she hear a certain annoyance in the question of the analyst? She still hasn't said the most important (and interesting) thing—can't she stay just a little longer?

---

65. Of course, this attitude can also manifest itself clinically in other ways. Thus the hysterical patient can always choose partners who display little or no independence, and who are emotionally and otherwise completely dependent upon her. She is then the object that fulfills their imperfection. The hysterical patient can easily imagine to herself (consciously or unconsciously) that such partners signify nothing without her, and she will consequently support them selflessly, sparing no necessary effort to make their career succeed, for example, in a way that never would have been possible without her.

66. Lacan claims that the neurotic wants ". . . to assure himself of the existence of the Other" (E 322/16, EF 825).

Just as the hysteric wants to know who she is for the analyst, so too she is in search of knowledge about herself. "Can't you say what's the matter with me yet?" "I've been coming to you for so long and you still haven't told me why things are so difficult for me." The analyst, however, does well not to address this question directly—whatever his answer might be, it will immediately be questioned and disputed, for the hysteric is in search of a hiatus in (the knowledge of) the Other that she can fill herself. She hopes to be an exceptional case, one that can thereby complete the knowledge of the analyst.[67]

The Phantasy of the "Ideal" Father in
Hysteria and Obsessional Neurosis

Where does the origin of the neurotic relation to the Other lie? Freud teaches us that neurosis must be understood in terms of an unresolved or insufficiently resolved oedipal problematic.[68] At a certain moment in the oedipal crisis, every child turns to a father who is worthy of love because he is "omnipotent."

---

67. Obviously, however, this "hope" need not necessarily be consciously experienced as such.

68. "In fact, the image of the ideal Father is a phantasy of the neurotic. Beyond the Mother, the real Other of demand, whose desire (that is, her desire) one wishes she would assuage, there stands out the image of a father who would close his eyes to desires. . . . The neurotic's wished-for Father is clearly the dead Father. But he is also a Father who can perfectly master his desire—and the same can be said of the subject" (E 321/28–36, EF 824). This quote immediately makes it clear that neurosis presupposes a triangular situation; the lack in the mother is explicitly attached to or connected with a third person—the father. This is not the case in perversion, and is only the case in an unstable fashion in phobia. We will return to this in more detail later.

According to Lacan, this "ideal father"[69] appears as the possessor of the (imaginary) phallus that is lacking in the mother, but at the same time, this father forbids the mother to the child. Since the mother belongs to father, it is not up to the child to satisfy her desire. Now, this "ideal father" is manifest not as the one who represents the law, but as the origin of the law—in other words, he is the "dead" father from "Totem and Taboo," whose symbolic character nevertheless is not appreciated.[70] The little child believes that it can find this father in reality—a belief that can, of course, take on various forms.

Thus the hysteric believes in an "ideal father," but she also "knows" that she never had such a father. In the history of the hysterical patient the presumed impotence (or absence) of the father is a constantly recurring theme[71]—the father is never up to the mark; he is not strong enough—and this impotence can greatly reinforce the fixation on the image of the "ideal father." The hysterical patient can then project herself as the redeeming angel, who must support the father in order to bring him the glory he never had. One thus understands the "logic" that underlies the complicated love life of the hysteric: the partners of the hysteric are idealized objects without lack (like the father she never had), objects that are expected to be "complete" and

---

69. Concerning the figure of the "ideal father," see "La figure du père idéal et ses incidences sur le rapport du sujet à la vérité" in Safouan 1974 pp. 44–51.

70. "The neurotic's wished-for Father is clearly the dead Father" (E 321/34, EF 824). The neurotic thus "recognizes" the Name-of-the-Father, but he has never learned to see the father-lawgiver as a pure signifier. He continues to dream of ("wish" for) an omnipotent father without lack, and for precisely this reason, he remains stuck in an imaginary interpretation of castration.

71. See Israel 1976. Obviously, we should ideally also take into account here the role of the mother of the hysteric in the genesis of this "knowledge." We do not have the necessary space here, however, and we refer the reader to the literature.

thus never for a moment caught in the grip of any desire they have not themselves willed.[72] At the same time, the hysterical patient "knows" that her love objects cannot fill such a tall order, and she thus searches unremittingly for signs of a desire that would point to the imperfection and incompleteness of her idealized partner. In this way, she can then take up her role as a redeeming angel. She is the object that can undo the Other's lack.

The phantasy of the "ideal father" not only plays an important role in hysteria; it is also of great importance for the problematic of the obsessional neurotic. The obsessional neurotic, as we know, exists only when he thinks. He cannot tolerate any lack; he is himself lord and master of his fate. This position is, according to Lacan, buttressed by a narcissistic identification with the "ideal father,"[73] which is determinative for every encounter of the obsessional neurotic with his object. For it is on the basis of this identification with the image of an omnipotent father figure that the obsessional neurotic tries to banish any lack from his life.

The narcissistic identification, however, inevitably turns the "ideal father" into a rival, and according to Lacan, that is the

---

72. "But he is also a Father who can perfectly master his desire . . ." (E 321/34–35, EF 824).

73. Lacan thus writes, "But he is also a Father who can perfectly master his desire—*and the same can be said of the subject*" (E 321/34–36, EF 824; my emphasis). On this point, see Safouan 1974, p. 45. The following incident forms a typical clinical illustration here. A student makes a comparison of two authors who, to his knowledge, have never been compared before. When he proudly presents the results of his research to his advisor, it turns out that the latter is totally unfamiliar with one of the two authors. The student goes away disappointed and sinks into a (fortunately passing) depressive state, thinking, "If he [the advisor] is not capable of a knowledge without lack, how will I ever be able to achieve it . . ."

origin of the ambivalence-conflict that typifies obsessional neurosis (Corveleyn 1988, p. 100ff, Freud 1909b). The neurotic ambivalence-conflict comprises intense concurrent positive and negative feelings towards the same person. From a topological standpoint, however, these feelings occur in different places: the strong feelings of hatred for the father-rival are forcefully repressed, as they are in conflict with the love for the same father. The love, however, cannot nullify the hatred—it only leads to its repression. In certain circumstances, that repression can go together with a reinforcement of the (conscious) feelings of love, and the ambivalence-conflict is consequently unconscious by definition; even then, however, it can show itself in aggressive obsessional thoughts that emerge suddenly to disturb the relationship with the loved person. This problematic of ambivalence implies, therefore, that the "ideal" father is the "dead" father—in accordance with the subject's rivalrous wishes.

The Ego in Neurosis

We have already discussed Lacan's critique of ego-psychology, but let us briefly recall the terms of that discussion. According to the ego-psychologists, there is an autonomous, conflict-free core in the ego, and the analysis should be directed to reinforcing this core, so that the ego can better connect with reality and master conflicts. According to Lacan, on the other hand, the ego must be understood as essentially a matter of alienation and misrecognition. We must now ask ourselves how these characteristics of the Lacanian ego come to expression in neurosis, for only thus can we really gauge the clinical value of Lacan's critique of ego-psychology. In this regard, let us first return to the neurotic phantasy.

The neurotic subject misrecognizes lack,[74] or (what comes down to the same thing) misrecognizes symbolic castration;[75] both the obsessional neurotic patient and the hysterical patient continue to believe in a world without lack. The obsessional neurotic subject, as we know, reduces his existence to his conscious existence, so that he is completely independent from the Other and neutralizes it. He wants to banish every reminder of limitation and lack from his life, and instead, by virtue of his identification with the "ideal father," he sets himself ($) up as the possessor of the (imaginary) phallus (-φ). The negation of the slash through the $ of the phantasy, which we mentioned above with regard to the obsessional phantasy, finds its origin here.[76]

As in the obsessional phantasy, in the hysterical phantasy too "the (-φ) slides under the $ of the phantasy." The hysterical subject ($) identifies with the object (-φ) that can undo the lack of the Other;[77] she thus recognizes the lack in the Other, but she sees it as her task to fill up this lack.

---

74. "In the case of the neurotic, the (-φ) slides under the $ of the phantasy, to the advantage of the imagination that is peculiar to it, that of the ego. For the neurotic has been subjected to imaginary castration from the beginning; it is castration that sustains this strong ego, so strong, one might say, that its proper name is an inconvenience for it, since the neurotic is really Nameless. Yes, it is beneath this ego, which certain analysts chose to strengthen still more, that the neurotic hides the castration that he denies" (E 323/17–24, EF 826).

75. ". . . the castration that he denies" (E 323/24, EF 826).

76. This is also the reason Lacan writes, "In the case of the neurotic, the (-φ) slides under the $ of the phantasy . . ." (E 323/17, EF 826). What this statement means in relation to hysteria—Lacan is here talking about neurosis in general—will be addressed directly.

77. In a text from the same year as "Subversion," Lacan will thus propose another formula for the hysterical phantasy: $\frac{a}{(-φ)} ◊ Ø$. The hysteric turns herself into the object (a) that can complete (-φ) the desire of the Other (Ø). See Lacan 1960–61, p. 289.

We can now understand why both the hysteric and the obsessional neurotic subject, each in their own way, exhaust themselves trying to adapt to the desire of the Other. First, the hysterical patient, who is permanently on the watch for signs of approval or disapproval from her friends and colleagues in the hope of obtaining an absolute affirmation, makes herself completely dependent on the desire of the Other. She finds a partner she can polish and develop far beyond his normal potential; she knows what he needs and lacks, and she tries to be precisely that for him. Of course, she can only assume this position by interpreting the desire of the Other within the order of demand ("I know what he needs/what is good for him")[78] and by completely subordinating her own desire to his. Thus the hysteric desires not "in her own name," but "in the name of the (presumed demand of the) Other."[79]

Generally speaking, the same applies *mutatis mutandis* to the obsessional neurotic, who identifies himself with the image of the "ideal father." This ideal father, or whoever incarnates him, is not only an example with which the subject equates himself, however. He is just as much a master, who posits the law to which the subject submits himself—not so much the representative of a law that transcends him, as he is himself the origin of the law he enunciates. Consider the example of the doctoral student who

---

78. One will recall here the passage cited earlier: "Indeed, the neurotic . . . is he who identifies the lack of the Other with his demand, Φ [the signifier of fulfilment as impossible] with D [an identifiable and determinable lack]. . . . As a result, the demand of the Other assumes the function of an object in his phantasy . . ." (E 321/4–7, EF 823).

79. This is one of the reasons Lacan writes that the neurotic does not have his own name (". . . the neurotic is really Nameless"). We will return to this idea in the following paragraph.

saw in his advisor a sort of demigod without lack:[80] the advisor is presumed to be all knowing. What, then, can this student do but conform to the advisor's demands and wishes? He will ask the advice of his learned master in all respects, and will always carry it out to the letter.

The obsessional neurotic is thus a follower, a slavish adept. As soon is he is in a situation where he must choose for himself—where he must speak in his own name without the support of his master—he is blocked. For this subject, speaking in his own name—or what amounts to the same thing, following his own desire—means putting himself in the place of the "ideal father," and there can be only one master.[81] In obsessional neurosis desire is reduced thus to the demand of the Other; the obsessional neurotic subject never desires "in his own name" ("[He] is really Nameless"). In fact, he almost finds it annoying that he *has* his own name, because it reminds him that he is summoned to his own desire, which does not dissolve into the desire of his master.[82]

---

80. See n. 73.

81. It is not difficult to discover aggression against the father behind the compliant character of the obsessional neurotic. Above we referred to the student who would prefer to stay at home than do an exam that was not "perfect," and we can now complete this picture: the obsessive student is a slavish student, who follows every lesson and takes painfully exact notes. At the crucial moment, however, he stays at home . . . and makes fun of the supposed ignorance of the teacher.

82. "[I]ts proper name is an inconvenience for it . . ." (E 323/21, EF 826). Figuring in the background here is a discussion concerning the status of the proper name, which we cannot deal with exhaustively. The proper name is a shifter, which "designates the subject, without signifying it." The assumption of this name is consequently equiprimordial with the assumption of the lack from which desire lives, and therefore implies that the subject can no longer interpret desire (and the lack) in terms of the demand of the Other (as in neurosis). Lacan has further worked out this theme in his commentary on

We can now better situate the "strong ego" of the obsessional neurotic and the hysteric. The obsessional neurotic subject is an "adapted" subject, and always has its affairs in order. It knows what it says. It has everything under control. This "strong ego" corresponds to the logic of the obsessional neurotic phantasy, in which the object *a* is understood as a part of the subject itself.[83] The hysteric, for her part, believes in a world without gaps—or more precisely, she believes in a completely complementary relationship between a man and a woman, and she believes that she herself can achieve that relationship.[84] For her, the incompleteness or the impotence of the father has no ground in principle; it is just a temporary incompleteness or shortcoming. This belief inevitably ties up with an ego dynamic in which the essential nature of every lack is misrecognized.

What good is it then, asks Lacan against the ego psychologists, to reinforce this ego in the analysis?[85] In the case of obsessional neurosis one can scarcely imagine how the ego could be made stronger, or where such reinforcement might lead. And even if we merely entertain the hysterical patient's demand for

---

Shakespeare's Hamlet (Lacan 1958–59, *Ornicar?* version): "Hamlet, the Dane" throughout the play rails against . . . the Dane! (His proper name is an inconvenience.) According to Lacan, it is precisely at the moment that he can call out before the grave of Ophelia, "I, Hamlet, the Dane," that he recovers his position as a desiring subject, and in the same moment, he realizes his name as a shifter. On this point, see Van Haute (in press).

83. "In the case of the neurotic, the (-φ) slides under the $ of the phantasy, *to the advantage of the imagination that is peculiar to it, that of the ego*" (E 323/17–18, EF 826; my emphasis).

84. We could also say in the terminology of Lacan's later work that the hysterical subject believes in the possibility of a sexual relation.

85. ". . . this ego, which certain analysts chose to strengthen still more . . ." (E 323/23–24, EF 826).

knowledge in the hope of getting her to understand something, we are barking up the wrong tree; the analyst will in any case only too quickly notice that he has done no more than put her in a position to realize her phantasy. Very quickly it will turn out that the knowledge of the analyst is deficient, and his analysand will come to his aid,[86] and if he repeats this "maneuver" too often, the analysand will turn her back on him in disillusionment and continue unabated with her search elsewhere.

Neurosis and the Jouissance of the Other

The neurotic subject does not recognize the castration to which it is submitted as a symbolic being; it attempts to banish every reference to castration from its life, and to conceal it beneath a strong ego.[87] And yet, Lacan writes, we ought not think that the neurotic subject only denies castration—quite to the contrary, it also clings tenaciously to it.[88] According to Lacan, what

---

86. For example, by producing new symptoms that can extend the knowledge of the analyst.

87. "For the neurotic has been subjected to imaginary castration from the beginning; it is castration that sustains this strong ego. . . . [I]t is beneath this ego . . . that the neurotic hides the castration that he denies" (E 323/19–24, EF 826).

88. "But, contrary to appearances, he clings to it. What the neurotic does not want, and what he strenuously refuses to do, until the end of the analysis, is to sacrifice his castration to the *jouissance* of the Other by allowing it to serve that *jouissance*. And, of course, he is not wrong, for although at bottom, he feels himself to be what is most vain in existing, a Want-to-be (*un Manque-être*) or a Too-much-of-it (*un En-Trop*), why should he sacrifice his difference (anything but that) to the *jouissance* of an Other that, let us remember, does not exist. Yes, but if by some chance it did exist, it would 'enjoy' it (*il en jouirait*) [i.e., the Other would enjoy the difference of the neurotic]. And that is what

the subject actually wants, and will go to any lengths to achieve, is to avoid *sacrificing* its castration to the *jouissance* of the Other.[89] For all that the neurotic subject feels like a failure and doubts the meaning of its existence,[90] it by no means wants its existence to serve the *jouissance* of the Other. In this section, we will explore this neurotic relation to the Other's *jouissance*.

We know that for Lacan, the processes of castration and entry into the symbolic order go completely hand in hand. The subject comes to be by inscribing itself in the order of signifiers, but there is a price to pay—there is no subject without a prior sacrifice. This sacrifice takes on concrete form in the castration complex; acceptance of castration detaches the subject from the first Other of the demand, and the subject thereby liberates itself from the grip of this Other, in which until then it was caught. From now on, the subject occupies its own place, and can develop its own desire and its own (sexuated) identity.[91] Desire is no longer in the grip of the mother, but is directed instead to other, symbolically validated objects.

---

the neurotic does not want. For he imagines that the Other demands his castration" (E 323/25–35, EF 826; translation modified).

89. "What the neurotic does not want . . . is to sacrifice his castration to the *jouissance* of the Other" (E 323/26–28, EF 826).

90. "[A]t bottom, he feels himself to be what is most vain in existing, a Want-to-be (*un Manque-être*) or a Too-much-of-it (*un En-Trop*) . . ." (E 323/29–31, EF 826). One thinks here of the fluctuations in self-esteem of the hysterical subject, who can never be sure if she measures up in the eyes of others; or of the obsessional subject, who sinks into depression when he is confronted with a "fault" in the knowledge of the one who for him incarnates the "ideal father."

91. Lacan refers to this when he speaks in the passage we are commenting upon here of "his [the neurotic subject's] difference" (E 323/31, EF 826).

The neurotic subject has also undergone castration and freed itself from the grip of the Other, at least in part. To the extent that it continues to interpret the problematic of castration in imaginary terms, however, it can also continue to believe in a world without limitations. The neurotic subject continues to believe that the *jouissance* of the Other is possible—or rather, it never entirely gives up the belief that it can help *make* it possible.[92] The realization of this lawless, limitless *jouissance*, however, is equivalent to the destruction of the subject,[93] for such a *jouissance* is of its essence beyond the symbolic, in which alone the subject can exist.

And in fact, *jouissance* is present in neurosis—a permanent threat to every relationship with the Other. We ought not to think of this threat too abstractly; what is at stake here is not a metaphysical problem. Recall, for example, the basic position of the hysteric, who offers herself but does not give herself. This hysterical sexuality in fact stands under the sign of the possibility of an unlimited and infinite bodily *jouissance* of and by the Other, for the hysterical subject sets herself up as the object that can complete the Other—or else make the *jouissance* of the Other possible, which amounts to the same thing.

The hysteric can only think of this *jouissance* as an assault upon her own bodily and sexual integrity, however. She fears that the Other requires from her an actual bodily sacrifice in order to

---

92. The neurotic is, in other words, not convinced of the fact that the Other does not exist: "Yes, but if by some chance it did exist . . ." (E 323/32–33, EF 826).

93. "[W]hy should he sacrifice his difference (anything but that) to the *jouissance* of an Other which . . . does not exist[?] Yes, but if by some chance it did exist, he would 'enjoy' it (*il en jouirait*)" (E 323/31–33, EF 826). The neurotic fears having to sacrifice his existence as a bodily subject with his own identity ("sacrifice his difference") for the *jouissance* of the Other ("if by some chance it did exist, he would 'enjoy' it [the neurotic's difference]").

realize his *jouissance*,[94] and she therefore fears becoming a mere instrument in the hands of the Other, underwriting that *jouissance*. Lacan writes in this regard that the hysterical patient—and the neurotic subject in general—imagines that the Other wants her castration in order to realize his own *jouissance*,[95] and this explains why hysterical patients so readily experience sexuality as rape, or as something disgusting and physically overwhelming—they are anxious about being passively delivered over to a *jouissance* that can submerge and destroy them.

What is true of the hysteric, however, is just as true *mutatis mutandis* of the obsessional neurotic. The obsessional neurotic patient from our example, who tries to affirm his independence from the (sexual) desire of the Other at any cost, fears becoming prisoner to *jouissance*—he fears, that is, being drawn into a movement over which he will lose all control, and in which he will disappear as a subject.

Thus we can also understand the true significance of Freud's famous dictum that neurosis is the inverse of perversion:[96] he means that the unconscious phantasies of the neurotic subject have a perverse content, and it is precisely on account of their

---

94. "What the neurotic does not want . . . is to sacrifice his castration to the *jouissance* of the Other by allowing it [castration as a violation of its bodily integrity] to serve that *jouissance*" (E 323/26–28, EF 826).

95. "For he [the neurotic] imagines that the Other demands his castration" (E 323/34–35, EF 826).

96. "*To return to the phantasy, let us say that the pervert imagines himself to be the Other in order to ensure his jouissance*, and that it is what the neurotic reveals when he imagines himself to be a pervert—in his case, to assure himself of the existence of the Other. It is this that gives the meaning of the perversion that is supposed to lie in the very principle of neurosis. The perversion is in the unconscious of the neurotic as phantasy of the Other" (E 322/13–19, EF 824–825; my emphasis). We have already commented on the first part of this passage (which I have italicized) in the section on perversion.

perverse content that these phantasies have to be repressed. To simplify somewhat, we could thus say that according to Freud, the neurotic subject dreams of what the pervert does. Now Lacan in a sense reverses this idea. For him, the perversion that lies at the basis of neurosis[97] has to do not so much with unconscious perverse desires in the neurotic subject, but rather a phantasy of what the Other wants *from* him.[98] In other words, the neurosis is for Lacan a defense against the supposed perversion *of the Other*. By way of illustration, recall the example of the hysteric: on the one hand she turns herself into the object of the desire of the Other, whose lack she wants to remedy;[99] on the other, the realization of this project would mean that she would become an instrument in the Other's pursuit of *jouissance*. She fears that the Other desires her to take up the position that is characteristic of perversion.[100]

---

97. "[T]he perversion that is supposed to lie in the very principle of neurosis" (E 322/17–18, EF 825).

98. "[T]he perversion is in the unconscious of the neurotic as phantasy of the Other" (E 322/18–19, EF 825).

99. "[She wants] to assure [her]self of the existence of the Other" (E 322/15–16, EF 825).

100. Lacan refers to this when he writes, "[T]hat . . . is what the neurotic reveals when he imagines himself to be a pervert—in his case, to assure himself of the existence of the Other" (E 322/13–16, EF 825). The neurotic sets himself up as the object of the Other's desire (he wants "to assure himself of the Other": he wants to make the Other complete and so bring him into being), but he thus risks becoming a mere instrument of the Other's *jouissance* and ending up in the position of perversion ("when he imagines himself to be a pervert"). This is what the neurotic resists at all costs. The perverse position is in the first place a phantasy about the Other; it concerns the neurotic's phantasmatic fear of what the Other has in store for him. In this way, the neurotic reveals that the perverse position involves the realization of the *jouissance* of the Other ("assuring his *jouissance*": the perverse subject wants nothing other than to be the instrument of the Other's *jouissance*).

We might now describe the leitmotif of neurosis as follows: "No *jouissance* for the Other" (Fink 1997, p. 128). Yet if the aim is to *deny* the Other's *jouissance*, why does Lacan write that in neurosis the phantasy "takes on the transcendental function of *ensuring* the *jouissance* of the Other, which passes this chain [the phantasy can be described as a chain or sequence] on to me in the Law" (E 324/2–3, EF 826; my emphasis)?

The following hypothetical (but not unimaginable) example can cast some light here (Fink 1997, p. 129). An obsessional neurotic writer or academic works for posterity, sacrificing everything that could bring him satisfaction in the here and now to write as many novels or papers as possible. He wants to be remembered as a great author, or as a learned man; he wants his name never to be forgotten. He wants, we could also say, to conquer death and finitude. Now, the name that this hypothetical patient will save from oblivion—the name of an idealized father?—functions in a sense as the Other, who lays down the law and whose *jouissance* is assured by the accumulation of publications.[101] "Something" that he has no hold over, something to which he is delivered over, drives this hypothetical patient ever onward, in a frenetic attempt to live on after death. We cannot say that this patient derives pleasure from this battle of attrition, if we understand by pleasure what we usually understand by it; the restless pursuit of timeless fame could well be a true path of woe for him. But in exactly this way, he realizes the *jouissance* of the idealized Other with whom he identifies—despite himself and without knowing it. The obsessional neurotic

---

101. ". . . the transcendental function of ensuring the *jouissance* of the Other, *which passes this chain on to me in the Law*" (E 324/2–3, EF 826; my emphasis).

subject does not act on his own account, but for an Other whom he wants to emulate, and to whom he proudly shows off the results of his diligent labors.[102]

JOUISSANCE, THE LAW, AND THE PLEASURE PRINCIPLE

In the course of this chapter, this much at least should have become clear: in Lacan, the term *jouissance* refers to a situation in which the subject is delivered over to an Other in which it risks being destroyed, albeit in a number of very different ways.[103] The psychotic subject is delivered over to the anonymous *jouissance* of the Other, in which it disappears; the hysteric is afraid of being sacrificed on the altar of the *jouissance* of the Other (in this case sexual), in which she as a subject would be destroyed; and the obsessional neurotic patient, as in our example, organizes his sexual life in such a manner that any loss of control is excluded—for him too, depending upon and yielding to the Other as the cause of his desire would equal his very destruction as a subject.

---

102. The following passage also refers to this: "Indeed, the Law appears to be giving the order, 'Jouis!,' to which the subject can only reply 'J'ouis' (I hear), the *jouissance* being no more than understood" (E 319/6–8, EF 821). The subject is here in the grasp of a cruel super-ego, which drives him without his realizing it. This is also the reason Lacan describes *jouissance* here as "under-stood" (*sous-entendue*) [this nuance is lost in Sheridan's translation—Trans.]; here it is a matter of the *jouissance* of the Other, of which the subject is more the victim than anything else. This cruel super-ego is the product of an identification with the "ideal father."

103. However, the subject can still represent this situation to itself on a phantasmatic level as a blissful state, in which every lack is cancelled.

Different as these problematics may be, in every case the subject, despite itself, is or fears to be drawn into *jouissance* and lost—for *jouissance* occurs "beyond" the symbolic, and I can exist as subject only within the symbolic, which protects me against the pull of the first Other / the mother. Thus *jouissance*, according to Lacan, takes no account of what we normally call "pleasurable" or "pleasing" (*plaisir*); pleasure presupposes an involvement of the subject, which is put out of play per se in *jouissance*. In this sense, *jouissance* stands at cross-purposes with the concern for one's own well-being and welfare, a point we could also express by saying that *jouissance* puts the pleasure principle out of play. This inevitably raises the question of how we must understand the relationship between the pleasure principle and the *jouissance* of the Other.

According to Freud, the psyche is automatically regulated by the pleasure principle. In this context, Freud identifies pleasure with a discharge of tension, and unpleasure with an increase in tension. For him, the dominance of the pleasure principle implies that humans strive in principle to keep psychic tension as low as possible, or at least constant, and in this sense, the Freudian pleasure principle is an *unpleasure* principle—it is directed primarily to the avoidance of unpleasure (increase in tension).

In our current context, we need not go into the significance of this pleasure principle for Freud's work, and into the many problems that it raises in that context. We will satisfy ourselves instead with the assertion that Lacanian *jouissance* seems to be at odds with Freud's formulation of the pleasure principle.[104]

---

104. This does not mean, however, that we could speak in a meaningful way about a "*jouissance* principle" that would stand opposed to the "pleasure principle." For *jouissance* inevitably has an essentially destructive connotation, and is thus more of an anti-principle.

How can we understand the frenetic efforts of the obsessional neurotic academic we discussed earlier, for example, in terms of the Freudian pleasure principle? Do we do justice to the phenomenon if we say that the patient is striving for "pleasure" in the normal sense of the word? And is it not even more difficult to understand the "pleasure" he strives after in terms of a reduction of tension? What reduction of tension could be the aim of his accumulation of publications and distinctions? Again, the *jouissance* of the Other we discussed in relation to psychosis seems even less amenable to description in terms of "pleasure"; the psychotic subject is drawn into a maelstrom in which it is destroyed, and it is anything but clear how that could adequately be understood in terms of a "reduction of tension" or "the pursuit of pleasure."

Lacan defines the pleasure principle primarily as a principle of homeostasis: the human organism (any organism?) tends of its nature, as it were, to maintain an optimal level of tension. When the tension rises too high, the organism seeks to discharge it; when it drops too low, the organism will undertake efforts to bring it back up to the mark. The pleasure principle, in consequence, stands under the sign of the interests of the organism (and of the ego). Lacan thus assumes that already on the level of life as such—that is to say, the (mythic) point Δ on the elementary cell of the graph—there is (or should be) a principle of regulation at work guarding the interests of the living. In the spontaneous movement of life, for example, pain (unpleasure) reminds us that we have overstepped a certain limit, and may be placing our continued existence in danger.

This homeostatic principle thus implies that the organism is characterized by a minimal self-attachment, on the basis of which every enjoyment has to be kept within bounds. Whenever the organism tries to overstep a certain (physiologically determined) boundary of *jouissance* (e.g., by stretching *jouissance* beyond a certain point or continuously intensifying it), the homeostatic mechanism intervenes to protect the organism against itself, and a possibly unlimited pursuit of *jouissance* in which it would forget its own "self-interest." This mechanism is thus a first and "natural" barrier against every attempt to realize an unlimited and measureless *jouissance*.[105]

Let us now return to the relation of *jouissance* to the law of castration and the signifier. As we know, the subject must both escape the grip (of the *jouissance*) of the Other, and also give up the dream of ever being able to attain such a *jouissance* for itself. A law is therefore needed to call a halt to this *jouissance*—the law of the father or of castration. The law of the father must keep the subject from being drawn into that movement of *jouissance* in which it will be lost, and it is precisely because and insofar as this law is carried through either not at all (psychosis) or only insufficiently (neurosis and perversion) that the subject remains in the grip of a nameless *jouissance* that threatens to destroy it. Just as the pleasure principle prevents the organism from overstepping certain (physiologically determined) boundaries, so too the law of castration must protect the subject of the signifier from the *jouissance* of the Other.

It seems, consequently, that we find here the same formal homology between life (the body) and language that we discussed earlier in relation to the object *a* and the phantasy. However, the law of castration is no mere duplicate of the pleasure principle as we have described it, for the problematic of the overstepping of a boundary acquires a whole new meaning from

---

105. "But it is not the Law itself that bars the subject's access to *jouissance*. . . . [I]t is pleasure that sets the limits on *jouissance*, pleasure as that which binds incoherent life together . . ." (E 319/9–12, EF 821).

this law, and from confrontation with the Other.[106] The "pre-subject," which is at first completely absorbed in the movement of the (pre-textual) life (Δ), is now a split subject ($), and must set itself apart from the *jouissance* of the Other.[107] The law of castration, moreover, places bodily *jouissance* under the dominion of the phallus;[108] *jouissance* is thus joined to concrete presentations and signifiers, or—what amounts to the same thing—it is staged in phantasies that themselves always refer, directly or indirectly, to sexual difference and the problematic of sexuation.[109]

---

106. The complete passage that we are discussing here thus runs as follows: "But it is not the Law itself that bars the subject's access to *jouissance*— *rather it creates out of an almost natural barrier a barred subject.* For it is pleasure that sets the limits on *jouissance*, pleasure as that which binds incoherent life together, until another, unchallengeable prohibition [the law of the father] arises from the regulation that Freud discovered as the primary process and appropriate law of pleasure" (E 319/9–14, EF 821; my emphasis). In our opinion the phrase "another . . . prohibition arises from the regulation" (*une autre . . . interdiction s'élève de cette régulation*) suggests that this new prohibition repeats a (logically) earlier regulation, and the phrase "the regulation that Freud discovered" refers grammatically to "pleasure as that which binds incoherent life together." This implies precisely that Lacan interprets the Freudian pleasure principle as a homeostatic principle. This principle, however, only obtains its true psychoanalytic significance in connection with the law of castration. We will return to this.

107. "But it is not the Law itself that bars the subject's access to *jouissance*—rather it creates out of an almost natural barrier a barred subject" (E 319/9–10, EF 821).

108. As a result, sexuality must be understood as a curtailment of the *jouissance* of the Other. Only when the law of castration is carried through in an incomplete fashion does the threat of this *jouissance* continue to hang over sexuality, for example, in hysteria.

109. This is also why in later texts, Lacan calls this limited bodily *jouissance* "phallic"; for reasons we already know, this "phallic" *jouissance* is a defense against the "*jouissance* of the Other."

The law of castration thus makes impossible any total and undifferentiated enjoyment that might draw the subject along and threaten to destroy it; above all, it forbids the subject from absolutizing objects into something that can fill in *jouissance*. For there is no object that can put an end to the movement of desire; no object can undo the lack indicated by the phallus. The law of the father and of castration thus reformulates a boundary that already pre-existed at the level of life as such, this time on the level of the subject of the signifier. At the same time, it also changes the meaning of that boundary so that it now refers to the *jouissance* of the Other, which itself cannot be thought apart from the intervention of the signifier.

The law of castration commands us to maintain our desire, and in fact it is this law that drives the subject ever onward in the endless movement from one signifier to another. More concretely, the mother is prohibited as object of desire, and the subject must now direct itself to symbolically sanctioned objects.[110] Naturally this does not exclude every satisfaction; however, every momentary satisfaction is limited, and the primacy of the signifier implies that new signifiers will immediately drive me onward towards new experiences of satisfaction, each just as limited as the last. The law of castration does not prohibit desire, but it demands from us that we maintain this movement, and the human subject must consequently abandon unlimited and destructive *jouissance* in order to make a limited (sexual) *jouissance* possible.[111] The law of the father demands that we

---

110. It is to this that the expression "another . . . prohibition" refers in our current passage.

111. "Castration means that *jouissance* must be refused, so that it can be reached on the inverted ladder (*l'échelle renversée*) of the Law of desire" (E 324/11–12, EF 827).

exchange the *jouissance* of the Other for desire.[112] In this sense, desire and the law of castration have an essentially defensive significance both in pathology, and in normality; their task is to protect us from the *jouissance* of the Other.[113]

Thus it becomes clear that the pleasure principle, which Freud claims regulates the primary processes of the unconscious, cannot be understood in terms of a simple reduction in tension. According to Lacan, unconscious desire stands rather under the sign of the law of castration. We recall here what we wrote above concerning perversion and neurosis: in perversion, the subject tries despite everything to establish a law that would make *jouissance* impossible; neurotic patients—hysterical or obsessive—cling to castration in a distorted fashion, because otherwise they fear being drawn into the dynamic of a *jouissance* that as much as they seek, they fear, because it would affect their bodily integrity. In other words, perversion and neurosis are each in their own way strategies to maintain desire against the incursions of *jouissance,* no matter what it takes.

The pleasure principle, which according to Lacan clearly must be understood as structurally homologous with the law of castration, achieves this by obliging the subject to continue to desire in accordance with the law of the signifiers. It thereby impedes the subject from transgressing a certain boundary in its pursuit of *jouissance,* by obliging it to yield to the endless movement from one signifier (representation) to another. If we

---

112. "The true function of the Father . . . is fundamentally to unite (and not to set in opposition) a desire and the Law . . ." (E 321/31–33, EF 824).

113. "For desire is a defence (*défense*), a prohibition (*défense*) against going beyond a certain limit in *jouissance*" (E 322/21–22, EF 825). "What analytic experience shows is that, in any case, it is castration that governs desire, whether in the normal or the abnormal" (E 323/36–37, EF 826).

want to describe this process in Freud's economic terms (increase and discharge of tension), we can by no means say that its guiding principle is to keep tension as low as possible, for the law of desire requires us to pass from one signifier to another, and thus to *maintain* a certain rhythm. What counts, we could also say, is not the reduction of tension as such, but the "cadence of desire."

NE PAS CÉDER SUR SON DÉSIR:[114]
TOWARDS A DIALECTIC OF DESIRE?

Let us look once more at the relation between *jouissance* and the law of castration. What is the significance of the acceptance of castration and the installation of the phallus as the signifier of lack? Does it mean that the dream of a *jouissance* without limits simply disappears, and that the subject henceforth devotes itself to the movement of the signifier without reserve? Would this not inevitably mean that for such a subject everything is just as meaningful as everything else—and therefore just as meaningless? If it all comes down to keeping desire in movement, then does it matter any more what desire is directed at, or which signifiers determine it?[115]

----

114. "Do not give up on your desire."
115. We can further illustrate this by way of what we wrote above (the section in Chapter 6, "The Significance of the Phantasy," pp. 133–140) concerning the relation between desire and the articulable properties or perfections of the other. If I were only interested in the properties of the other—if my desire were aroused exclusively by these properties—then every other would simply be exchangeable with all those who have comparable properties. Each of these "others" would then be just as interesting as the others—or as uninteresting.

Let us recall what we wrote above[116] concerning the "representative of representation" (the mother). There we claimed that once the child has accepted that it can only access this "representative of representation" via substitutes, the presentation disappears into the unconscious, though this does not mean that this "representative" stops functioning as the ultimate mainspring of human desire. True, we must free ourselves from the mother in order to exist as subjects at all; but even after we have freed ourselves from her grip, the "memory" of that first fundamental attachment continues to be active in the unconscious as the center of gravity around which the unconscious presentations revolve. This implies that in the unconscious the subject remains unavoidably and structurally attached to (the dream of) a *jouissance* uninhibited by any law, beyond the lack that is instituted by the symbolic. This reference to *jouissance* thus determines the tension of psychic life; it is the (impossible) final term of desire, to which we remain attached by means of the (substitutive) signifiers of the unconscious.

How can we reconcile this thought with the idea that human existence is nothing outside of the chain of differentially determined signifiers or with the thought that it also aims at *jouissance*, when *jouissance* is of its essence beyond that chain?[117] Recall, first, that the subject accepts that desire can only find satisfaction by means of signifiers through symbolic castration, which transforms the phallus into the signifier of an impossibility. However, symbolic castration does not thereby liberate us from

---

116. See the section in Chapter 5, "Further Characterization of Desire: The Transitional Object" (pp. 119–123).

117. Lacan does not really give an answer to this question in "Subversion." In what follows we nevertheless attempt to formulate a solution—inevitably summary—on the basis of our foregoing reading.

every reference to an (impossible) *jouissance* as the end term of desire; it merely means that the subject "realizes" that it can aim at this end term solely via substitutes. In the order of signifiers, total fulfillment is impossible.

This also means, however, that a reference inevitably arises to something lying beyond this order, something primordially excluded from it; precisely because no signifier is capable of making up the lack, the order of signifiers evokes a fascination for that which lies beyond it. Phantasies are precisely the staging of this ineffable, unrepresentable something.[118] They turn around a point that it is impossible to represent, but that holds measureless fascination for us for just this reason[119]—for we suspect in it a fullness never given us in our everyday existence.

We thus cannot understand human existence in terms of an exclusive reference to the order of signifiers, and even less can we do so in terms of an exclusive reference to *jouissance*. We live out our existence, rather, in terms of an essential tension between these two poles. Precisely for this reason, we continually attach special significance to new objects, in a perennial dream of existence complete and without lack; on the other hand, we are confronted again and again with the limitedness of these objects of desire, and with the futility of our hope to be anything other than stretched between those poles—the equiprimordial determinants of our existence. Humans are in this sense an "in-between-being" whose existence is carried on

---

118. This is why the phantasy is inscribed on the graph of desire on a line that runs over ($\$\lozenge D$) and S($\emptyset$). The phantasy, so we could say, stages something whose impossibility is indicated by the slash through O.

119. What interests me in this specific woman or man is never exclusively her or his articulable properties (see n. 115), but rather something that I cannot articulate in language and that is announced or evoked by a trembling voice or a fleeting gaze.

in a dialectical relation between two antithetical terms: *jouissance* and castration. Human being is desire.

Neurosis must be understood in this perspective as the constant and painful attempt to maintain this dialectical relation, and the same holds *mutatis mutandis* for perversion and even psychosis. Due to structural considerations, the imaginary interpretation of castration means that one of the two terms inevitably threatens to gain the upper hand over the other: the neurotic subject fears the *jouissance* of the Other, in which it would disappear as subject, and its whole existence is directed to making this *jouissance* impossible and thereby saving desire. In this sense, pathology teaches us that the first commandment of any truly human existence is: *Ne pas céder sur son désir* (Lacan 1959–60, p. 319).

Conclusion:
The Primacy of
Sexuality, or
Against Adaptation

What can we learn today from Lacan? It is clear that Lacanian psychoanalysis raises numerous questions; Lacanian psychoanalysis is and will remain controversial, and many of the problems raised by Lacan's work remain unresolved. For example, we pointed to obscurities in Lacan's theory of psychosis;[1] and the great importance Lacan gives to the Name-of-the-Father, the phallus, and the castration complex have also been the cause of much debate. Whatever one might think of these controversies, however, and whatever position one wants to adopt in regard to them, it is clear that Lacanian psychoanalysis is an important point of reference in various debates—for example, discussions concerning the crisis of fatherhood and the primacy of the phallus. Even if we do not always agree with Lacan, his thought undoubtedly helps us to articulate this problematic more clearly and to define what is at stake. If only for this reason, it would be unwise to simply turn our backs on Lacanian thought.

Lacan has perhaps become best known as a defender of the primacy of the symbolic and of language. There is, he never tires of repeating, no subjectivity outside of language, and the status of the subject must be reconsidered in terms of its dependence on language. As we have already suggested, this idea is closely linked to the ontological dualism that characterizes Lacan's thought: for Lacan it is clear that language and subjectivity on

---

1. Here we could add that the absence of any reference to the "border-line-problematic" is undoubtedly somewhat strange for the Anglo-Saxon trained psychoanalyst. See Gurewich and Tort 1998.

the one hand, and the body on the other, are in principle two distinct orders, each following its own logic.

In this respect, Lacan repeats a thematic that has fundamentally defined French philosophy in the twentieth century. Kojève (1949), for instance, distinguishes in principle between the order of nature and the order of labor and of history; although labor and history are, of course, always directed to nature which is transformed by them, nature is of a fundamentally different order to them. Labor and history undergo a dialectical development, while nature of itself—which is to say insofar as it is not taken up in human activity—simply coincides with itself. In an entirely analogous way, Sartre (1969) distinguishes the *en soi*, which "is what it is," from the *pour soi*, which "is what it is not and is not what it is." It is thus the *pour soi* that introduces negativity into the *en soi*, which of itself is mere identity. Even if the *pour soi* cannot be thought apart from the *en soi*, and remains always directed to it, it is nevertheless a question here of two different orders, each governed by two different principles.

Our discussion of the elementary cell of the graph of desire, and of the way in which Lacan brings together the body and language, teaches us that Lacan departs from one and the same premise.[2] The order of signifiers is always and unavoidably oriented to the order of corporeality, which it determines; nevertheless, two different orders are in principle at stake here, each of which must be understood according to its own principles and logic. Lacan weakens the opposition somewhat by pointing to the structural homology between the two orders, but ultimately this makes little difference to his point of departure.

---

2. The reader will no doubt remember that this is the basic reason the two arrows in the elementary cell of the graph run in opposite directions.

The experience of loss that comes about on the level of the body only acquires meaning in terms of the order of the signifiers that is grafted onto it. Like "nature" in Kojève, and the *en soi* in Sartre, the body in Lacan makes no positive contribution to the production of meaning.

What attitude should we adopt towards this Lacanian point of departure? It would be all too easy to reject this ontological dualism in the name of one ideal of unity or another. Rather, we must first ask ourselves what motives led Lacan to embrace, *mutatis mutandis,* the Kojèvean-Sartrean schema. Or to put it differently: What is the strategic significance of this ontological dualism for Lacan's engagement with the psychoanalytic and philosophical traditions? Above all, we must ask ourselves how Lacan concretely works out this ontological dualism in his metapsychology. Only thus can we avoid overlooking the stakes of Lacan's thought, and its continuing importance, in any critique of him we might make.

The aim of Lacan's ontological dualism is to preserve a crucial insight of Freudian psychoanalysis, and breathe new life into it. That is to say, Freud (1930) not only shows that the origin of neurosis must be sought in sexuality; he also adds that something in sexuality itself "denies us complete satisfaction and leads us along other paths" (p. 105). In other words, it is not merely the "pressure of culture" that makes a harmonious experience of sexuality impossible and predestines us to neurosis ("other paths"), but the very way we are constituted as sexual beings. There is an "incommensurability" between the human subject and its drives, such that it can never really live in peace with them, and in this sense, a harmonious relation with oneself and with one's environment is denied to humans in principle. Neurosis and psychic suffering in general thus cannot simply be understood as difficulties "adapting," since the relations of the subject to itself and to its environment are basically marked by the impossibility of adaptation—that is precisely what constitutes our humanity. This, in turn, implies that the aim of the psychoanalytic cure cannot be thought of in terms of the repair of a lost harmony or lost coadaptation.

We can claim, without exaggeration, that Lacan's whole *oeuvre* is one sustained reflection upon this basic insight of Freud, and in a certain sense, Lacan intends nothing more than this when he describes the subject as essentially "split." We would be mistaken to detect this thematic only in Lacan's work after the fifties, when the notion of the split subject appears, however—it is already present from his earliest publications on the mirror-stage, and the introduction of the mirror-stage and the imaginary, in the thirties, was already intended to secure psychoanalysis against any ideology of adaptation.

In his text on the mirror-stage, Lacan uses a number of observations from child psychology in order to show that what is really at stake in the relation between the child and its specular image is "an ontological structure of the human world" (Lacan 1949; E 2, EF 94). The jubilation of the child when confronted with its specular image is not because it recognizes itself therein, but is grounded in its formative impact—the child *sees* a *Gestalt* where, because of its biological prematurity, it cannot yet *be* one, and this *Gestalt* offers the child a "self" that fundamentally differs from the vague and poorly delineated "self" of proprioceptive experience. On the basis of this identification with the specular image, the child can develop a firm and sharply delineated feeling of self. It is in the other, Lacan writes, and through identifying with her, that the infant for the first time experiences itself as a firm and well-delineated unity.

But if this experience is at first sight only beneficial, it quickly displays its more problematic aspects. Just as much as

"I" love the image in which I recognize myself, I hate it, for this image is both myself and the other at the same time—it is indissolubly a *heteron* that robs me of myself at the same instant I find myself in it. I am the other. The ego is the effect of an essential alienation that the subject cannot undo without obliterating itself in the same movement. "[The] ego," so Lacan claims, "hangs over the abyss of a dizzy Assent in which one can perhaps see the very essence of anxiety" (Lacan 1953, p. 15).

The biological prematurity that lies at the origin of the identification with the image is accordingly only a symptom of a more essential and indissoluble "primordial Discord" (*Discorde primordiale*; Lacan 1949, E 4) between human being and nature. For the identification with the specular image, on the basis of which the infant hopes to compensate for this prematurity, cannot but make it a prisoner in its own home—which in fact can thereby never *be* its "own." The "primordial discord" between human being and nature resounds throughout the entire history of the subject, and in a sense, this history is no more or less than the sustained attempt to undo this fundamental break between the ego and itself (and the environment), or at least to put it out of sight.[3] The ego is essentially misrecognition. The autonomy that it prides itself on, and in which it seems to find its destiny, the control and domination over its environment for which it strives, both work to conceal the ego's fragile nature. Every harmony and accord between the ego and itself or the ego and the other is always necessarily under threat, and the threat originates

---

3. Which is why Lacan also writes that "[The] history of the formation of the individual [translation modified: (*l'*)*histoire de la formation de l'individu*] . . . is a drama whose internal thrust is precipitated from insufficiency to anticipation . . ." (E 4, EF 97); he never mentions any possibility of remedying the discord.

not in external circumstances that might have been otherwise, but in the constitution of the ego itself. Every harmony is secondary in relation to a more fundamental disharmony that determines the genesis and destiny of the ego.[4]

In his work from the fifties and early sixties, Lacan claims that the imaginary is essentially dependent upon and determined by the symbolic.[5] The imaginary is no longer a response to a real lack, but to a lack introduced by the symbolic, for entry into the symbolic is equiprimordial with the birth of a desire that cannot be satisfied by any object. This desire is essentially incarnated; the reference to the order of signifiers only means anything insofar as we immediately add that it is always grafted onto the order of corporeality, to which it gives meaning. Or perhaps better: on the basis of the negativity of the signifier, precisely those parts of the body that can give concrete content to the symbolic lack are cut out, and indeed, the determination of the various erogenous zones, and objects *a* that are bound up with them, cannot be thought apart from the differential structure of the signifier. These erogenous zones—the places where the body alternately and endlessly opens and shuts—and the objects *a* are characterized by a structural homology with the working of the

---

4. For this whole problematic in relation to the work of Merleau-Ponty, see Visker 1999, p. 220ff.

5. Here we want to suggest that Lacan's theory of the Borromean knots, which he developed mainly in the seventies, is already anticipated in part in "Subversion." In this theory, the three orders of the symbolic, the imaginary, and the real are represented by three circles knotted together in such a way that one cannot undo one of them without separating all three. In such a model it no longer seems possible to say that one order dominates the others. Located where the three circles overlap is the object *a*, which thus forms the "pivot" around which the three orders turn. It would lead us too far astray to further work this problematic out here, however.

subject of the (differential) signifier, which only shows itself at the moment that it once again withdraws or is lost. The subject thus acquires a concrete corporeal form in its relation to the object *a*, which is to say, in the phantasy ($⊘a$).

All of this means that for the subject of the unconscious, the body is not primarily the capacity on the basis of which that subject—for instance, as an essentially meaning-instituting being—is engaged with the reality surrounding it.[6] On the contrary, the body is above all the locus of an experience of irreversible *loss*. Lacan can thus conceive of the subject as both essentially incarnated, and as delivered over to an insatiable desire. This desire is essentially out of joint, at least in the sense that it is caused by an object—the object *a*—that fundamentally disorders phenomenal reality, rather than having consistency with it; it is thus borne along by a dynamic that always carries it beyond the order of phenomenality.[7] Desire, as a result, cannot be understood in terms of adaptation to this reality. Only in the imaginary do we believe that such a completion is possible, or (what amounts to the same thing) that there is an adequate object for desire, for in the imaginary the essential incompleteness and "inadaptation" of the subject of desire is misrecognized. The idea of a closed universe, in which subject and object can at least in principle be brought into accord, is no more than an imaginary illusion.

It would nevertheless be a mistake to believe that the function of the imaginary consists exclusively in concealing the "pri-

---

6. One might think here of the early work of Maurice Merleau-Ponty (and indeed his later work as well), which characterizes the body primarily as an "I can."

7. This is the basic reason Lacan describes desire as essentially a desire unto death (*désir de mort*). Desire carries us out of ourselves and beyond the order of meaning, or of what can appear meaningful to us.

mordial discord" between the subject and the various objects in which it seeks satisfaction. For it is only too clear that the loss of certain objects only affects the subject because and insofar as it is also concerned with its own completeness or wholeness; the inscription of the order of signifiers in the order of the body, and the determination of the various objects *a*, thus presupposes the dynamic of the mirror-stage and of the imaginary. Not only does this significantly relativize Lacan's famed primacy of the symbolic—and its dualistic point of departure?—but it also makes it clear that the operation of Lacan's three orders (the imaginary, the symbolic, and the real) can only be thought in their mutual implication. The imaginary refers to the order of the signifier (the symbolic) as its condition of possibility, while conversely, the symbolic can only graft itself onto the body on the basis of a constitutive reference to the imaginary and the mirror-stage. The real, finally, refers to what in principle cannot be integrated into this dynamic, and the object *a* is a permanent memorial to this impossibility, so that the three orders revolve, as it were, around the object *a* as a sort of vacuum-point holding them together.

Of course, Lacan's ideas on the relation between the body and language pose numerous problems. For example, he repeatedly writes that language creates meaning *ex nihilo* (Lacan 1959–60), implying that the production of meaning in language is in no respect dependent upon a reality outside of language—and thus not dependent on the body either. Let us take the example of the distinction between "man" and "woman" that we discussed earlier.[8] One can agree with Lacan that the absoluteness of this

---

8. See the section in Chapter 1, "A Few General Remarks on Lacan's Theory of Language" (pp. 7–19).

distinction—I am either one or the other—is grounded in the symbolic; but does this also mean that the symbolic is the sole ground of the distinction *per se*? Must we not say, rather, that the symbolic attaches itself to inchoate meanings that have already come into being on the level of intersubjective experience of the body as such? And that the articulation of these meanings in language—we could also say "anticipations of meanings"—takes them up into a logic that is not merely a duplicate or extension of what was already given on the level of the lived body? Language indeed has its own autonomy, which cannot be reduced to, or derived from, reality outside of language; but this does not mean, or at least does not necessarily mean, that language could function completely independently of this reality (*creatio ex nihilo*).

Lacan seldom, if ever, made this problem an explicit theme of reflection, and probably he did not really find it necessary to do so; for at bottom what he really wants to show is that the body and "reality" in general inevitably fail us when it comes to crucial questions like our identity as either "man" or "woman." The way this and other "existential" problematics acquire meaning for us is primarily dependent upon the symbolic structures in which we are taken up, and outside of which subjectivity cannot exist. Whether the distinction between "man" and "woman" is not already outlined on the level of the lived body as such is a question simply subordinate to this; it seems of little or no importance for the message Lacan wants to convey to us.

Because of his differential definition of the signifier and the ontological dualism Lacan inherits from Kojève, Lacan characterizes the body primarily in terms of its negative moments. The central role of the object *a* is inseparable from this. What we called the "inadaptation" of the subject—the fact that it is essentially borne along by a dynamic that carries it beyond the phenomenal—cannot be thought apart from the constitutive role of the object *a* for subjectivity; the object *a* is like a permanent memorial to the loss that gives life to desire. It gives minimal bodily content to the lack introduced by the symbolic, of which the phallus is the privileged signifier—and this immediately implies that the objects *a* can only fulfill their role in reference to the phallus. In this sense Lacan, like Freud, founds the fundamental "inadaptation" of the subject in the very nature of sexuality, which is in turn intrinsically dependent upon the symbolic. Desire has no adequate object because and insofar as it stands under the dominion of the phallus, which is to say, because and insofar as it is sexual. The importance of Lacan's ontological dualism thus becomes clear: it makes it possible to think the intrinsic interweaving of the sexual character of the unconscious and the essential inability of the subject to adapt.

Just as it is for Freud, for Lacan the unconscious is essentially sexual. The way Lacan founds this idea immediately implies a novel solution for the debate between Freud and Jung concerning the role of sexuality in pathology in general, and in psychosis in particular.[9] In order to understand psychosis, Freud first consulted what his analyses had already taught him about neurosis; psychosis, he claimed, must in principle be understood in terms of an unbearable conflict between the demands of an intrinsically sexual drive and those of the ego, on the model of neurosis. As he worked this idea out, he was subsequently forced to understand the ego itself as a libidinous and therefore sexual construct.

---

9. A detailed treatment of this problematic here would carry us too far astray. I will thus confine myself to what is necessary to understand what is at stake in Lacanian thought. For more detailed discussion of the Freud–Jung debate, see Vandermeersch 1991, Van Haute 1997.

This conceptual shift not only forced Freud to abandon his original drive-dualism, according to which psychic life is governed by an opposition between sexual drives and drives of self-preservation; it also led him into numerous insoluble aporias. For example: according to Freud, the libidinous investment of the ego implies a de-sexualization of the libido. Although the libido is de-sexualized, however, it nonetheless remains in itself essentially sexual, and it is anything but clear what such a non-sexual/sexual energy might mean.

Jung, on the other hand, was compelled by the confrontation with the problematic of psychosis and the apparent untenability of some Freudian doctrines to reject the sexual character of the libido. For him, libido is a general psychic interest, and is not of itself sexual; it only *becomes* sexual when it is directed at an explicitly sexual object. Nothing stops the libido from choosing an object other than a sexual one, however, and realizing itself, for example, as "will to power." According to Jung the libido, then, is thus not of itself sexual, but is always qualified anew by its object, and from this perspective he contests the essentially sexual etiology of psychosis and of pathology generally.

Lacan's intervention in this debate is intrinsically determined by the way he conceives the relation between sexuality, the body, and the signifier, by which the institution of the primacy of sexuality (of the phallus) is equiprimordial with the acceptance of the metaphor of the Name-of-the-Father and with the entry into the symbolic. Since the psychotic subject, unlike the neurotic subject, has never been able to take this step, the psychotic problematic is not characterized by a conflict within the order of sexuality as such.

The problematic of neurosis (and of perversion), by contrast, refers to a problematic relation to the law of the father—which has thus in this case acquired meaning. The (however partial) acceptance of this law establishes the primacy of the phallus and of sexuality. From now on the problematic of *jouissance,* which is decisive for pathology, is sexualized,[10] and for that reason, too, the conflict with which the neurotic subject wrestles *does* pertain primarily to sexuality.[11] The dilemma that dominated the debate between Freud and Jung[12] is thus resolved: Freud is right to claim that sexuality is of decisive importance for the neuroses, and Jung is right to deny it for psychosis.

All this makes it clear that Lacan's ontological dualism is not just a questionable inheritance from twentieth-century French philosophy. On the contrary: Lacan uses this dualism in a particularly original manner, to rethink Freud's basic intuitions and to found them in a new way. One is not obliged to follow Lacan in everything that he says, but one cannot deny that his *oeuvre* forms an indispensable contribution to the "return to Freud"—and that return is more than necessary for contemporary psychoanalysis.

---

10. But what precisely does the term "subject" mean here, when Lacan also makes subjectivity intrinsically dependent upon entry into the order of language?

11. See the section in Chapter 8, "The Three Moments of the Oedipus Complex" (pp. 233–238).

12. And perhaps the whole later psychoanalytic tradition?

References

Adriaensen, M. (1992). *Over de subjectwording.* Leuven, Belgium: Acco ("Idesça").

André, S. (1986). *Que veut une femme?* Paris: Navarin. English translation: *What Does a Woman Want?,* trans. S. Fairfield. New York: Other Press, 1999.

Aulagnier, P. (1991). Remarques sur la structure psychotique. In *Un interprète en quête de sens,* pp. 267–286. Paris: Payot.

Baas, B. (1996). L'élaboration phénoménologique de l'objet *a:* Lacan avec Kant et Merleau-Ponty. *Cahiers philosophiques de Strasbourg* 4:13–41.

Bataille, L. (1987). *L'ombilic du rêve. D'une pratique de psychanalyse.* Paris: Seuil.

Benvéniste, E. (1966/1974). *Problèmes de linguistique générale I/II.* Paris: Gallimard. English translation: *Problems in General Linguistics,* trans. M. E. Meek. Coral Gables, FL: University of Miami Press, 1971.

Bernet, R. (in press). Gaze, drive and body in Lacan and Merleau-Ponty. In *Psychosis. Phenomenological and Psychoanalytical Approaches,* ed. J. Corveleyn and P. Moyaert. Leuven, Belgium: Louvain University Press.

Borch-Jacobsen, M. (1991). *Lacan: The Absolute Master,* trans. D. Brick. Stanford, CA: Stanford University Press.

Broekman, J. M. (1973). *Strukturalisme. Moskou-Praag-Parijs.* Amsterdam: Athenaeum-Polak & Van Gennep.

Buckley P., ed. (1986). *Essential Papers on Object-Relations.* New York/London: New York University Press.

Cassiers, L. (1988). Perversie en psychopathie. In Vergote et. al., 1988, pp. 250–281.

Conté, C. (1992). *Le réel et le sexuel: de Freud à Lacan.* Paris: Points hors ligne.

Copernicus, N. (1974). *De Revolutionibus.* Hildesheim, Germany: Gerstenberg.

Corveleyn, J. (1988). Hysterie en dwangneurose. In Vergote et. al., 1988, pp. 52–104.

De Waelhens, A. (1978). *Schizophrenia: A Philosophical Reflection on Lacan's Structuralist Interpretation,* trans. W. Ver Eecke. Pittsburgh, PA: Duquesne University Press.

Dor, J. (1985). *Introduction à la lecture de Lacan.* Paris: Denoël. English translation: *Introduction to the Reading of Lacan,* ed. J. Feher Gurewich, trans. S. Fairfield. New York: Other Press, 2000.

Evans, D. (1998). From Kantian ethics to mystical experience: an exploration of "jouissance." In *Key Concepts of Lacanian Psychoanalysis,* ed. D. Nobus, pp. 1–28. London: Rebus.

Fairbairn, W. R. D. (1986). A revised psychopathology of the psychoses and psychoneuroses. In Buckley 1986, p. 74.

Ferenczi, S. (1952). A little chanticleer. In *Sex in Psychoanalysis,* trans. E. Jones, pp. 240–252. New York: Basic Books.

Fine, A. (1997). L'observation du petit Hans 'revisitée' par Jacques Lacan. In *Peurs et phobies,* ed. A. Fine, A. Le Guen, and A. Oppenheimer, pp. 67–90. Paris: Monographies de la revue française de psychanalyse, P.U.F.

Fink, B. (1995). *The Lacanian Subject: Between Language and Jouissance.* Princeton, NJ: Princeton University Press.

———— (1997). *A Clinical Introduction to Lacanian Psychoanalysis: Theory and Technique.* Cambridge, MA: Harvard University Press.

Florence, J. (1997). Onbewuste verleiding, gesuggereerd onbewuste. *Psychoanalyse/Psychanalyse* 11:9–26.

Freud, S. (1900). The interpretation of dreams. *Standard Edition* 4/5.

———— (1901). The psychopathology of everyday life. *Standard Edition* 6.

———— (1905). Fragment of an analysis of a case of hysteria. *Standard Edition* 7:3–122.

———— (1908). On the sexual theories of children. *Standard Edition* 9:207–226.

———— (1909a). Analysis of a phobia in a five-year-old boy. *Standard Edition* 10:3–149.

———— (1909b). Notes on a case of obsessional neurosis. *Standard Edition* 10:153–320.

———— (1911). Formulations on two principles of mental functioning. *Standard Edition* 12:215–226.

———— (1912–13). Totem and taboo. *Standard Edition* 13:1–162.

———— (1914). On narcissism: an introduction. *Standard Edition* 14:69–102.

———— (1915). The unconscious. *Standard Edition* 14:161–215.

———— (1917). On transformations of instinct, as exemplified in anal eroticism. *Standard Edition*, 17:125–133.

———— (1918). From the history of an infantile neurosis. *Standard Edition* 17:3–123.

———— (1921). Group psychology and the analysis of the ego. *Standard Edition* 18:67–143.

———— (1927). Fetishism. *Standard Edition* 21:149–157.

———— (1930). Civilization and its discontents. *Standard Edition* 21:59–145.

———— (1933). New introductory lectures on psycho-analysis. *Standard Edition* 22:3–182.

———— (1937). Analysis terminable and interminable. *Standard Edition* 23:211–253.

———— (1940). The splitting of the ego in the process of defence. *Standard Edition* 23:273–278.

———— (1974). *L'homme aux rats. Journal d'une analyse,* trans. E. R. Hawelka. Paris: P.U.F.

Green, A. (1995). *Le complexe de castration.* Paris: P.U.F.

Gurewich, J., and Tort, M., eds. (1998). *The Subject and the Self: Lacan and American Psychoanalysis.* Northvale NJ: Jason Aronson.

Guyomard, P. (1998). *Le désir d'éthique.* Paris: Aubier.

Hassoun, J. (1998). In the beginning was sexual difference. In Gurewich and Tort 1998, pp. 145–154.

Hegel, G. W. F. (1977). *Phenomenology of Spirit,* trans. A. V. Miller. Oxford, UK: Oxford University Press.

Heidegger, M. (1962). *Being and Time,* trans. J. Macquarrie and E. Robinson. London: Blackwell.

———(1977). *The Question Concerning Technology and Other Essays,* trans. W. Lovitt. New York: Harper & Row.

Hiel, A. (1990). Inhibitie, inassertiviteit en obsessionale neurose. *Psychoanalyse/Psychanalyse* 6:162–170.

Israel, L. (1976). *L'hystérique, le sexe et le médecin.* Paris: Masson.

Jakobson, R. (1963). *Essais de linguistique générale.* Paris: Gallimard.

Kojève, A. (1949). *Introduction to the Reading of Hegel,* trans. J. H. Nichols. Ithaca, NY: Cornell University Press, 1980.

Kristeva, J. (1996). *Sens et non-sens de la révolte. Pouvoirs et limites de la psychanalyse I.* Paris: Fayard.

Lacan, J. (1948). Aggressivity in psychoanalysis. In Lacan 1977, pp. 8–29.

——— (1949). The mirror stage as formative of the function of the I. In Lacan 1977, pp. 1–7.

——— (1953). Some reflections on the ego. *International Journal of Psycho-Analysis* 34:11–17.

——— (1954–55). *The Seminar. Book II. The Ego in Freud's Theory and in the Technique of Psychoanalysis, 1954–55,* ed. J.-A. Miller, trans. S. Tomaselli. New York: Norton, 1991.

——— (1955–56). *The Seminar of Jacques Lacan. Book III: The Psychoses,* ed. J.-A. Miller, trans. R. Grigg. New York: Norton, 1993.

——— (1956). The function and field of speech and language in psychoanalysis. In Lacan 1977, pp. 30–113.

——— (1956–57). *Le Séminaire. Livre IV. La relation d'objet, 1956–57,* texte établi par J.-A. Miller. Paris: Seuil, 1994.

———— (1957a). The agency of the letter in the unconscious or reason since Freud. In Lacan 1977, pp. 146–178.

———— (1957b). On a question preliminary to any possible treatment of psychosis. In Lacan 1977, pp. 179–225.

———— (1957–58). *Le Séminaire. Livre V. Les formations de l'inconscient, 1957–58*, texte établi par J.-A. Miller. Paris: Seuil, 1998.

———— (1958). The direction of the treatment and the principles of its power. In Lacan 1977, pp. 226–280.

———— (1958–59). *Le Séminaire. Livre VI. Le désire et son interprétation, 1958–59*, published in part in *Ornicar?*, pp. 24–27 (1981–83). Partial account: Le désir et son interprétation, compte rendu par J.-B. Pontalis. *Bulletin de psychologie* 13 (1959). Partial English translation: Desire and the interpretation of desire in *Hamlet*, trans. J. Hulbert. *Yale French Studies* 55/6:11–52 (1977).

———— (1959–60). *The Seminar of Jacques Lacan. Book VII: The Ethics of Psychoanalysis*, ed. J.-A. Miller, trans. D. Potter. New York: Norton, 1992.

———— (1960). The subversion of the subject and the dialectic of desire in the Freudian unconscious. In Lacan 1977, pp. 292–325.

———— (1960–61). *Le Séminaire. Livre VIII. Le transfert, 1960–61*, texte établi par J.-A. Miller. Paris: Seuil, 1991.

———— (1962–63). *Le Séminaire. Livre X. L'angoisse, 1962–63*. Unpublished.

———— (1964). *The Seminar. Book XI. The Four Fundamental Concepts of Psychoanalysis*, ed., J.-A. Miller, trans. A. Sheridan. New York: Norton, 1977.

———— (1966). *Écrits*. Paris: Seuil.

———— (1972–73). *Le Séminaire. Livre XX. Encore, 1972–73*, texte établi par J.-A. Miller. Paris: Seuil. English translation: *On Feminine Sexuality: The Limits of Love and Knowledge*, trans. B. Fink. New York: Norton, 1998.

———— (1977). *Ecrits. A Selection*, trans. A Sheridan. London: Routledge.

Lacoue-Labarthe, P., and Nancy, J.-L. (1990). *Le titre de la lettre*. Paris: Gallimard.

Laplanche, J. (1980). *Castrations, symbolisations (problématiques II)*. Paris: P.U.F.

Laplanche, J., and Pontalis, J.-B. (1988). *The Language of Psychoanalysis*, trans. D. Nicholson-Smith. London: Karnac Books and the Institute of Psycho-Analysis.

Lévi-Strauss, C. (1949). *Les structures élémentaires de la parenté*. Paris: P.U.F. English translation: *The Elementary Structures of Kinship*, trans. J. H. Bell and J. R. von Sturmer, ed. R. Needham. Boston: Beacon, 1969.

————— (1950). Introduction à l'œuvre de Marcel Mauss. In M. Mauss, *Sociologie et anthropologie*, pp. ix–lii. Paris: P.U.F. English translation: *Introduction to the Work of Marcel Mauss*, trans. F. Baker. London: Routledge and Kegan Paul, 1987.

Merleau-Ponty, M. (1968). *The Visible and the Invisible*, ed. C. Lefort, trans. A. Lingis. Evanston, IL: Northwestern University Press.

Moyaert, P. (1982). De grondstuctuur van de taal. Een kritische analyse van de vooronderstellingen van Chomsky in het licht van de problematiek van Derrida en Lacan. *Tijdschrift voor Filosofie* 44:232–265.

————— (1988). Schizofrenie en paranoia. In Vergote et al., 1988, pp. 227–249.

————— (1994). *Ethiek en sublimatie*. Nijmegen, Netherlands: SUN.

M'Uzan, M. de (1977). *De l'art à la mort. Itinéraire psychanalytique*. Paris: Gallimard.

Nasio, J.-D. (1995). *L'hystérie ou l'enfant magnifique de la psychoanalyse*. Paris: Payot.

Ogilvie, B. (1987). *Lacan. La formation du concept du sujet*. Paris: P.U.F. ("Philosophes" series).

Rey-Flaud, H. (1994). *Comment Freud inventa le fétichisme . . . et réinventa la psychanalyse*. Paris: Payot.

Safouan, M. (1974). *Etudes sur l'œdipe*. Paris: Seuil.

Sartre, J.-P. (1969). *Being and Nothingness*, trans. H. Barnes. London: Routledge.

Saussure, F. de (1978). *Cours de linguistique générale*, éd. critique préparée par Tullio de Mauro. Paris: Payot. English translation: *Course in General Linguistics*, ed. C. Bally and A. Sechehaye, trans. W. Baskin. New York: McGraw Hill, 1959.

Sokal, A., and Bricmont, J. (1997). *Impostures intellectuelles*. Paris: Editions Odile Jacob.

Tatossian, A. (1997). La phénoménologie des psychoses. *L'art du comprendre*, juillet/numéro double hors série, pp. 5–151.

Thoné, A. (1999). *Van passiviteit naar passie. Eros and Lichamelijkheid in het werk van Emmanuel Levinas*. Unpublished doctoral dissertation, K. U. Nijmegen.

Vandermeersch, P. (1991). *Unresolved Questions in the Freud–Jung Debate on Psychosis, Sexual Identity and Religion*. Louvain, Belgium: Leuven University Press (Louvain Philosophical Studies 4).

Van Haute, P. (1990). *Psychoanalyse en filosofie. Het imaginaire en het symbolische in het werk van Jacques Lacan*. Leuven, Belgium: Peeters.

——— (1995). Naamgeving kinderen: een in alle opzicht schadelijk voorstel. *Trouw*, 27 September.

——— (1997). Narcissism, mimesis, psychosis: the Freud–Jung debate revisited. *Journal of the British Society for Phenomenology* 1:3–20.

——— (1998). Death and sublimation in Lacan's reading of *Antigone*. In *Levinas and Lacan: The Missed Encounter*, ed. S. Harasym, pp. 102–120. New York: SUNY Press.

——— (in press). Entre phénoménologie et psychanalyse: Lacan, lecteur d'Hamlet. In P. Marrati, ed., *Phénoménologie et psychanalyse*, ed. P. Marrati. Louvain, Belgium: Leuven University Press.

Van Haute, P., and Geyskens, T. (2002). *Spraakverwarring: het primaat van de seksualiteit bij Freud, Ferenczi en Laplanche*. Nijmegen, Netherlands: SUN.

Vergote, A. (1984). Le fantasme de la castration dans l'homosexualité et la paranoïa. *Psychoanalyse/Psychanalyse* 2:57–69.

——— (1997). *La psychanalyse à l'épreuve de la sublimation*. Paris: Cerf.

Vergote, A. et al., eds. (1988). *Psychanalyse. De mens en zijn lotgevallen.* Kapellen: De Nederlandsche Boekhandel / Uitgeverij Pelckmans.

Verhaeghe, P. (1999). *Does the Woman Exist?: From Freud's Hysteric to Lacan's Feminine.* New York: Other Press.

———— (1994). *Klinische pyschodiagnostiek vanuit Lacans discourstheorie.* Leuven, Belgium: Acco.

———— (1999). *Love in a Time of Loneliness.* New York: Other Press.

Verminck, M. (1996). De naam van de moeder? *Streven* July-August, pp. 588–596.

Visker, R. (1999). A Western problem? Merleau-Ponty on intersubjectivity. In *Truth and Singularity: Taking Foucault into Phenomenology*, pp. 201–231. Dordrecht, Netherlands: Kluwer (Phaenomenologica 155).

Winnicott, D. W. (1975). *Jeu et réalité. L'espace potentiel*, trans. C. Monod and J. B. Pontalis. Paris: Gallimard. English original: *Playing and Reality.* New York: Basic Books, 1971.

Zilbach, J. (1998). Toward a separate line of female development: on adolescence. In Gurewich and Tort 1998, pp. 127–144.

Index

www.ingramcontent.com/pod-product-compliance
Lightning Source LLC
Chambersburg PA
CBHW022347280326
41935CB00007B/104